W9-ACZ-383

THE
MANHATTAN
NOBODY KNOWS

THE
MANHATTAN
NOBODY KNOWS
≡ AN URBAN WALKING GUIDE ≡
WILLIAM B. HELMREICH

PRINCETON UNIVERSITY PRESS
PRINCETON AND OXFORD

SAYVILLE LIBRARY

Copyright © 2018 by Princeton University Press

Published by Princeton University Press,
41 William Street, Princeton, New Jersey 08540

In the United Kingdom: Princeton University Press,
6 Oxford Street, Woodstock, Oxfordshire OX20 1TR

press.princeton.edu

Cover and frontispiece photographs by Antony Bennett
Interior photographs by Christopher Holewski
Cover and interior design by Amanda Weiss

All Rights Reserved

ISBN (pbk.) 978-0-691-16699-5

Library of Congress Control Number: 2017958315

British Library Cataloging-in-Publication Data is available

This book has been composed in Adobe Caslon Pro, Futura Std
and HWT Unit Gothic

Printed on acid-free paper. ∞

Printed in China

10 9 8 7 6 5 4 3 2 1

To my mother

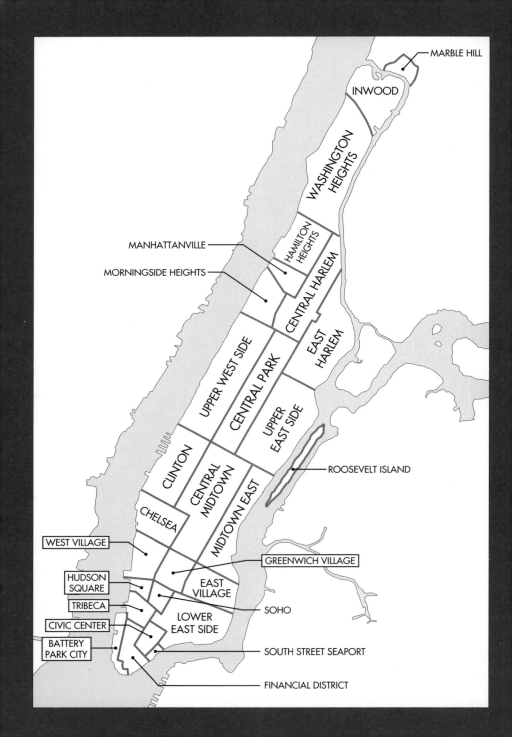

MARBLE HILL

INWOOD

WASHINGTON HEIGHTS

MANHATTANVILLE

MORNINGSIDE HEIGHTS

HAMILTON HEIGHTS

CENTRAL HARLEM

EAST HARLEM

UPPER WEST SIDE

CENTRAL PARK

UPPER EAST SIDE

ROOSEVELT ISLAND

CLINTON

CENTRAL MIDTOWN

MIDTOWN EAST

CHELSEA

WEST VILLAGE

GREENWICH VILLAGE

HUDSON SQUARE

EAST VILLAGE

TRIBECA

SOHO

LOWER EAST SIDE

CIVIC CENTER

BATTERY PARK CITY

SOUTH STREET SEAPORT

FINANCIAL DISTRICT

CONTENTS

INTRODUCTION

MY LOVE FOR WALKING THE CITY can be traced back to a game my father played with me as a child, called "Last Stop." On every available weekend, when I was between the ages of 9 and 14, my dad and I took the subway from our home on the Upper West Side to the last stop of the line and walked around for a couple of hours. When we ran out of new last stops on the various lines, we did the second, then third to last, and so on, always traveling to a new place. In this way, I learned to love and appreciate the city, one that I like to call "the world's greatest outdoor museum." I also developed a very close bond with my father, who gave me the greatest present a kid can have—the gift of time.

The island of Manhattan is a world-famous place. When people say, "I've visited New York City," 90 percent of the time they are referring to the best-known of the city's boroughs. And by a similar margin, they have spent most of their time exploring and experiencing this island's major attractions and sites. Almost always, they've taken in a Broadway show. They've walked down Fifth Avenue and strolled through Lord & Taylor, Bergdorf Goodman, Saks Fifth Avenue, and Henri Bendel. In the Financial District, they toured the New York Stock Exchange. They rode to the top of the Empire State Building and viewed the gigantic Christmas tree at Rockefeller Center, where they might also have seen a show put on by the Rockettes. And if they've seen other parts of Manhattan, they've usually done so by bus or a boat trip around the island. For food, they might have tried a Sabrett hot dog or a halal chicken and rice dish, both sold by street vendors; or an overstuffed pastrami sandwich at the Stage Door Deli in Midtown or Katz's Deli on the Lower East Side, popping into Russ & Daughters as well while they're in the neighborhood. They may also have indulged in lox, sable, or herring at Zabar's on the Upper West Side. For upscale dining, perhaps they visited one of the many options—"21" Club, Bouley, Jean-Georges, Sparks Steak House, Daniel, Le Bernardin, and Il Mulino.

There's nothing wrong with a trip like that. After all, this is what has made the Big Apple so special. And when they return home, tourists want to tell their friends and family that they saw the sights that everyone has heard of and knows about. But is this all that's worth seeing? What is there for those who want to explore the rest of Manhattan? For people who want to combine seeing the well-known with the unknown? Or for those who've seen the regular sights several times but want to see the city from a completely new perspective?

That's why I have written this book—to reveal Manhattan in all its beauty, complexity, and mystery; to demonstrate to visitors that it has so much to offer beyond its most famous locations. This is true of every one of its many neighborhoods, from the northernmost to the southernmost areas, and from east to west across the island. Some of the points made here are true, in varying degrees, of other cities too, while other points are unique.

Take Marble Hill, for instance. To walk through its quaint curved streets and take in its many private, wood-framed homes with peaks or cupolas, is to get a firsthand view of what Manhattan looked like in the nineteenth century. It's the borough's northernmost section and seems so far away from the noise and high-octane activity that people think of when Manhattan is mentioned. Since the community is not on Manhattan Island itself, it's logical to think it should be part of the Bronx. But that's not the case, due to some very interesting historical and geographical changes.

Washington Heights is a hilly neighborhood consisting almost exclusively of apartment buildings constructed on rocky terrain, some of it exposed for six stories clearly visible to the naked eye. Here, I learn about former secretary of state Henry Kissinger's teenage home, and in the area around Jumel Terrace, I discover old wooden houses in their more or less original incarnation. I'm also saddened to learn that the site of Malcolm X's assassination, the

Audubon Ballroom, is not being cared for in the way it should be. This reminds me that I was waiting for a bus outside the ballroom at exactly the time it occurred. (Later in this book, I share the details of what I saw that day.)

Morningside Heights has two neighborhood institutions with great food—V & T Pizzeria and the Hungarian Pastry Shop. Frank Vela, one of V & T's owners, has a fascinating tale about his life as an immigrant in the 1940s and his experiences with Giovanni Buitoni, the famous spaghetti manufacturer.

The point is that all of these communities have their own mini-histories, with stories and places that will entice and delight explorers of the island. But this is equally true of the Manhattan people come to see, its central core, which visitors feel certain they know. I myself wondered if there was anything new I could say about the better-known places. After all, this town offers many tours of all varieties (food tours, literary tours, etc.) and Manhattan is only twenty-two square miles. Moreover, as the sociologist and tour guide Jonathan Wynn points out in his wonderful book, *The Tour Guide*, Manhattan guides are very adept at pointing out the "odds and ends of urban life."[1] As it turned out, discovering new odds and ends wasn't so hard.

Midtown Manhattan, for example, which includes many famous places, like Carnegie Hall, the Empire State and Chrysler Buildings, Times Square, the New York Public Library, and the Theater District, has lots of other places worth seeing. Take the Alwyn Court, an elegant apartment building. Even the majority of New Yorkers have never noticed or even seen it. Nearly every inch of its exterior is encrusted with fire-breathing salamanders, flowers, urns, statues, dragons. No description of this building, either inside or out, can do it justice. It must be seen to be appreciated. There's also a building on W. 58th Street that, when viewed a certain way, gives the distinct impression that half of it is falling down. The Diamond District on 47th Street is a familiar place for visitors, but it's the conversation with a businesswoman there that provides insight into its inner workings.

Greenwich Village is often thought of as a center for entertainment. Every evening as well as all day on weekends, MacDougal and 3rd Streets are filled with throngs of people looking for a good time. But the Village also has a darker, lurid side. How many people know the story of 18 W. 11th Street, where five Weathermen terrorists built a bomb factory in the basement? Three were killed in an explosion there, leaving only two Weathermen to face the music for what they had plotted to do. And what about the "House of Death," at 14 W. 10th Street, where attorney Joel Steinberg beat his six-year-old daughter to death in one of the city's most notorious murder cases? And that's not the only reason for this townhouse's name. Shortly after telling of the ghosts she saw there, a resident, Jan Bryant Bartell, died under mysterious circumstances. She and several others swore they had seen Mark Twain wandering the premises attired in a white suit.

The neighborhood is also home to the Central Bar, where Irish and British expats hoot, holler, and curse as they watch home soccer games on "the telly." For chess set collectors and players, the Chess Forum on Thompson Street is a must. To me, it was special because as a college student I had the honor of losing to Bobby Fischer, an anecdote recounted in this book.

Every neighborhood has its special location that, over time, becomes embedded in the collective memory of those who have been there. At "Rock" Plaza it's the Christmas tree, and Bleecker Street is where it's at in the Village. And in the Wall Street area it's the bull sculpture on Broadway, while in Times Square, the bright-red glass stairs at the TKTS booth on 47th Street is a major attraction. People often need an image to capture what they've experienced, but there's much more to these neighborhoods. To truly understand the history of the Financial District it's necessary to connect with the people who live and work there. One of them would be Paul Quinn, the owner of Jim Brady's saloon and restaurant over at 75 Maiden Lane. He'll tell you how they moved the bar of the world-famous Stork Club, now defunct, to his premises. But more than that, this insightful raconteur will explain what the area was like before and after 9/11; how deserted it became and how and, even more importantly, why thousands of young families now live here.

All this is just a tiny sampling of what this book presents. But it isn't limited to a description of the relatively unknown bricks and mortar of the city's jewels and treasures, fascinating as they may be. A city cannot be understood purely in terms of its colorful history or fascinating architecture. Its heart and soul are the people who inhabit it. They are literally the repository of its essence, and this book presents the most interesting conversations I was fortunate enough to have had with some of the hundreds of people I met in my journey through its many streets. What they say is what makes the city come alive to the reader.

In Inwood, a neighborhood in upper Manhattan, I meet Sabas, an eighty-two-year-old man who lives in a cave. Most people would think of him as a homeless man, but he really isn't. The cave *is* his home, and by choice. I say to him: "Well, you have a million-dollar view of the forest from here." His answer is exquisite: "I do. I do. I see the leaves falling. I see them come down like ballet dancers. Each one is turning and twisting and bending, caressing the air. It's a loving situation. And no two fall in the same way, so I'm overwhelmed. I'm overwhelmed." I ask if I can give him anything. His response says it all: "Why would you have to give me anything? I have everything I need. And I have my Korean War veteran's pension. It's not much, but it's enough. The creator takes care of me because I obey his natural laws."

In Washington Heights, I meet Theo, a young Greek American, who owns Jumbo Pizza and Coffee Shop. This place lives up to its name, serving up the largest slices of pizza I've ever seen. He's following in his father's path, one that epitomizes the ambition of immigrants in this city. Nearby, the journey takes place in reverse. The Brotherhood/Sister Sol at 143rd Street takes Harlem kids to other parts of the world. As Nando Rodriguez, a coordinator, tells me: "We recently took a group of kids to Brazil. In this country we think of

slavery as a US thing. But now they learn it existed in Brazil too."
Organizations like this enrich and change lives in these poorer parts
of the city. For the children who go, the experience is something they
are likely to remember for the rest of their lives.

In a Harlem restaurant, a waiter tells me about his background:
"My mother is Gabonese and French, and my father is Polish and
Chinese. I guess I'm just an American." These multicultural families
are on the rise, especially in New York City but nationally too. I
also learn about them from students in my classes at City College.
On the Upper West Side I come across Jacob's Pickles. Sounds like
a pickle joint, but it's much more. It has sour cukes, kosher cukes,
pickled carrots, and many other dishes and a wide selection of beers
and biscuit dishes. I chat with the proprietor, who tells me why he
opened this eatery: "I always loved pickles. It was my passion. That
and beer. I see pickles, beer, and biscuits as the ultimate comfort
food." His comment reflects a very New York thing—the right to
take your ultimate fantasy, put it out there, and see who will buy into
it. It can be a place loaded with pinball machines that you can play
and pay for by the hour or by the game. It can be a shop where you
choose from many varieties of mayonnaise mixed with items you
never thought would be a good mix. The pickle idea seems to be a
winner, judging from the number of customers there.

Then there are people whose game seems to be a bit more out of
touch with the masses. Yet they too survive, albeit with a smaller customer base. Take Jack Seidenberg, owner of an antiques emporium in
Greenwich Village which, with its absolutely stunning merchandise,
looks like a museum. Alas, he has few customers these days.

"How's business?" I ask him.

"Well, I make a living. My father started this business in 1940.
It's in my blood. But with everybody shopping virtually and rents
going up, more and more stores are vacant. So it's a struggle."

"And yet, you're happy."

"You know, I have people who come in here and wake me up
from my lethargy. They say to me: 'You must have such a wonderful

life, being surrounded by all these beautiful works of art.' And I'm thinking about the next sale, but they set me right, and stop me in my tracks, stop me from thinking despairing thoughts." Jack's dilemma is one faced by thousands of small-business owners. They are conflicted by the love they have for their work or the fact that this is simply what they know how to do and by the realization that it may all end badly.

New Yorkers are what makes this city what it is. Often, they rise to the occasion. Others do not, but they are at least passive identifiers. And this raises an interesting question. Is there something that binds Manhattanites together? I think so, and it starts with an acute consciousness of place. They know that they live and work in one of the most renowned places on the planet. About 80 percent of Manhattanites work in their home borough, which means their relationship with the city is all-encompassing, in a 24/7 way. It's one of the factors that unites them in terms of what they see, do, and think about.

Clearly a wealthy resident of Park Avenue and 86th Street experiences Manhattan differently than someone from Park Avenue and 118th Street. The former may dine in a fancy restaurant while the latter works in the kitchen. But the point is that New Yorkers at every level interact with each other almost daily. The cabbie or Uber driver talks politics or shares personal information with his or her passenger.[2] People from different walks of life wait on line to get into a Knicks game and a conversation happens. As a result, everyone learns about the lives of others. Some learn more because they are interested and willing to share information and stories. Others, a bit suspicious or simply introverted, gain less, but almost everyone's horizons are broadened in varying degrees over time. This creates a shared identity, one that's far more common in a crowded and diverse city.

But what accounts for that sense of commonality? First and foremost, there is an awareness of a common history, some of it bad, some of it good. A perfect case in point is what happened in

Manhattan on 9/11. Just as people did nationally when John F. Kennedy was assassinated in 1963, one of the most frequent questions New Yorkers ask each other is "Where were you when 9/11 happened?" This creates a bond of shared tragedy that, in effect, breaks the ice among people looking for a way to do so. A second choice may be where people were during the days when the "Son of Sam" terrorized the city. There's also a positive way to engage: "Do you remember going to Coney Island?" "Remember how the Mets almost won the World Series?"

A second factor has to do with daily topics of conversation that are relevant to all New Yorkers. This includes the subways, safety, the weather, or thoughts about the police or the mayor—loaded but still avidly discussed subjects, even among strangers. If people are in agreement on these subjects, that's fine, though less interesting. If they're not, it's at least an area of shared experience. Since my method in this book was to approach total strangers and encourage them to talk to me, these and other similar topics were of crucial importance, and they worked for me as they do for other Manhattan dwellers.

No matter where they live in Manhattan, many people are proud to tell others that they reside in this internationally known borough. Someone who lives in a public housing project on the Lower East Side is still the resident of a borough with great cachet. I grew up in a modest neighborhood in Manhattan, not Riverside Drive or Central Park West, but between Columbus and Amsterdam Avenues, above 96th Street. But when, as an adult, I told people that I was raised in Manhattan I could see they were impressed. As for those who live in the finest areas of the borough—the Upper East Side, Sutton Place, Chelsea—they know they're at the top. It is the dream of many a suburbanite from Long Island or New Jersey to retire and live "in the city."

In the larger context, New Yorkers have multiple, overlapping identities. First, we have the neighborhood, be it the Upper West Side, Gramercy Park, Hamilton Heights, or Clinton. Second, there's the borough, whichever one the person lives in. And then we have

New York City, any and every part of it. These categories are used in many ways—to impress, to identify with, to make a comment about why they are who they are. In this last case, New Yorkers are apt to see themselves in the way that they think others see them: brash, smart-alecky, edgy; aggressive but also cool, hip trend-setters. And these are just some of the ways they describe themselves. Sometimes they use what they know to be stereotypes as a way of setting themselves apart, as in "I'm not your typical New Yorker."

The neighborhoods often intersect or overlap in very interesting ways. Many Manhattan residents have chosen to live somewhere because they can get to their place of work, also in Manhattan, more quickly. Thus residents of Washington Heights, now called Hudson Heights to improve the value of the real estate (it just sounds better), select it because the A train is a quick ride to Midtown or the Financial District. Others live in Harlem because it's close to Columbia University, where they work. A woman living all the way up near 96th Street and Park Avenue feels violated because she can see from her apartment one of the world's tallest apartment buildings all the way down on 57th Street, and she doesn't like the way it looks. A man from Manhattanville works as a security guard in a Midtown museum. All day long he interacts with people who are regular museum visitors. Few of them come from his neighborhood. Observing them broadens his horizons. A social worker from the West Village travels to a low-income neighborhood in Marble Hill, where she engages on an intimate level with poor residents living in a public housing project. In short, Manhattanites know there are many different "Manhattans," but they are all part of one geographically connected and incredibly complex borough.

In essence, the great equalizer in Manhattan is *accessibility*. People think of the tremendous cultural jewels of Manhattan, like the theater, opera, concerts, sports events—not to mention its fine restaurants and expensive jewelry and clothing stores—as beyond the reach of all but the wealthy and upper-middle class. But it's not true. They don't need a substantial bank account to buy a low-end item at Tiffany's, where a chain in sterling silver sells for $50, and other items are available for under $200. They can eat in Il Mulino and select carefully from the menu offerings. They can stand on the cancellation line to get discounted tickets for a Broadway show. They can go to the same Knicks game that Spike Lee attends; they just can't afford to sit in the box seats, unless, of course, they know an employee at the Garden. Even a reservation at Rao's,[3] one of the city's hardest restaurants to gain entry to, is achievable, that is, if they're cousins of the Puerto Rican chef who works there. And they can certainly visit the Empire State Building or the Statue of Liberty. In fact, some of the best things—relaxing or jogging in Central Park, various concerts everywhere—are free. The only difference is they can't do it on a regular basis.

Still, the warm glow from that occasional pleasure can last for years in the form of "Yes, we ate at Nobu [or Marea] and it was great." They can reminisce about that great rock concert they went to, or that dress they bought at Saks Fifth Avenue. In short, it isn't necessarily about how often you do something but simply the fact that you did it. They even have an economic edge over one category—the tourists. They don't have to pay airfare to get here, nor do they have to find a hotel because they're here already. The ability, however infrequently, to do all these things makes them feel that they too are real New Yorkers. People who live in the rest of the country can't do them so easily.

And what of Manhattan's future? It certainly looks bright, what with 65 million tourists a year visiting the city, most of them focusing on Manhattan. So long as the crime rate remains low, it will remain that way. Yet, it does have some unique problems. One is that commercial and residential interests compete intensely with each other for the limited space that's available. The city must find creative solutions that balance these critical needs. Another issue is affordable housing. In order for the hundreds of thousands of people employed in the service industries that keep the city functioning to get to work, they must live within a reasonable commute.

Fortunately, the nearness of the Bronx, Brooklyn, Queens, and even Staten Island reduce the urgency of this issue. But the rest of the city is rapidly gentrifying as well, and the day of reckoning when hard decisions must be made is not far off. In New York City the number of homeless people continues to rise despite the city's continuing efforts to address the problem. Mass transit is yet another problem, one that grows more urgent as more and more people pour into its aging and deteriorating stations and trains. Band-Aid solutions won't work here, but major repairs and construction take time, effort, and planning that will inconvenience millions.

Despite issues of this sort, Manhattan has both survived and thrived. Its people and leaders have always had a can-do, no-nonsense attitude that problems can and must be dealt with and solved. The classic example of recent times has been the response to 9/11, but other examples abound. For instance, in 2017, Mayor Bill de Blasio wanted the city to retain control of the schools. When it became clear that part of the solution required making a deal with the charter schools, which he disliked, he gritted his teeth and came to an agreement. Also in 2017, he compromised when he realized that the railroads into the city required extensive repairs. Janette Sadik-Khan, the sometimes controversial commissioner of transportation under Mayor Michael Bloomberg, was widely respected as an innovative commissioner who knew what she wanted and got it done quickly.

To write this book, I re-walked most of Manhattan, which I had systematically gone through when I walked it for *The New York Nobody Knows*. In doing so, I wore out two pairs of Rockport shoes. I didn't walk every block as I had done before, but I covered most of them, traversing 721 miles as measured by my pedometer. Simply walking 51st Street from west to east is about 2.5 miles, so the miles add up very quickly. Portions of some avenues or streets were sometimes revisited if subsequent information about them made it necessary. As opposed to, say, Brooklyn or Queens, which have many larger and more spacious areas, Manhattan is very dense everywhere, both in area and in terms of population, so the blocks tend to have much more to see on them. This requires walking more slowly and looking very carefully at everything.

It took me eleven months to complete this project. Manhattan is a compact borough, and with parking at a premium, I relied almost exclusively on mass transit, which worked out very well. I began my walks at 230th Street and systematically walked every neighborhood, from that northernmost part to the southern tip of the island at State and South Streets. I walked the streets in the daytime and at night; during the week and on weekends; in the heat, which in 2016 was really bad at times, and in the cold, which wasn't bad at all that mild winter.

Even in the few years since my first book on this topic appeared, many changes have occurred—new buildings, restaurants, community gardens, bike paths, and so on. Because of both this and my desire to write a genuinely new book, almost everything in it is new material. The approach was also different, and this played an even bigger role in why so much of the material is new. The focus and structure of the book was to create a walking guide that allows the reader to cover *every single neighborhood.* This means that there must be a certain number of pages on every community, regardless of how interesting—or uninteresting—it may seem at first. That forces the writer to work hard to uncover new material. What surprised me was that every area *is* interesting. Sometimes I just had to look at things more closely and be more creative.

Some of the places described here may no longer be there when you take your walks. The city is always changing. But no doubt, there will be new places to explore of equal or even greater interest. Most of the borough is safe, but for the few areas that aren't, the appendix has useful tips on how to walk them. To find specific places and people, consult the index.

There's a street map for each community, and you can walk it in any order you'd like, searching out whatever moves you. I don't know where walkers will begin their walks or what they will or will not want to see. Therefore, you can start and end anywhere, and the letters are not a guide to the order in which you should see places. To cover every area, it was necessary to be selective about what was chosen for discussion. But what I picked is also meant to whet your appetite, to entice you into wandering these streets on your own, where you're likely to make new discoveries.

Post offices, community district leaders, police precincts, and local schools often differ on the precise boundaries of neighborhoods, as do experts who have carefully studied the city. In drawing these maps, I relied primarily on my own walks and personal knowledge and, for corroboration, on Kenneth Jackson's *The Encyclopedia of New York City*, plus some entries in Wikipedia, mostly as a fallback. A small portion of the historical material in the book was also corroborated by Jackson's book and Wikipedia. Most of it, however, comes from my knowledge of the subject gained from forty years of teaching the New York City course at City College and CUNY Graduate Center. The best discussion regarding boundaries appears in a 2012 *New York Times* article.[4]

There are two critical ways in which this guidebook differs from the typical one. First is *its focus on impromptu conversations* with people from every walk of life. These people breathe life and energy into the material. By listening to what they had to say, I gained a much deeper understanding of what Manhattan is all about—its complexity, the joys and struggles of its inhabitants, the challenges its residents face, and what helps them get through life. This enhances the reader's and/or walker's ability to see life as the people who live there do.

Sometimes I told people I was writing a book and at other times I simply engaged them in conversation. Whenever I recorded what was being said on my iPhone, I informed people of that. No one objected, as I explained that what they were saying was very important in terms of understanding the city. New Yorkers are actually a very friendly, if sometimes gruff, lot and are often pretty chatty once they get going. I attended community events, concerts, and parties; hung out in parks; stood on street corners; frequented bars and restaurants; and did all the things necessary to appreciate the pulse and heart of this wonderful place.

The second major distinction between this and most other guidebooks is *its focus on the unknown parts of the city*. Clearly, they aren't completely unknown, but they are unknown to most people who live or visit here. I deliberately ignored the sites that appear in other guidebooks. It's not that these places aren't critical in making the city what it is. They are, but they've already been covered. The goal here was to discover new, hidden aspects of Manhattan. Hopefully, readers will find the effort to have been worthwhile.

And now, we begin our journey.

MARBLE HILL

INWOOD

WASHINGTON
HEIGHTS

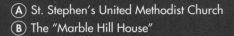
(A) St. Stephen's United Methodist Church
(B) The "Marble Hill House"

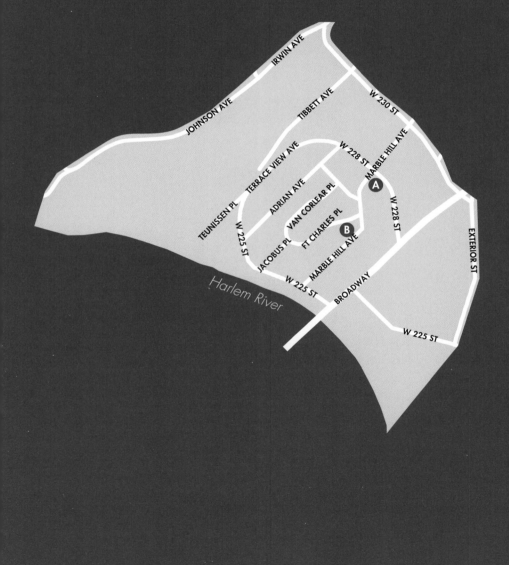

MARBLE HILL

WHAT DETERMINES WHERE A NEIGHBORHOOD BELONGS? I begin my walk through Manhattan with Marble Hill, where this question is very appropriate. While legally part of Manhattan or, if you will, the County of New York, it is geographically completely separated from it. Instead of being part of Manhattan Island, it is the only portion of the borough located on the North American mainland, right next to the Bronx. Though it has a Bronx zip code, most of the city's administrative offices that serve it are in Manhattan. Attitudes about the placement, some of them quite passionate, vary among the residents, so it's probably best to start at the beginning.

Built on a natural base of soft rock, dolomite marble, the hill, with its commanding view, was important for its strategic value during the Revolution. The hill was dubbed Fort Prince Charles by British forces, and one of its most beautiful, winding, and quiet streets still bears that name. The legal separation from Manhattan came in 1897, when the Harlem River boundary was moved some blocks south by the construction of the Harlem River ship canal, due to an increase in ship traffic. Now boats could go all the way around Manhattan and on a route that also reduced the distance from the Hudson River to Long Island Sound. In 1914, the northern border was filled in. For many in this uppermost section it was a tragedy, for Marble Hill was now literally left high and dry and with a less classy, even humdrum, address in their eyes.

Sociologically, this can be seen in a somewhat different light. The sociologist W. I. Thomas famously said: "If men define situations as real, they are real in their consequences." To which a philosopher's rejoinder might be: Does defining them as real *make* them real? Today, this area is largely Hispanic and black, but this is true of both the Bronx and Manhattan, so ethnically speaking, this part of town would be a reasonable fit in either borough.

Marble Hill has its own shopping areas, but they don't help in the conversation about where Marble Hill belongs. If you closed your eyes and walked this part of Broadway and then Inwood's Dyckman Street, listening to the sounds of the neighborhood, its blaring music, languages spoken, heavy traffic, or opened them and looked at the stores, you could be in either the Kingsbridge part of the Bronx, immediately north, or in Inwood, immediately south.

Sure, some people will say the fact that Marble Hill is physically separated from Manhattan by a bridge puts it in the Bronx. But isn't Roosevelt Island part of Manhattan too? So, in the end, we yield to the legal, geographical, and political definitions and the decision made by the New York Legislature in 1984 to consider it part of Manhattan.

The official boundaries are 230th Street on the north, Exterior Street to the east, the Harlem River on the south, and Johnson and Irwin Avenues on the west. It's a mostly residential area with apartment buildings, many of them in the Art Moderne style, others of old wood frame, and private Victorian homes, in varying conditions. West of Broadway, the overall effect, augmented by its numerous winding, hilly streets, is that of a quaint, rustic village, but not completely, because there are some apartment buildings here too. Some of the nicest streets to wander around on are Terrace View Avenue, which partially encircles the buildings and other streets on the hill; Adrian Avenue, Van Corlear Place, Fort Charles Place, and Marble Hill Avenue. The Promenade, on 225th Street, has apartments with gorgeous views of the Hudson River and the Palisade Cliffs, as do some of the Art Moderne buildings with their corner casement windows in the area. East of Broadway, things are very different. You have bustling shopping streets, mostly on Broadway, 225th Street, and 230th Street. There's also the NYCHA (New York City Housing Authority) Marble Hill Houses, built around 1950, which today are home to black and Hispanic low-income residents.

Those familiar with Marble Hill's location think of a small area between 225th and 228th Streets with circular streets. It is that too, but there's more to it geographically. From Broadway, I begin by walking east on 225th Street toward the Major Deegan Expressway, a short distance away. Here, there are many chain stores of the inexpensive variety—T. J. Maxx, Sports Authority, etc.—as well as fast-food places and one of two Starbucks that service the community. I approach a man in a flowing white robe, or kaftan, who's also wearing a large, white, crocheted skullcap, or kufi, on his head. He's selling aromatic oils of many kinds across the street from the Marble Hill Houses. It turns out he's from Senegal.

"Are these any better than, say, Chanel No. 5?" I ask as an opening conversational gambit of sorts.

"Oh, yeah. They are better, because the oils are natural and pure."

I take a whiff of one and it smells quite nice. But then, looking at the name, "Weekend," I exclaim: "Oh no! Today is Thursday. I'll have to wait until the weekend for my wife to be able to use it!"

He laughs and continues his sales pitch: "And instead of paying one hundred, you can get it for ten, twenty dollars, depending on the size you choose."

He has a point. This is not a wealthy or even middle-class area. People here don't have the money for expensive perfume. This oil has a pleasant fragrance and is cheap, so even if the bottle is quite plain-looking it's a great deal. Ten minutes away in upscale Riverdale, it's a different universe.

Returning to the west side of Broadway and walking up 230th Street, I make a left on Kingsbridge Avenue and, after a block, enter the old part of Marble Hill that overlooks the water. St. Stephen's United Methodist Church on the corner of 228th Street and Marble Hill Avenue, built in 1897, is one of the oldest structures in the area. The entrance has diagonal, red-painted wooden slatted doors and features a beautiful rose window. It has adapted to better serve the changing demographics of the neighborhood, offering services in both Spanish and English.

I meet Derek Winslow as he's walking out of his multi-apartment building at 61 Marble Hill Avenue and express my admiration for

A gorgeous church from 1897 adapts—Spanish and English services.

A Catskills vacation hotel? A one-family in Marble Hill.

what was once a single family home built by a real estate agent in the 1890s.The black half-timbers surrounding the white squares that make up the building have a Tudor appearance, but the style isn't really Tudor. Nonetheless, it's a pretty house. It's one of the oldest homes in the area and some call it the "Marble Hill House." Derek gives his views regarding Marble Hill: "It's a great area, very quiet, pretty safe, with real character as far as the houses go. I love the stones near the bottom of the curved brick apartment building across the street. It's also convenient to the city with the IRT number 1 train nearby."

That's a pretty accurate description. I walk to Fort Charles Place and see numerous private wood-frame places with peaks or cupolas, usually covered with protective shingles. People are relaxing in the early evening, chatting or enjoying an outdoor meal in their small gardens. In terms of peace and quiet, it's a most un-Manhattan-like place and definitely worth the trip.

HENRY HUDSON BRIDGE

Hudson River

Harlem River

HENRY HUDSON PKWY

Inwood Hill Park

(A)

(B)

INDIAN RD
W 215 ST
W 214 ST
PARK TERR W
PARK TERR E
W 218 ST
W 217 ST
W 213 ST
W 212 ST
W 211 ST

BROADWAY
W 220 ST
W 219 ST
9TH AVE
W 216 ST
W 215 ST

Isham Park

PAYSON AVE
SEAMAN AVE
COOPER ST
BEAK ST
CUMMING ST
ACADEMY ST
BROADWAY
VERMILYEA AVE
ISHAM ST
W 207 ST
10TH AVE

(G)

(C)

(D)

(F)

(E)

SHERMAN AVE
W 204 ST
POST AVE
NAGLE AVE
DYCKMAN ST

W 207 ST
W 206 ST
W 205 ST
W 204 ST
W 203 ST
W 202 ST
W 201 ST
9TH AVE
10TH AVE

Harlem River

(A) Cave of Sabas
(B) Site where Peter Minuit bought Manhattan for $24
(C) Dichter's Pharmacy
(D) Dyckman Farmhouse Museum
(E) MamaSushi Restaurant
(F) Mamajuana Restaurant
(G) La Marina – celebrity place

INWOOD

THE BOUNDARIES OF THIS AREA ARE THE HARLEM RIVER to the north and east, Dyckman Street on the south, and the Hudson River along the west. The US Postal Service considers Fairview Avenue to be Inwood's southern border. However, as a trip to the area will confirm, most residents consider Dyckman Street and not Fairview Avenue to be the southern border of Inwood and the longer they have lived there the more emphatic they are about it. That includes Yours Truly, who had lived in Washington Heights for seven years. This may be, in part, because the topography immediately below Dyckman "feels" like Washington Heights. For example, "the Heights" has many buildings on both sides of Broadway that have five or more stories' worth of concrete support foundation *before* the actual basement begins, and that includes Fairview Avenue and the surrounding streets. Second, Dyckman is a major thoroughfare and Fairview is a minor street. Third, most authoritative sources, including *The Encyclopedia of New York City*, also consider the southern border to be Dyckman.

Beginning in 1906, when the IRT train began running here, Inwood became a neighborhood of apartment buildings, many of them in the Art Deco style. Its growth accelerated with the arrival of the A train in 1932. The main ethnic population groups living here were Irish and Jewish until the arrival of Dominicans in the late 1970s. This pattern accelerated over the next few decades, and today the area is predominantly Dominican, augmented by increasing numbers of more recently arrived Mexicans.[5] The public housing project, Dyckman Houses, is where Kareem Abdul-Jabbar grew up. In recent years, however, the area has begun to gentrify, especially north of Dyckman Street and west of Broadway. Its reputation as a dangerous neighborhood stems from the 1970s, but overall, it's one of the safer areas in the city. It has two wonderful parks, Inwood Hill Park and Fort

Tryon Park, the latter belonging mostly to neighboring Washington Heights. The main commercial thoroughfares are Broadway; Dyckman Street, which has some nightclubs; and 207th Street.

I begin my walk on Dyckman Street, near the Hudson River, where it meets Riverside Drive, and turn left. These are the last two blocks of Riverside, which begins its northward path on Manhattan's West Side. Most people living on the Upper West Side, in Morningside Heights, and in the Washington Heights parts of Riverside Drive have no idea that this is where it ends. It's a peaceful quiet street, and I notice some fancy cars parked here, including a black high-end Jaguar sedan.

Retracing my steps on Riverside and returning to Dyckman, I head east and turn left in two blocks onto Payson Avenue and soon enter Inwood Hill Park, which runs along the left side of Payson. The park has 196 acres of a naturally preserved park, complete with many shady paths, often covered with a thick canopy of leaves. There are huge trees with gnarled branches, thick underbrush along the sides of the path, and, intermittently, cliffs and giant boulders. There's an occasional jogger or dog walker, but it's nothing like the crowds in the upper part of nearby Fort Tryon Park. The well-maintained soccer, tennis, and baseball fields, as well as a large man-made pond, are nearby, but I can't see, or even hear the noise from, these recreational facilities. It is here that I meet and speak with a most interesting individual.

Walking along one of these trails, my reverie is interrupted by a faint noise, which sounds like the crackling from one of those now extinct transistor radios. My hunch turns out to be right, for as I follow the noise along a dirt path, ascending a steep rocky incline, I recognize the sound of a voice reporting the news. Simultaneously I spy, between low-hanging branches, a small elderly man relaxing beneath the overhang of a rock formation. His place is not visible to those strolling along the concrete walkway below. I call out to him in greeting, and he responds affirmatively in a thin reedy voice:

Grand entrance to cave-home of Sabas.

"How are you doing today?" "Fine. Why not?" By now I'm standing in front of his cave, or lair. He's a small fellow and is actually dressed like a gnome—a peaked woolen hat, a red and black jacket, green pants, and soft, suede-like moccasins. He's surrounded by black and white smallish garbage bags, a number of which seem to contain clothing, bottles, and assorted detritus.

"I'm the creature from the creation," he tells me, smiling.

"That's great to hear. I'm just turning on the tape recorder, so I won't forget what you're saying. You have a nice home here, and it's got a great view; but you can't stay here in the winter, can you?"

"Why not? What's the problem?"

"Problem? Well, it's so cold then."

"All my neighbors are here—squirrels, birds, raccoons. We all hang out together."

"You remind me of the Garden of Eden, when people lived happily with all living things. Are you a New Yorker?"

The palace grounds of an urban cave-dweller.

"Yeh. From all around here."

"I see you have this nice yellow sombrero here to protect you from the sun. What about shopping? How do you get your necessities back to your place?"

"It's not easy, but I manage."

"Did I just happen to catch you at lunch or are you here all day?"

"No, I wander around the hills and elsewhere in the city. But I move between civilization and the primordial. And it's very easy to slip from one to the other if you're in wooded areas within the city."

"Do you like the primordial better?"

"Well, it's healthier."

"Is it dangerous here at night?"

"God knows. I'm here. It's like asking a squirrel, 'Is it dangerous?' It depends on who you meet, I guess. I haven't experienced crime at night."

"What's your name?"

"Sabas, and it's a name with a very interesting history.[6] It's from the fifth century, originally descended from the Egyptian pharaohs. And they built many monasteries in the Middle East."

"Did you serve in the Korean War?"

"Yes. I was drafted. Afterwards I gambled. And you win, and you win, and you win, and you win, and then you have some money. That's how you manage to eat. I wasn't rich, but I always had money in my pocket. I'm eighty-two years old. I used to live on 135th Street between Amsterdam and Broadway, paying $78 a month. I had rent control. No more, though."

"You should visit me at City College, where I teach."

"Well, I camped out in St. Nicholas Park behind the college for many years. It was a wild area. I had a wonderful experience there about twenty-five years ago, going down the stairs. The students were coming up, 1,000 students, I'd guess. It was a windy day. Birds love to fly in windy weather. So, I'd be watching them fly, trying to follow these birds, which way they were going, up, down, sideways, for about ten or fifteen minutes, and when I looked down all the students were gone, nowhere to be seen. I had been concentrating so hard on the birds that I forgot they were there! And I laughed and laughed hysterically. It was so funny to me. And I collapsed laughing for five minutes."

"You seem to love life."

"I've enjoyed my life. I've had a great life. I sleep here at night and it's beautiful. I take a quick dip if it's 50 degrees. It's very stimulating and refreshing."

"But you must wear warm clothing in the winter."

"How dare you ask that? Are you suggesting that I go nude in the winter? Of course, I wear clothing. But I don't always stay here. I have many, many locations. I don't want to suffer. But I always return here. When I see these snow-clad hills, I'm happy. I prepare the area in the autumn with leaves that I can lie on under a tree or in a cave. I've been doing this at least half my adult life. And it's warm. There's no wind in here."

"When you hear the radio and catch the news, what do you think about what's going on in the world?"

"Why would I want to listen to that? It's mostly bad. I want to think about good things."

"Well, you have a million-dollar view of the forest from here."

"I do. I do. I see the leaves falling. I see them come down like ballet dancers. Each one is turning and twisting and bending, caressing the air. It's a loving situation. And no two fall the same way, so I'm overwhelmed. I'm overwhelmed."

"That's beautifully put. Before I leave, let me ask you if you need any money. Can I give you something?"

"Why would you have to give me anything? I have everything I need. And I have my Korean War veteran's pension too. It's not much, but it's enough. The creator takes care of me because I obey his natural laws."

"I'm going home. Maybe I can call you sometime."

"I don't have a phone. I'm antiquated."

This is, when all is said and done, a beautiful man. Sabas has carved out a life for himself that is the essence of simplicity. Allowing for the rough patches he has had throughout his life and probably still has, his outdoor existence is like a modern-day urbanized version of Thoreau's at Walden Pond. His description of the leaves falling is quite literally "poetry in motion." He is peaceful, friendly, rational, and at one with his environment. As in the story about the students, he is able to find joy even in seemingly inconsequential events. He isn't really homeless. He has a home in a cave, and it's all he needs or wants. He's apparently in good health, perhaps better than most eighty-two-year-olds. When I look into his twinkling blue eyes, I see a happy, contented person. The ancient book *Sayings of the Fathers*, compiled almost 2,000 years ago, states: "Who is rich? He who is satisfied with what he has." And is this not true of Sabas?

History lives in these parts. As I walk to the park entrance, I stop at a plaque proclaiming the rock to which it is affixed to be the legendary precise location (a contradiction in terms!) where Peter Minuit reportedly purchased Manhattan Island in 1626 from the Lenape Indians for $24 (actually, 60 Dutch guilders) and some trinkets, and where a tulip tree grew to be 120 feet tall, with a girth of twenty feet.

At the corner of Seaman Avenue and W. 207th Street, by the park exit, I stand in front of an elderly black man with a full white beard. He is sitting at a long folding table in front of the park and conducting a Bible study class. Seated before him are three women; two are Hispanic and the third is African American. He is reading from a Hebrew-English Bible, one typically used by Orthodox Jews. His religion seems to be a mix of Judaism and Christianity. To emphasize that, perched on his head is a black crocheted skullcap with a white cross stitched into it.

"We study Jesus," he tells me. "Why did he come into this world? What was his mission? Either he's a liar or he was God. So we have to dissect this frog, figure out what's true and what's not."

"You're wearing this unusual skullcap with a cross on it."

"Ah, yes," he exclaims with a smile as his eyes open wider. "Isaac asked his father, 'We have wood and the flint, but where's the sacrifice?' Abraham's answer is everything: 'God shall provide the answer for himself.' Only God can do that. So whatever hung on that cross is God. Any other view is an abomination. And to be a true Jew, you must follow every letter of the law. We fast on Yom Kippur, and our hearts are truly broken when we have sinned."

This man's voice, appearance, and persona are both warm and charismatic. He has been here for years. He harms no one, and he has his devoted followers. Like the Jehovah's Witnesses near the Inwood train station, he is part of a veritable army of religious devotees of a variety of faiths who sort of patrol the streets looking for people willing to hear their message. They are part of the tapestry that makes up this city and gives it the reputation it deserves as a world center for freedom of expression.

In two blocks I turn left onto Broadway and come to Dichter's Pharmacy. It also houses a soda fountain that serves delicious ice cream cones at low prices. Continuing back down Broadway to W. 204th Street, I pass the well-known Dyckman Farmhouse Museum, named after the family that once inhabited this two-story Dutch Colonial. I swing right onto Dyckman and head west, toward the river. This part of the street has nightclubs and restaurants like Mamajuana Café at #247, featuring mostly Hispanic food, but there's also a sushi place, MamaSushi at #237; both draw large crowds on the weekend. Locals complain about the noise emanating from La Marina, a club by the Hudson River that draws celebrities like Jay-Z and Beyoncé. These places are an attraction both for gentrifiers and for middle-class Dominicans who like to return to where their American lives began, a combination of nostalgia and remembering how far they have gone on the road.

I turn around and go back east along Dyckman. After Broadway, I begin passing many low- and medium-priced stores. One that stands out has the familiar masks of comedy and tragedy above the shop window, but they're reversed. The store sells sports hats, and the connection between that and the neon sign outside is unclear. The Chinese owner thought it looked nice, and so there it is. There aren't always explanations for what turns out to be best described as a mere whim.

Entering a Yemeni grocery store, I conclude my trip on a more somber note. The owner, thinking I might be, as he put it, "CIA or FBI," pulls out his driver's license to prove to me that "I am legal," in case I suspect otherwise. This is a reminder that many residents in this metropolis are haunted daily by the prospect of possible arrest and deportation. Others with similar concerns may be found in the Mexican joints along Tenth Avenue that are a harbinger of Inwood's newest and fast-growing group of immigrants.

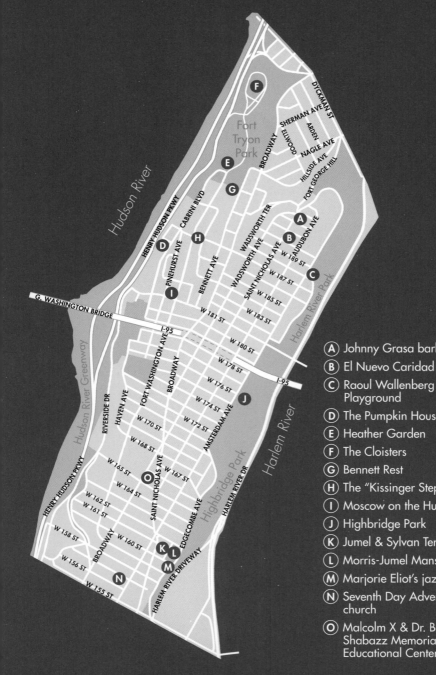

(A) Johnny Grasa barber shop

(B) El Nuevo Caridad

(C) Raoul Wallenberg Playground

(D) The Pumpkin House

(E) Heather Garden

(F) The Cloisters

(G) Bennett Rest

(H) The "Kissinger Steps"

(I) Moscow on the Hudson

(J) Highbridge Park

(K) Jumel & Sylvan Terraces

(L) Morris-Jumel Mansion

(M) Marjorie Eliot's jazz parlor

(N) Seventh Day Adventist church

(O) Malcolm X & Dr. Betty Shabazz Memorial & Educational Center

WASHINGTON HEIGHTS

THIS IS A LARGE, SPRAWLING AREA IN UPPER MANHATTAN bounded on the north by Dyckman Street, the Harlem River on the east, 155th Street on the south, and the Hudson River along the west. Until the early 1900s it was mostly estates and quite rural. But once the subway lines were able to reach it, it became a favorite of developers. Throughout most of the twentieth century, Broadway was a dividing line here, both economically and ethnically. The poorer folks lived east of the avenue and the middle classes predominated on the west side. The white population was mostly Irish and Jewish, with many of the latter consisting of refugees from Germany and elsewhere in Europe. Greeks also moved to the community in the 1950s and 1960s. By the 1960s, the area east of Broadway had become quite Hispanic, most of them Puerto Ricans and, to a lesser extent, Cubans. Soviet Jews arrived in the 1970s, but the major demographic shift in the mid-1970s was the influx of large numbers of Dominicans, who eventually became the largest group. The area east of St. Nicholas Avenue from about 163rd Street south to 155th Street remained a black enclave.

Today, the area is mostly Dominican to the east (the largest such concentration in the United States), with a small community of Orthodox Jews who live around Amsterdam Avenue and Laurel Hill Terrace and are affiliated with Yeshiva University's campus there. The Irish and Jews are mostly gone as distinct ethnic groups, but there are still a few synagogues, churches, and schools to accommodate the few who remain west of Broadway. The major development today is an increase in a young population of gentrifier types who find the western side, dubbed Hudson Heights by realtors, both attractive and convenient. They include Jews, Italians, Irish, Hispanics, Chinese, Koreans, and people of many other backgrounds whose common denominator isn't ethnicity or race, but rather young, hip, and professional. There's also a tiny upscale section that has long been home to professional and entertainment personalities. You'll find it from 155th to 158th Street between Riverside Drive and Riverside Drive West.

The primary commercial thoroughfares are Broadway, St. Nicholas Avenue, and 181st Street. There are no prominent upscale department stores, but there are small versions of them, as well as boutiques, eateries, and taverns, plus a major hospital around 168th Street, New York Presbyterian. For R & R, the main parks are Fort Tryon Park, Riverside Drive, and Highbridge Park, all with stunning views, plus walking and biking paths.

As I begin my walk on Hillside Avenue where it intersects with Fort George Hill, Nagle Avenue, and twenty yards from bustling Dyckman Street, I'm struck by how quickly Hillside becomes residential and very quiet. The same is true for the surrounding small streets—Sickles, Ellwood, Arden, and Thayer Streets, Bogardus Place, and Broadway Terrace, hilly and lined with solid-brick prewar apartment buildings, most of them in good shape.

I turn right off Hillside, onto Broadway where I can make out traces of the past, one of which is the former building of Congregation Ohav Sholaum on Broadway, north of Nagle Avenue. Today, it is home to the New York Child Resource Center, but the Star of David is still visible, high above the entrance, as is the cornerstone that reads, "1950." The names and signs of Irish bars are still present on some of the avenues, though their clientele and fare have changed for the most part because of the large Dominican population now residing here. Inevitably, much has faded into obscurity over the decades. The large bowling alley near Broadway and Sherman Avenue that I frequented as a teenager, Manhattan Lanes, is now a parking garage with not a shred of evidence of its previous life visible from the street.

Along Broadway, I enter the eastern edge of the lower part of Fort Tryon Park at Nagle Avenue and walk along a shaded path lined with large rocks, tall trees surrounded by grass and small bushes that are not as well tended as the well-known upper section, which is home to the Cloisters and offers gorgeous views of the Hudson River and the city. This area is perfectly safe in the daytime, but not at night. This part of Fort Tryon runs along Inwood, but because its main upper part, entered from Fort Washington Avenue on the south, is geographically part of Washington Heights, the park as a whole is not considered part of Inwood.

At Dyckman Street I swing right and complete the circular route I've taken at Hillside, but this time I go up the urban treadmill known as Fort George Hill. Invigorating on a cool day, I climb a street about nine-tenths of a mile beginning on Sherman Avenue and ending at the intersection of St. Nicholas Avenue and Wadsworth Terrace. The Dominicans are the dominant group in this area. People can be seen sitting by the windows, looking out on the street as if it were an entertainment venue. They also include mothers keeping an eye on their children. On almost every block, on a nice day, men are sitting around on folding chairs and stools, playing dominoes, conversing animatedly in rapid-fire Spanish as they mix and deal the smooth red, white, and black tiles. There are bodegas on almost every corner. Run by Dominicans, these have replaced the candy stores of an earlier, mostly Jewish and Irish generation. In a modern-day version of ethnic succession, many of the Hispanic owners are themselves being supplanted by Yemenis. They're different in that they sell fruits, vegetables, and meat, but they also offer candy, soda, small packets of aspirin, toothpaste, and batteries. Men hang out in front of the stores and inside.[7]

Near 193rd Street, I stare at a most unusual barbershop located at 1632 St. Nicholas. Called Johnny Grasa, it has a twelve-foot-high glass display window, including the entrance door, which is framed by a nice wood design. In front of the window are two dark urns, connected by three bright-gold chains attached to golden brass rings. An American flag is on the left side, visible inside the shop. There's a statue of a bald-headed man who, at first glance, looks

One-of-a-kind music-themed barber shop—with instruments.

like he might have been "scalped" by the barber. It turns out to be a Halloween joke, a head that pops up and grins wickedly at whoever's looking.

I walk in and say hello to the barber at the first chair. He turns out to be the owner, Johnny, since that's usually the owner's station. Johnny looks at me a bit suspiciously, wondering what an "Americano" like me is doing here—not surprising, as the clientele in these places is almost exclusively Dominican. But that look is quickly replaced by a broad smile as I tell him that his shop is beautiful. As I've learned, a nice compliment goes a long way when interviewing people.

"I see you've got all these instruments hanging on the wall—a trumpet, a keyboard, a guitar, and in pretty good condition. Why?"

"They're mine. I like to play music; so this way I can look at them when I work." Johnny takes great pride in his place, and while it looks expensive, haircuts are a bargain at only $15. I engage in some banter with the other fellows, and then take my leave.

I see and enter a restaurant on 191st Street and St. Nicholas Avenue in Washington Heights called El Nuevo Caridad. It features photos of the owner, Miguel Montas, with famous ballplayers, mostly New York Mets and Yankees. The Formica tables are laminated with photos of players. Some forty-odd menu offerings—a mix of Spanish, West Indian, and generic food—are named after the players, most of them Hispanic and some of them eternally famous, like retired Giants pitcher Juan Marichal. It reminds me of Larry David's Los Angeles deli, where the sandwiches are identified by the names of famous Hollywood actors and personalities. By eating here, customers get deferred status from the players who have also dined here.

A few blocks south and east I enter Raoul Wallenberg Playground, which runs south on Amsterdam Avenue from 188th Street. Encountering the Park and Recreation Manager, I ask him: "Who was Raoul Wallenberg?" He knows something about him but not much: "He was a man who saved Jews, I think." "Has anyone ever

asked about him?" "Yes, sometimes I get the question, and I'm thinking about doing a history of who he was, like they often do in parks."

There's a real opportunity here. During World War II, some
Jews fleeing the Holocaust were given refuge by the Dominican
Republic, settling in the town of Sosua. Wallenberg, a Swedish dip-
lomat, saved thousands of Jewish lives by issuing them protective
Swedish passports. This commonality could strengthen the bonds
between the Jewish and Dominican communities living in this area
by bringing them together on the theme of helping those in need.
From here I walk south to 181st Street and turn right, heading
past Broadway.

The area from 181st Street north to Fort Tryon Park and west
of Broadway to the river is generally known as Hudson Heights
rather than Washington Heights. It's an invention by realtors designed to give the area cachet. It sounds better by creating an image
of living in a place overlooking a scenic and historic river. In fact,
other business enterprises have long used this approach here, as they
have done elsewhere. For example, the Hudson View restaurant on
the corner of Fort Washington Avenue and 181st Street definitely
doesn't have even a smidgen of a view of the river, and it's unlikely
it ever did unless a person could see through ten brick buildings, but
that's business. You hype what you have.

At Fort Washington Avenue, I swing right and walk up to 187th
Street, where I turn left. There's no shortage of Art Deco buildings
in New York, but the one at 822 W. 187th near Chittenden Avenue
is truly exquisite, from the design on the doors and the exterior to
the intricate markings in the lobby. And don't miss the etched clipper ship on the silver elevator doors. I continue west and turn left
on Chittenden, where I enjoy gorgeous views of the Hudson and the
Palisades of New Jersey. At 16 Chittenden on the corner of 186th
Street, there's a brick private home resting on a steel reinforced cliff
that overlooks the Hudson River, a true *pièce de résistance*. The home
is also known as the Pumpkin House, so named because from the
paths along the Hudson River far below or from boats in the river,

it looks like a jack-o'-lantern when lit up at night, because of where the windows are. Talk about the importance of location!

I can actually see the demographic changes in the population by looking at the stores on 187th between Pinehurst and Fort Washington Avenues. There are ads for art and music workshops, yoga classes, and the like. There's Waterford crystal for sale. Signs in local cafés plead for people to help owners find their lost Yorkies and West Highland terriers. There's a pricey upscale grocery store, Frank's Market. The process is different, however, than in Brooklyn's Bushwick or Greenpoint because the area was always solidly middle class, even upscale. The young professionals moving in now are simply joining an existing older community of a similar socioeconomic level, not really transforming it. Rather, they are bringing in their own tastes and style of life.

At Fort Washington Avenue, I turn left and soon arrive at Fort Tryon Park, one of the city's most beautiful parks. Its appeal can immediately be appreciated upon entering it at 193rd Street and Fort Washington Avenue. There, resplendent in all its glory, is the Heather Garden. I stroll through it and enjoy the 500 or so varieties of shrubs and perennials—-dogwoods, tulips, hibiscus, azaleas, peonies, thistle, and much more. At the beginning of the garden there's a sign:

Let no one say, and
say it to your shame,
That all was beauty
Here, until you came.

A great no-littering exhortation!

The park has the Met Cloisters, a branch of the Metropolitan Museum of Art and home to almost 5,000 works of medieval art in a reproduced medieval stone monastery. The building is actually a reconstruction of five European abbeys, dismantled and shipped to New York City, and then reassembled into a new configuration. It has a very nice restaurant, called New Leaf, and many benches on which to relax, but it's the totality of the place that makes it so special. At every turn, it seems, there are breathtaking vistas of the city on one side and the Hudson River on the other, along the stone walls that line many of the walkways. You can see hills and valleys within the park, huge outcroppings of boulders, tall trees—all of which give the visitor an unparalleled feeling of peace and quiet hard to find in Manhattan.

I exit the park at Fort Washington and head down to 187th Street. This whole area, sometimes called "Frankfurt on the Hudson," was once home to thousands of German Jews, most of whom fled the Nazi regime in the 1930s.[8] One of its most prominent residents was Henry Kissinger, who grew up here and attended George Washington High School. The 132 stone steps at 187th Street near his apartment building on Fort Washington Avenue, known as the "Kissinger Steps," led down to Overlook Terrace, and Henry walked them every day to get to the school, located on Audubon Avenue and still there to this day.

I trip down the stairs to Overlook Terrace and then to Bennett Avenue, where I make a left, walking up to 192nd Street. Have you ever heard of Bennett Rest? Probably not, unless you're a local. It's not a park; it's not a restroom; and it's not a playground. It's situated on Bennett Avenue near 192nd Street and shaped in a semicircle, around which are arranged ten benches where I can sit in the shade beneath a tree or in the sun, close my eyes, and listen to the blue jays and robins serenading me or each other. Behind is a steep six-story rocky incline. Ascend it with caution.

Turning around, I head south on Bennett to 181st Street and make a right. Just beyond Fort Washington I see a shop purveying Russian food. I'm surprised that it's here since it's not really a Russian neighborhood. It's called "Moscow on the Hudson," perhaps after the 1984 film starring Robin Williams, about a Russian circus musician who defects to the United States while visiting there. My conversation with the manager, a young fellow with beautiful black curly hair, is revealing.

"Why is this store here? Are there are Russians living here?"

"Not many, but we have some, especially in the building on the corner. But most of our customers are online and we deliver. They come from all the way down on Gold Street in the Financial District, to the 70s and 80s on the West Side."

"How long have you been here?"

"About sixteen or seventeen years. There used to be two other Russian stores here, but they closed."

"Why?"

"Why? Because whatever they sold for five dollars we sold for three. That's business."

As I survey the place, I see it has hundreds of items for sale—cheeses, meats, vegetables, canned products of all types, and even fresh cakes and pies. In the age of the Internet, location isn't all that important. You can take orders from anywhere, including Europe or Asia, and have them shipped directly from the source, largely eliminating the need to make calls and even trips to distributors or manufacturers.

A main shopping area in this part of the Heights is 181st Street, especially from Broadway east to Audubon Avenue. Here I pass by many affordable stores. One offers a real bargain for men's suits: buy one, get two more for free. Sweaters are $10 apiece, but be warned—they're 100 percent polyester. Outside one of the stores, a Hispanic woman dressed in bright blue sings the praises of Jesus, off-key but sincere-sounding. Whichever way I turn onto St. Nicholas Avenue, I have to carefully thread my way past the merchandise arrayed in almost chaotic fashion along the sidewalks, where Dominican vendors try to tempt me with bargain-basement prices, offering up shoes, dishwashing liquids, shirts, pants, brooms of every description, toys, and so on. The scene is reminiscent of what the Lower East Side's Orchard Street used to look like in the '50s and '60s. And it's but a few blocks east of Hudson Heights, reminding me that the contrasts offered by this city are even sharper because of their close proximity to each other.

Highbridge Park along Amsterdam Avenue, whose main entrance is on 173rd Street, has been around forever. It has a huge swimming pool and an indoor recreation center, but its newest feature is the footbridge, which has been refurbished and reopened to the public, leading across the Harlem River to the Bronx. The footbridge had been closed for decades for safety reasons. In the 1980s, the neighborhoods on both the Manhattan and the Bronx side were crime- and drug-infested areas. As one knowledgeable person told me: "The authorities got tired of people being thrown off the bridge, so they closed it." Today you can walk it in peace, strolling on a red-brick walkway with a herringbone design. Because of its unsavory past, perhaps, the fence along each side is about twelve feet high. The views of the city, both north and south, are really nice. I would see the same views from other bridges with vehicular traffic but I couldn't take in the sights from a car in heavy traffic, especially if I was driving.

On the return walk to the Manhattan side, there's a great direct view of the Art Moderne–style water tower, built in 1934. As I stand there looking at it, I'm reminded of a different time, when I was nineteen. Seeking adventure, I joined a group of friends one evening at the base of the tower and pried away a round, wood-slatted cover on the rocky ground. We descended, about ten of us, via a rope ladder and found ourselves inside an old water tunnel. We walked some fifty blocks, lighting up the tunnel with our flashlights. Seeing a manhole cover, we pushed it up and found ourselves in Mount Morris Park (now renamed Marcus Garvey Park) in the heart of Harlem.

This was not long after the Harlem riots of July 1964, and tensions in the community were running high. No white person in his right mind ventured there at night, but we had let the manhole cover close shut and could not reopen it. All of us were white, and we split up and made our way to the Upper West Side, about a half-mile away, sticking to the shadows and avoiding people. We met up at 122nd Street and Broadway, unharmed and greatly relieved to have made it back to relative safety. In a way, it was a typical Gotham adventure. You do something crazy, flirt with danger, and have a story to tell to your children.

Back in the present, the shortest way back to Amsterdam Avenue from the walkway involves a 97-step climb up a staircase through Highbridge Park—great exercise if you want it. There's also a sculpture garden in the park, with some unusual creations. When I last saw it, these included a gorgeous evening dress with sequined panels and ruffles constructed out of empty potato chip bags, and an unidentified sculpture with flags and hundreds of tiny bells that looked sort of Tibetan. Many New York parks have exhibits like this, which give artists a valuable opportunity to showcase their talents.

South of the park, I head down Amsterdam Avenue for about ten blocks until I reach St. Nicholas Avenue, where I veer left and come to the area surrounding Jumel Terrace, another interesting place to visit. While familiar to many local residents, it's unknown, as I discovered, to most New Yorkers. Tucked away just east of St. Nicholas Avenue, it can be accessed most easily by climbing some stairs between 161st and 160th Streets. I found myself on Sylvan Terrace, a block of old wooden houses in a landmarked historic area. This may account for the fact that the neighborhood in the immediate vicinity remained stable enough during the bad times and was then poised to help gentrification along. It had a core, in other words. The brownstones around here are also well maintained and the tree-lined streets look very good. Today it's racially mixed, and the houses on Sylvan Terrace sell for $1 million each or more. Nearby, the Morris-Jumel Mansion attracts visitors interested in Revolutionary War history and the sites of important events from the period. Nearby, at 555 Edgecombe Avenue by 160th Street, there's an unusual place to hear free jazz on Sunday afternoons. That would be at the home of Marjorie Eliot, in her parlor, Studio 3F. Check the Internet for exact times.

On 157th Street, between Amsterdam Avenue and Broadway, I come upon a Seventh Day Adventist church that I knew had taken over a site where an Orthodox synagogue had previously existed more than a half-century earlier. This happens quite often, but there was a difference here. The Adventists' form of Christianity contains many similarities to Judaism. They take the Bible literally. Thus, they do not work on Saturday, observing it as the Sabbath. Nor do they eat pork. Taking over a synagogue therefore meant something to them. It was a sanctified place. Indeed, as I entered the sanctuary, I saw that much of the original interior had been beautifully preserved—the pews, the windows, even the social hall.

I speak with a Hispanic member who is modestly dressed in a long skirt, just like the Orthodox: "Every Friday night we eat dinner together in the social hall. We don't work on the Sabbath, we don't cook, and we don't buy anything, although we turn on lights and we drive. We follow the Old Testament. Whatever it says, we do. We only eat kosher food—no pork, no shrimp or lobster. We have 200 members, mostly Dominican and a few Puerto Ricans."

"Since you have many Jewish practices, how do you feel about the fact that this was once a synagogue?" I ask.

"Well, we feel a special holiness about this place because it was a synagogue before and many of the customs and laws we have are the same as the Jews. After all, they also observe the Sabbath."

Malcolm X was assassinated in Washington Heights in the Audubon Ballroom, at 166th Street and Broadway. An educational center with an imposing entrance has been created in his memory. Called the Malcolm X and Dr. Betty Shabazz Memorial and Educational Center, it's an interactive museum and an event space. I show up on a weekday at noon, the only visitor besides two French tourists, and speak with someone affiliated with it. "We have some visitors," she says, "but it's not promoted enough. Money has been a problem. And so we're forced to rent it out for straight-up parties—you know, drinking, cocktail dresses, sweet sixteens, you name it. I don't like it. I mean, this is like sacred ground." As a product of the 1960s, I strongly sympathize with her. To those who grew up in this era, the man was an inspiration, a person who overcame great hardship, only to be gunned down in the prime of his life.

I go upstairs and enter the ballroom. Beautiful murals on the walls movingly present Malcolm X's story. It is a somber place, one that invites reflection as you read the highlights of his life and his impact. A statement by Malcolm X under the last known photograph of him, dated February 18, 1965, reads: "I am only facing the facts. And I know that any moment of any day or any night could bring me death." People are always interested in that sort of thing because it makes them feel that now they're in the know, that they are acutely aware of how prophetic his statement was just a few days before his untimely death.

The whole experience of seeing the memorial feels eerie to me because I was waiting for the uptown number 3 bus on that Sunday afternoon, February 21, 1965, along 165th Street, just east of Broadway, when I saw two men racing by me with a crowd of perhaps forty or fifty people in hot pursuit. I instinctively stepped back as far as I could inside a doorway as they went by. Malcolm X was eulogized on February 27th, and Ossie Davis spoke at his funeral before a crowd of about twenty thousand people. He was buried in Ferncliff Cemetery in Hartsdale, New York. Years later, I met one of Malcolm X's daughters on a TV show, and when I told her what I had seen on that fateful day, she questioned me very closely about it. "What did the men look like?" she asked. I answered as best I could. I couldn't have known if the two people I saw actually shot him or were being chased for some other reason. Today, it is widely agreed that the perpetrators were supporters of Elijah Muhammad who were angry with Malcolm X for having broken with their leader.[9] For many, it seems somewhat unimportant to know which people or factions gunned him down. That knowledge has been overwhelmed by the tragedy that a man who might have united blacks and whites never got a chance to change or at least deeply affect the course of history.[10]

HAMILTON HEIGHTS

MANHATTANVILLE

MORNINGSIDE HEIGHTS

CENTRAL HARLEM

EAST HARLEM

Hudson River

W 155 ST
W 153 ST
W 154 ST
W 150 ST
W 151 ST
RIVERSIDE DR
W 149 ST
AMSTERDAM AVE
ST. NICHOLAS AVE
ST. NICHOLAS PL
W 147 ST
BROADWAY
W 145 ST
EDGECOMBE AVE
W 143 ST
W 141 ST
CONVENT AVE
HAMILTON TER
HAMILTON PL
ST. NICHOLAS AVE
W 139 ST
HENRY HUDSON PKWY
W 137 ST
W 135 ST
St. Nicholas Park
EDGECOMBE AVE

Riverbank
State Park

(A) City Tabernacle Seventh
Day Adventist Church

(B) Friendship Garden (Bette Midler)

(C) Harlem Public

(D) The Hand Pulled Noodle

(E) Jumbo Pizza & Coffee Shop

(F) Mural of Langston Hughes,
Duke Ellington, & Billy Strayhorn

(G) Our Lady of Lourdes Church

(H) City College of New York

(I) Riverbank State Park

(J) Former home of James Bailey of
Barnum & Bailey Circus fame

(K) Apartment building where
Thurgood Marshall, W.E.B. Du Bois,
Roy Wilkins and other black
luminaries once lived

HAMILTON HEIGHTS

THE BOUNDARIES OF THIS UPPER MANHATTAN COMMUNITY located within West Harlem are 155th Street on the north, Edgecombe Avenue on the east, 135th Street on the south, and the Hudson River on the west. It's named after Alexander Hamilton, who lived here in a home known as Hamilton Grange, now relocated to 141st Street between Convent and St. Nicholas Avenues. From the end of the nineteenth century until the 1930s and 1940s, it was a largely white area. It then began to attract more black residents and remained a black area through the 1960s and 1970s, when many middle-class blacks lived in the brownstones that make up a good part of the housing stock. Today, the population is predominantly Dominican, residing primarily west of Amsterdam Avenue. The remaining black population is east of Amsterdam.

A major change has been added to this mix in the past eleven years, as young, mostly white students, artists, musicians, and even some young families have moved to the area. They live scattered throughout the area, along the side streets east and west of Broadway, the commercial thoroughfare in the area along with Amsterdam Avenue. Commercially, it's a hodgepodge of Hispanic-run groceries, restaurants, clothing stores, and the like, interspersed with boutiques, wine bars, pubs, and neutral places like AT&T outlets, fast-food places, veterinarian offices, and pharmacies. Glass/metal apartment boxes are being built more frequently in the last several years, and the trend is toward gentrification. One major presence in the neighborhood is Riverbank State Park on 145th Street and Riverside Drive, which sort of unifies the neighborhood. The Drive is a popular place for everyone, and its constant pedestrian traffic makes it a fairly safe place for all. Hamilton Heights is also home to City College of New York.

A well-known subsection is Sugar Hill, which extends roughly from 145th to 155th Street and from St. Nicholas to Edgecombe Avenues. Called "Sugar Hill" to emphasize the "sweet life" that existed there, it has been the subject of books, films, and songs and has many beautiful homes. Many well-known and wealthy African Americans lived there at one time or another, including W.E.B. Du Bois, Cab Calloway, Duke Ellington, and Thurgood Marshall. It's worth noting that in recent years people have begun referring to Hamilton Heights, Manhattanville, and even Morningside Heights, as part of west, or greater, Harlem.[11]

If you thought that gentrification in these parts is only occurring in Central Harlem or in Hudson Heights, think again because it's definitely happening here, in Hamilton Heights. Passing by a vest-pocket park near 147th Street, I see a group of white and black mothers with their pricey carriages, supervising their toddlers. Don, a tall and fit black man, is originally from Connecticut. He's walking his cute Pomeranian along Riverside Drive in the 140s and is an IT entrepreneur who works downtown. There seems to be a dearth of pit bulls here in contrast to what it was like fifteen years ago, when I walked up the Drive. Down-to-earth, he talks enthusiastically about his neighborhood: "This area's great. It's quiet and safe. There's affordable housing, but a lot of it is market rate and quite expensive. Apartments near me, by 157th Street, are going for 1.7 million. There's all sorts of pubs and restaurants opening up here. Entire blocks are changing before you know it, store rents are going up. Movies are made here all the time now in these streets."

A walk along 147th Street between the Drive and Broadway provides ample evidence of what has transpired. Almost every brownstone is well tended. Potted plants and gardens are beautifully arranged in front of most homes, a good example being #628. A red brick house with inviting bay windows, it has a wrought-iron terrace and an array of chrysanthemums, hydrangeas, hibiscus, coleus, impatiens, and roses that look like they belong in a *House & Garden* photo spread. The entire row of houses ascends, almost romantically, up a steep hill. The detailing around the cornices and doorways is often exquisite. One has a coffered checkerboard pattern on the second floor, painted in rainbow colors. I ask two young white males about the area and they confirm the dramatic change, telling me that everything's being brought in—"shops, new apartment buildings on Broadway, and dog parks" in preparation for the expected wave of well-heeled residents.

One of the many attractive side streets both east and west of Broadway is 150th Street. As I walk east toward Amsterdam Avenue, I take a look at the pink marble facade of the City Tabernacle Seventh Day Adventist Church with a nice wooden entranceway. There's a large ornate archway over it with intricate designs of leaves and branches. Above that the rose window is closed off, and instead of the stained glass there's a camera—a true sign of the changing times, notwithstanding the eternal nature of religion. There are Corinthian columns and a tiled roof as well, along with stained glass windows.

Farther down are some beautiful brownstones and limestone homes in various styles, well preserved and well tended. And near Amsterdam there's a surely one-of-a-kind community garden, dubbed the Friendship Garden, founded by Bette Midler and funded by the New York Restoration Project and also by a grant from the Broadway musical *Wicked*. It has hanging impatiens, shrubs, tomato plants, benches to sit on, tables, and a nice cobblestone walkway. But it's the theme that draws you in. Built into the wrought-iron gate are two images of witches—one dressed in white, the other in black—because *Wicked* is a play about the Wizard of Oz. All of the lampposts in the garden have the word OZ at the top. The painting on the garden wall features the field of poppies associated with *The Wizard of Oz*. It was certainly creative thinking to approach the play's producers and offer them free advertising in exchange for some funding.

The Wizard of Oz lives—"far from" the madding crowd.

The building next to the garden was once home to the Joseph Loth Fair & Square Ribbon Factory, established in 1893 and running a full block between 150th and 151st Streets on Amsterdam Avenue. If you stand next to the garden on 150th Street, you can see the original, very weathered sign reading "Fair & Square" on the back of the building. It's a reminder that this was once a manufacturing town. The red-brick building still stands and now houses a charter school.

One of the best-known pubs around here with good food is Harlem Public at 3612 Broadway, near 149th Street, with a hipster-type ambience that nevertheless attracts people of all ages and is crowded even during off-hours. More unusual is a small place at 3600 called the Hand-Pulled Noodle. "Come watch us pull your noodle, slap your ribbon, and chop your ding-ding," reads the signboard outside the place. It sounds somewhat obscene, perhaps, but it's actually an insider description of how their noodles are made, and I'm able to watch how the kitchen workers do this. The ding ding noodles are not the usual variety of noodles, as they are folded several times and chopped into a knot. They're native to the northwest Chinese province of Xinjiang. Regular noodles and dumplings are also available. The wallpaper features Chinese newspapers and the seating is simple, with red metal stools along wooden counters. The place is packed both at lunch and in the evening, with the line out the door. And if you're not in the mood to wait, they even deliver. A young bearded man eating there gives me his take on the neighborhood: "I'm a designer and I've been living here for three months because the rents are cheap. I got a 400-square-foot two-bedroom for $1,800 a month, but I can tell you if you pay any less it gets really grim— bad building, sketchy laundry situation. This is true of everything from 135th to Inwood in the 200s, although up there it's often not good. And no matter where you live up here it's gonna be noisy because this part of town is heavily Dominican, but you can live with that."

Standing at 147th Street and Broadway, I see a sign across the street near 148th for Jumbo Pizza and Coffee Shop at 3954 Broadway. Does "jumbo" really mean giant slices? Is jumbo necessarily good? Yes on both counts, it turns out. The slices are gigantic (and fresh) and the taste is outstanding, according to a sampling of customers with whom I spoke. And the price is right, $2.25 a slice. Plus, it's clean and attractive-looking. I chat with Theo, the young owner of Greek heritage, who tells me he opened the place two years ago. He was following in his father's footsteps, who owned pizza shops in upper Manhattan for many years: "We're doing very well. We have the local market, but we also do orders from as far away as Columbia University. The City College basketball team also orders from us. And we have the coffee shop because then it's a complete A to Z restaurant." Places like this are what make a neighborhood gel in its earlier stages, when there's a mix of students and artsy types. Then, when and if it becomes upscale, they morph into more expensive eateries or they sell it to someone else who can do that. And sometimes, if they are renting the space, rent increases may drive them out. But until then, they stand out, they become hangouts, and they serve good food at low prices.

On the south side of 142nd Street between Hamilton Place and Amsterdam Avenue, there's a mural depicting important figures in black history—Langston Hughes, ostensibly reading his poetry from a sheet of white paper; a portrait of the bandleader and composer Duke Ellington; Billy Strayhorn, who collaborated with Ellington for about thirty years; and an unidentified woman holding some books. The mural's lead artist was Frank Parga, a well-known painter who has done murals throughout the city. Cross the street and on the next block at 467 W. 142nd Street, you'll see Our Lady of Lourdes Church, a fine example of Victorian Gothic architecture, built around 1903.

The Brotherhood/Sister Sol is located at W. 143rd Street and is an excellent example of the many community organizations that exist throughout New York. Funded by a variety of foundations and corporations, its dedicated staff provides a home away from home for kids who come from broken families, providing love and comfort. But it also has many programs that help youngsters grow academically and professionally. Those who benefit from its services come mostly from Harlem and range in age from seven to twenty-seven. It's a true success story, with 88 percent of the youngsters graduating from high school and 85 percent admitted to college. I speak with Nando Rodriguez, the Environmental Program Coordinator, who gives me a more personal portrait of what the group does.

"We run all sorts of activities for the children. We recently took a group of kids to Brazil for a month. And they prepared for six months before they went. We think of slavery as a US thing. But now they learn it existed in Brazil too. It would normally cost about $5,000 to take someone there, but for them it's free. We have art projects here. They take a picture of themselves and then create a self-portrait. We have taken teenage gang members and turned them into college grads."

"What about the garden? It looks like there's a lot happening here."

"There is. We grow all sorts of stuff and they learn that things can grow here just like they do on a farm and just like rich suburban residents do in their gardens. And they learn responsibility by working on projects. We have a rock-climbing wall, turtles and fish, and a waterfall. We teach them about hydroponics. The garden is named in memory of Frank White, who many years ago chased gang members from the block who wanted to take it over. Tragically, he was shot to death in a drive-by." This last comment illustrates how attempts to change the dynamics of a community in an area like this have faced incredible challenges. Those who reside here lived with danger every day in years past, and there are still pockets of crime.

The area between 144th and 141st Streets contains some of Hamilton Heights' prettiest side streets, with brownstones, limestones, and row houses of every description. Among the nicest are the Flemish and Tudor homes between 142nd and 145th Streets on Convent Avenue. They're right near City College of New York, and some of them are home to faculty members.

From 141st to 137th Street are the iconic buildings of City College's eleven-block campus. It's a Gothic masterpiece made of Manhattan dark gray schist, its buildings adorned with terracotta accents. It has recently been refaced and restored to its former glory. In front of the buildings on the right side there's a quad where students lie on the grass, enjoy lunch, and generally hang out. By coincidence, I spot the former Secretary of State Colin Powell having, as I learn, an impromptu conversation with some students who have stopped him just to talk. In 2013, the school inaugurated the Colin Powell School for Civic and Global Leadership, and he visits there whenever he can. As I walk through the campus I listen to the students as they chat animatedly with each other. The school is today considered an excellent academic institution and its student body includes many people who cannot afford private college tuition and who consider City College to be their Harvard. They represent 160 nationalities, speaking ninety languages. The college has also produced ten Nobel laureates.

This also happens to be the college where I have taught for forty-five years. Way back in 1973, when I first arrived, I found the college to be a polarized place. One indication of this was seating patterns in the school cafeteria. The tables were largely segregated, with Asian, white, Hispanic, and black students eating in separate groups. Today, it's the opposite. Students sit together and tensions are much less in evidence, though there are occasional flare-ups.

At 135th Street, I turn right and head over to Riverside Drive, turning right again to walk the drive along a beautiful promenade that runs in front of Riverside Park. People are sitting on park benches eating, reading, or people-watching, just as they do all along the Drive, from 72nd street all the way to 125th street. A half-mile north, I see the entrance to Riverbank State Park, located at 145th Street. It's one of the few parks run by the state and not the city. Unlike city parks, dogs are not allowed, but other than that it's a marvelous facility. It features an Olympic-size pool and a rink for both roller and ice skating, depending on the season. There's swimming all year round with classes and lessons, as well as a kayaking program. Cultural programs include art, band, guitar, keyboard, songwriting, ballet, dance, belly dancing, chess, quilting, and sewing classes. There's also a special sports program for "little athletes" that includes ice skating and ice hockey. In addition to all this, there's an 800-seat cultural theater for concerts and other performances, a 2,500-seat athletic complex, docking facilities for boats, playgrounds, and picnic areas. In short, it's a state-of-the-art facility with lots to do that serves an area made up of people from every socioeconomic level.

As I leave the park and continue my walk up the Drive, an elderly woman catches my eye. She's from Haiti, it turns out, and loves the neighborhood. "I'm a niece of former Haitian President Magliore and I've lived here a long time and things are really getting better. More middle-class and rich people are moving in and it's safer. But I worry about what will happen to the poor people." It's a legitimate concern. Hamilton Heights is part of a long swath of a low-income, predominantly Hispanic area stretching from W. 135th Street, starting in West Harlem, through Washington Heights, and then Inwood, a length of ninety blocks. What will happen to these people as the area becomes more upscale? The rents will rise way beyond what people can afford, as will prices in the local stores. Where will those displaced go? Will they only find living quarters in less-safe areas or in communities out in, say, Suffolk County, Long Island, where they'll be far away from the jobs they now have? Much will depend on the city's housing policies and the degree to which they are implemented.

At 147th Street, I turn right and go up a steep hill to the Sugar Hill area. If you want to see how verdant and lush some of the backyards are here, you need only stand on the eastern side of Convent

Avenue between 146th and 147th Streets and look at those that are visible from that vantage point. All manner of flora and fauna grow there, and people have flower boxes, latticed fences, soft electric globes to light up the evening, benches, and picnic tables. Black squirrels scamper up and down the trees—a whole life going on here that isn't visible from the sidewalks. I turn right from Convent at 147th Street toward St. Nicholas Avenue, and find myself passing what is one of the best examples of the brownstones that prevail here, along with row houses. The wooden doors are polished to a high sheen; the windows are crystal clear. Henri Fouchaux, perhaps the most outstanding architect in this part of Harlem, designed this graceful home at number 406 in 1898, and there are others of comparable quality on the block.

Strolling the streets in general can provide interesting opportunities for remembering history. For instance, on Convent Avenue and 150th Street, I see a large, crudely scrawled epitaph of sorts along the side wall of a tenement harking back thirty years or so. It reads: "Is Reagan wacker than crack?"—clearly referring to the crack epidemic of the '80s that ravaged communities up here and elsewhere in the city. And someone has updated it, crossing out "is" and replacing it with "was," almost as though they were doing an editing job! Across the street, catty-corner, there's a parking garage (457–459 150th Street) with two carved, white-painted heads of horses in front of it, denoting that it was once a horse stable. That would be from the early 1900s, and the horses were probably used for transport—hansom cabs and the like. Thus, the garage continues the tradition, but with autos replacing horses.

Two blocks east on 150th Street and in front of 10 St. Nicholas Place, I find myself staring at the magnificent home of James Bailey, a member of the dynamic Barnum & Bailey Circus duo. Completed in 1888, it was landmarked in 1980. Before it was purchased privately in 2011 and renovated, it had been, for a while, a funeral parlor, as I knew from driving past it many times. It's a one-of-a-kind, limestone, Victorian-style castle, with gables, turrets,

James Bailey's glorious mansion of Barnum & Bailey fame.

a tower, and sixty-six windows, a number of them made of stained glass. The interior had deteriorated over the years but is now being refurbished.

Outside the home I chat with Roy, a sixty-eight-year-old black man who was born and raised in this area. Now retired, but apparently in great shape, he's an avid singles tennis player, a sport I love and play: "Hey, what are you doing with these two tennis rackets?" "I just came from the Jungle [the Frederick Johnson Playground] near Seventh Avenue [Adam Clayton Powell Boulevard] close to 151st Street. Althea Gibson, Arthur Ashe played there. So did James Blake, the fella the cops threw down and mistreated the other week. They got rubber surfaces, which are good on your knees." Blake is a retired tennis star who was roughed up by a cop in 2015. In an unusual turn of events, he rejected a financial settlement for his complaint. Instead he requested that the police department establish a fellowship in his name as part of the agency that looks into cases of alleged police misconduct, and the department agreed to do so.

Roy invites me to play with him, an offer I accept, and we agree to meet. He was a retail salesman and graduated from a university in Virginia. The encounter demonstrates once again how easy it is to build rapport with people if you find something you have in common with them. He also takes pride in the fact that James Bailey lived in the neighborhood he calls home. Such homes and their history are part of what we mean when we say a community has character.

And that's equally true of the now somewhat faded structure at 409 Edgecombe Avenue at the corner of 155th Street. It's a thirteen-story neo-Georgian apartment building that was once quite nice, perhaps in the early twentieth century. Thurgood Marshall, W.E.B. Du Bois, Roy Wilkins, and other prominent African Americans lived here at various times, and the lobby has small photos of Marshall and Du Bois. It always had panoramic views of Harlem and the Bronx, including Yankee Stadium and the now gone Polo Grounds from the building. Inside, the elevators still have the old-fashioned gold dials that indicate what floor you're on. As I leave the building, I gaze down and across at the panoramic eastern view from Edgecombe of most of Harlem. It's a splendid end to a perfect day.

Ⓐ West Harlem Piers Waterfront Park
Ⓑ Dinosaur Barbeque
Ⓒ Cotton Club
Ⓓ Sweets Building
Ⓔ Mink Building

Hudson River

HENRY HUDSON PKWY
12TH AVE
RIVERSIDE DR

Ⓐ

W 135 ST

W 133 ST

W 132 ST

W 134 ST

Ⓑ

W 131 ST

BROADWAY

OLD BROADWAY

AMSTERDAM AVE

CONVENT AVE

Ⓒ

W 130 ST

W 125 ST

W 129 ST

OLD BROADWAY

W 130 ST

ST. NICHOLAS TER

W 126 ST

W 129 ST

CONVENT AVE

Ⓔ W 128 ST

Ⓓ

W 127 ST

MARTIN LUTHER KING BLVD

MORNINGSIDE AVE

W 126 ST

St. Nicholas Park

ST. NICHOLAS AVE

MANHATTANVILLE

THE BOUNDARIES OF MANHATTANVILLE ARE A BIT UNCLEAR. Depending on which agency, community board, or map you consult, they can overlap with Morningside Heights or even Central Harlem. For purposes of this discussion, which is to help the walker navigate the streets and neighborhood, they are defined as 135th Street on the north, St. Nicholas Avenue on the east, 125th Street on the south, and the Hudson River on the west. Such decisions are made here by observing it firsthand on the ground and determining, by what's there, how it can best be characterized.

West of Broadway, I find myself in an industrial and commercial area, several residential complexes, along with university buildings (both Columbia and CUNY). East of Broadway is more or less residential. The main shopping thoroughfares are Amsterdam and St. Nicholas Avenues, and 125th Street. This section, which was once home to factories, is now beginning to slowly gentrify, and many college students live here. Ethnically, the community is both Hispanic and black. There are many churches, both large and small, and a synagogue, established in 1911 and still functioning, on one-block-long Old Broadway.

There's a riverfront bike path entrance at 135th Street along the Hudson River adjacent to a relatively new and little-known park, the West Harlem Piers Waterfront Park, which is situated at about the same level as the river. I reach it by heading one long block west on 133rd Street from Broadway toward the river. Extending along Twelfth Avenue underneath the Riverside Drive viaduct, down to 125th Street, it has terrific views along the shoreline. I walk down Twelfth from 135th to 125th streets. The view of the Hudson River to the west and the New Jersey skyline is beautiful, especially when framed against the setting sun. I pass some nightclubs/cafes/beer gardens crowded with young people partying and drinking, followed by a large Fairway supermarket at 133rd Street. The avenue and the side streets leading up to Broadway become more industrial at 132nd Street. The large trestle above the street resembles something made from an old erector set. It looks very spooky and ethereal at night; as you walk along the cobbled road beneath your feet, you might find yourself glancing over your shoulder every few minutes. Broadway, between 135th and 125th Streets, is also deserted at night. It's lined with old buildings that were once factories and serve today as inexpensive office buildings, warehouses, or places for college offices.

Standing by the river, near 125th Street, I realize that when my parents took me to the old Palisades Amusement Park in New Jersey, we took a ferry from this spot. It was a reasonable alternative to faraway Coney Island. It was a fun place, made even more famous by a jingle whose first two stanzas were:

Palisades has the rides
Palisades has the fun
Come on over

Shows and dancing are free
So's the parking, so gee
Come on over

Anyone who grew up in mid-twentieth-century Gotham will remember Palisades Park with fondness. For me, however, the enduring memory was my father giving me some change to buy him a cup of beer. I was six years old, and the outraged vendor yelled at me: "Tell your dad to come here! Right now!" I got him and the man said: "You've got some nerve telling your little kid to buy a beer. It's against the law." To which my dad retorted: "I'm from Europe. Over there any little boy can buy a beer." "Oh yeah? Well, mister, you're in America now. Get used to it!" I never forgot this incident, one that I recall as having been bewildering to me. When I was a little kid, my father was the ultimate boss to me. But the man in charge of the beer was also an authority figure. I knew that because my father simply said, "Okay," and shortly afterward we went home. And I continued to enjoy beer at home when, on occasion, he'd pour me a glass.

Near 125th Street, a giant project is under way, with Columbia University constructing a complex of buildings that will likely bring much more life and energy to this little-known part of town. This is not to say that nothing is happening here now. There's the Dinosaur Barbeque on 125th Street, near the river, a favorite of both students and young families, as well as the Cotton Club, which is an attempt to connect visitors to the long-defunct Cotton Club that was located at 142nd Street and Lenox Avenue from the mid-1920s until 1935. Many celebrities headlined at the original establishment, including Billie Holiday, Cab Calloway, Fats Waller, Louis Armstrong, and Count Basie. At the new location there is a nightclub catering mostly to groups, and offering blues, jazz, swing, and a gospel brunch. It has a full-sized band, and if you close your eyes, you can imagine that you've gone back to the old days.

I turn around at 125rd Street and retrace my steps along Twelfth Avenue back to 133rd Street, where I make a right and walk two blocks over to Amsterdam Avenue. Turning left, I go two blocks and turn right onto 135th Street, continuing past Convent Avenue to where it dead-ends at St. Nicholas Terrace and make another right. Readers familiar with what City College of New York used to look like would probably be shocked to see it today. Sure, the north campus still has the emblematic Gothic buildings, like Shepard Hall, but the south campus is another story. I stroll down to 130th Street, marveling along the way at the spanking-new glass-and-steel towers that house the School of Architecture, named after Bernard and Anne Spitzer, former New York Governor Eliot Spitzer's parents. I pass some science research buildings and then, lo and behold, a residence for students at the college. Actually, it's been there for some

SAYVILLE LIBRARY

A former Harlem brewery—the Mink Building.

years, but most people I speak with who went to City or know the place are unaware of its existence.

I turn right at 130th and walk up and down the streets from 130th to 126th Street. The area west from Convent Avenue to Amsterdam Avenue and from about 125th to 131st Street was once a central location for factories and related industries. There was the Taystee Bakery, the Horton Pilsener Brewery, and even a candy research lab housed in the Sweets Building at 127th Street. Today this little neighborhood is being repackaged and re-imagined as the Manhattanville Factory District. Like the Cotton Club, it tries to link the present to a nostalgic past. The brewery was in the Mink Building, on Amsterdam, from 126th to 128th Street, so named because in the 1940s, long after the brewery closed, it became a winter storage facility for fur coats. The imposing red-brick structure still stands, and is now home to offices.

I chat with Jason, a community organizer walking down 126th Street, who sheds more light on this topic: "Columbia has donated millions of dollars to the community for various projects, and that's good, but I still worry about how the poorer folks will be able to pay the price for living here. A Chinese developer has bought one of the factories and plans to turn it into a luxury hotel. In a couple of years I certainly won't be able to afford this area the way things are going."

This neighborhood is clearly a work in progress, as there a few NYCHA housing projects like the Manhattanville and Grant Houses. But, as is always the case in the city, they will remain and developers will build around them. If you walk through the district, its potential is readily apparent. It's near a few subway lines, there's two-way 125th Street, Columbia is investing heavily, and private developers are getting involved as well. Ten years from now, it will probably have gone from gritty to chic, just like areas farther east in Central Harlem that were once seen as undesirable investments.

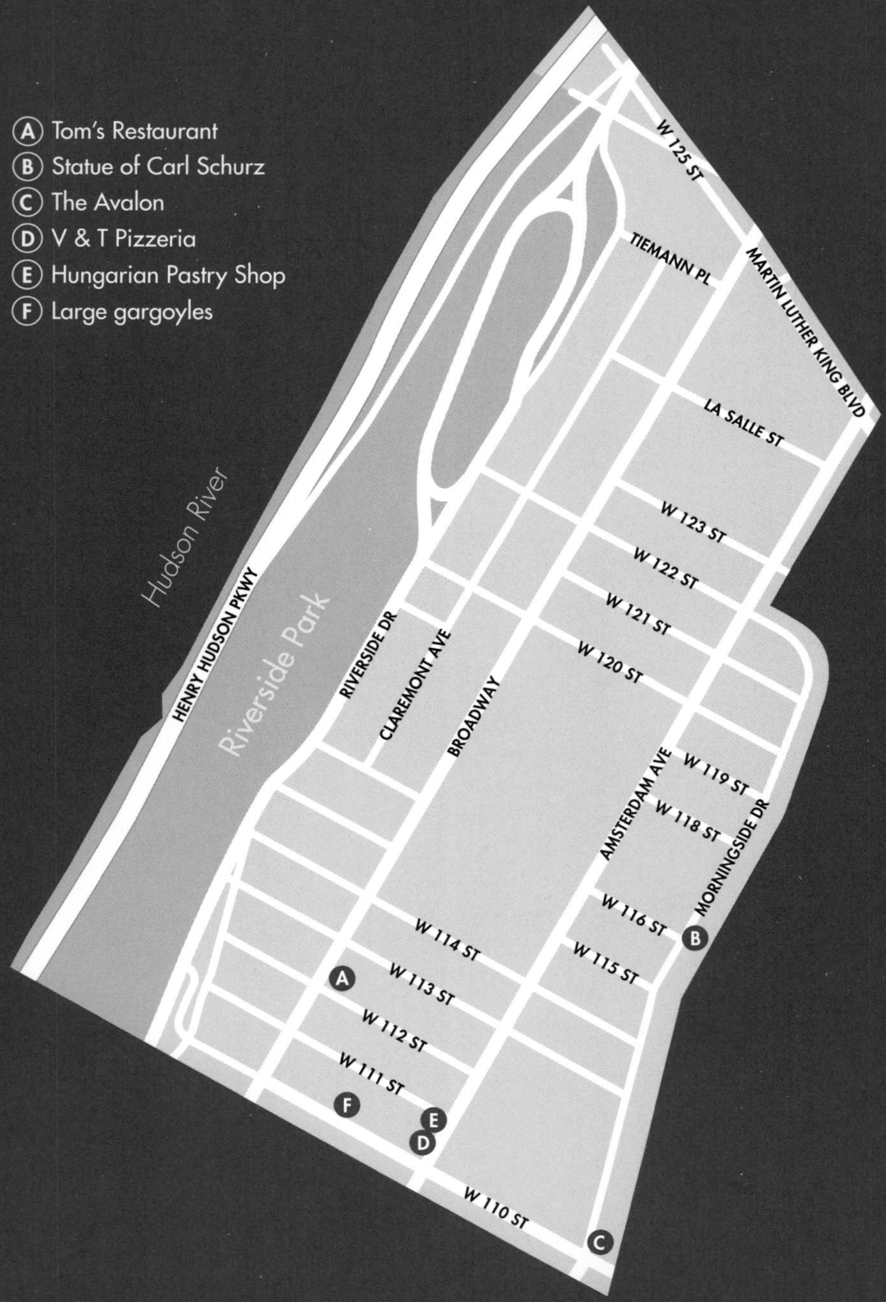

A Tom's Restaurant
B Statue of Carl Schurz
C The Avalon
D V & T Pizzeria
E Hungarian Pastry Shop
F Large gargoyles

Hudson River

HENRY HUDSON PKWY

Riverside Park

RIVERSIDE DR

CLAREMONT AVE

BROADWAY

AMSTERDAM AVE

MORNINGSIDE DR

MARTIN LUTHER KING BLVD

W 125 ST

TIEMANN PL

LA SALLE ST

W 123 ST

W 122 ST

W 121 ST

W 120 ST

W 119 ST

W 118 ST

W 116 ST

W 115 ST

W 114 ST

W 113 ST

W 112 ST

W 111 ST

W 110 ST

MORNINGSIDE HEIGHTS

THE BOUNDARIES OF MORNINGSIDE HEIGHTS are 125th Street on the north, Morningside Drive and Amsterdam Avenue on the east, 110th Street on the south, and the Hudson River on the west. The main commercial thoroughfares are, first, Broadway and, then, portions of Amsterdam Avenue.

Columbia University dominates this neighborhood. Many of the residential buildings are owned by the university and dedicated to housing for Columbia's students, faculty, and staff and, of course, there's the campus itself with many places of interest. In addition, there's the Riverside Church, Grant's Tomb, the Cathedral of St. John the Divine, Union Theological Seminary, Jewish Theological Seminary, Bank Street College of Education, Manhattan School of Music, and many other well-known tourist sites.

This area was the site of several battles during the Revolutionary era. It became urbanized in the early twentieth century when middle-class people, attracted by its many elevator buildings and attractive row houses, settled here. By the mid-1950s, however, Morningside Heights had declined, as many buildings became rundown single-room occupancy (SRO) residences. Having grown up five blocks from there, on 105th Street, I witnessed this turnaround as a child and remember how some of the side streets were considered dangerous after sundown. This is no longer true today, as the neighborhood is considered quite safe, day or night.

One of the most recognizable landmarks here is Tom's Restaurant at 2880 Broadway, on the northeast corner of 112th Street, which has been serving the community, especially Columbia students, for more than seventy years. The facade was featured on the television sitcom *Seinfeld* and is synonymous with the show because the sign appeared in so many episodes. In reality, only the exterior was displayed. The interior of the fictional Monk's Café was filmed on a set in the NBC studio in California. The name of that restaurant was inspired by a poster of the great jazz musician Thelonious Monk that hung in the office where Jerry Seinfeld and Larry David were creating their episodes.

Many of the side streets, especially those between Amsterdam and Riverside Drive from 111th to 114th Street, as well as those along the Drive, are worth seeing as the buildings are often one-of-a-kind and visually interesting. Riverside Park also has much to offer on the upper and lower levels, both recreationally and in terms of the buildings that line it from 110th Street to 123rd. And for a change of pace, simply walk through the Columbia University campus, with its many historic buildings and pleasant walkways.

Going south from 125th Street along Amsterdam Avenue, the first two blocks are sort of a transition from grittier Manhattanville to established Morningside Heights. As I walk uphill I observe the usual bodegas, takeout joints, and barbershops on the right and the NYCHA Grant Houses, whose residents frequent these stores, on the left. But just before 123rd Street I notice what at first glance looks like an inexpensive Chinese takeout joint called West Place, at #1288. The food *is* reasonably priced, but it's the decor inside that captures my attention. There are beautiful photos of the menu items on the walls, the tables are clean, and the chairs are made of polished wood with an attractive back. Large framed photos of Chinese landscapes add to the charm of this eatery. The clientele consists of what seem to be Columbia students—no surprise, since the university campus begins at 123rd Street.

As I speak with the women taking orders, I learn that this spruced-up place had made a decision to reach out to the well-heeled students and that the strategy has worked. Next door, at #1280, there's a much fancier Asian-fusion Nikko Hibachi Asian Fusion Grill restaurant. From there on, as I walk down to 110th Street, it's a typical middle-class neighborhood that most clearly resembles the adjacent Upper West Side. The structures are well maintained, and some of the buildings have doormen.

At 122nd Street, the beginning of Morningside Drive extends southward to 110th Street, with Morningside Park on the left. The buildings here are older, usually between six and nine stories, and they're mostly owned by Columbia and reserved for university faculty, staff, and, students. Given Columbia's overwhelming presence here residentially, you could call this entire area "Columbia Heights." The buildings are clean and nice on the inside with rugs, paintings on the walls, and chandeliers. Some even have plush leather chairs in the lobby. The neighborhood has an excellent panoramic view of Central Harlem. When I was a kid, my dad once chased a mugger into the park, a dangerous move, but he was simply reacting instinctively. Someone was in danger and needed help.

At 116th Street and Morningside Drive, on the eastern side of the street, there's a bronze statue of Carl Schurz, hat in hand, and described as "a defender of liberty." Indeed, he was, certainly as a US Senator from Missouri who opposed slavery. He lived in New York City for many years and wrote editorials for *Harper's Weekly* opposing imperialism. One could do a very interesting history of the city simply by writing about the lives of the people who are immortalized in statues. Generally speaking, the entire walk down Morningside Drive is relaxing and peaceful, away from the hubbub of Amsterdam and Broadway. As Bob, an acupuncturist wheeling his baby, tells me: "This is a great place to live in—convenient, safe, friendly, and still affordable. I love it. You're near everything."

In a sense, the Avalon, located at One Morningside Drive, on 110th Street, where Morningside morphs into Columbus Avenue, perfectly illustrates the pros and cons of living in a Manhattan neighborhood. It's a large, fairly new apartment building, a gleaming tower of twenty-first-century living. There's a concierge, a fitness center, indoor parking, nice-looking apartments, expansive views, and no roaches or other pests. It's convenient, with subway service and easy-to-flag-down cabs, good restaurants nearby, and

What's this U.S. senator from Missouri doing here in New York?

Morningside Park, with its nice paths and playgrounds. And it's fairly safe.

And yet this is by no means a perfect situation, as I learn from the residents. They lament the absence of balconies and the presence of some loud canines residing in the building. And the market-rate apartments aren't cheap. Depending on the features you choose, rentals range from about $3,000 and up for a studio to $7,000 and more for a three-bedroom apartment. But their problems mostly stem from their surroundings. Several hospitals are nearby, which means loud sirens from ambulances at all hours. There are homeless people on the block who, while not aggressive, can be loud and boisterous at times. And there are even occasional shootings and muggings in the area east of the building. The truth is, these are the usual pros and cons of city life, and urban residents have to decide if it's worth it.

I head west on 110th Street, where my next stop is the venerable V & T Pizzeria, which has been at Amsterdam between 110th and 111th Streets for some forty years. Its pizza is considered quite good. I meet Frank Vela (the titular "V"). Mr. "T" is gone, but there's another partner, an Albanian man named Leka Gjolaj. This is no accident, as Albanians are today prominently involved in New York's pizza industry, and in every borough. "What's your secret?" I ask Frank. "How come so many people like your pizza?"

"It's the sauce, which comes from California. And we really make our own dough. Plus, we have New York water," he tells me. "People are just addicted to the food. Also, today the area's much better." Frank sees himself as a community resource and provider: "We've served food over the years to Columbia, St. John the Divine, and St. Luke's." It's this kind of larger self-perception that makes the long hours and hard work of running a retail store worthwhile. He's a very genial seventy-six-year-old man with thick, flowing gray-white hair, dressed casually and very at home in his surroundings. I tell him I'm writing a book about Manhattan and he says: "Really? I wanna write a book. Can you tell me how it's done?" This is not the first time I've been asked that question. I look at him and think that maybe he has an interesting story to tell and that perhaps he could fulfill the second requirement of successful book writing—an interesting *way* of telling his story. I ask him to describe something interesting that happened to him. Frank does not disappoint.

"My father came to the US from Naples in 1939. He was a barber, but he didn't enjoy cutting people's hair because he felt it was beneath him. So one day he dressed to the nines and went to the World's Fair. There he met a man from Italy who said to him, 'I'm a businessman and I'm looking for someone to promote my business. You're in America a little while already so maybe you can help me.' So my dad, who spoke four languages, helped him. The man's name was Giovanni Buitoni, the maker of Buitoni sauce and spaghetti. Here's the climax to the story: My father said to him, 'You have to open a restaurant in New York.' He found a place on Broadway in Times Square. The space was maybe thirty feet wide. And together with this engineer, my father developed this unique restaurant and it was called Buitoni's. To make up for the lack of space, they built a conveyor belt coming around a horseshoe-shaped bar. They'd call into a microphone: 'Two meatballs for a spaghetti dish.' Then it was put on a blue plate and the meatball placed in a pocket-shaped mound of spaghetti so it wouldn't fall off from the vibrations on the conveyor belt. And this is the can-do spirit of a New Yorker. This is what it's all about."

In truth, it's not the inventiveness so much as what it exemplifies—that New Yorkers are innovative and driven. Not only that, but the way the partners met is indicative of this spirit. An immigrant has a chance encounter with someone and finds a way to make things happen. Moreover, the repetition of the story to someone else validates its inner meaning. It certainly resonates with me, who grew up with Buitoni as literally a household name.

A few doors up Amsterdam is the equally famous Hungarian Pastry Shop, where the apple strudel with raisins is, as they say, "to die for." The outside wall has beautiful paintings—a yin-and-yang

Hideously expressive faces follow you as you walk by on 110th Street.

type portrait in yellow, blue, and red, with Hungarian words on it. Other paintings depict angels gathered for—who knows?—perhaps a convention! Inside, the place is really crowded for a Sunday afternoon at 3:00 p.m. People sip cappuccino or tea at small tables. The front room has a glass counter filled with mouth-watering pastries—éclairs, strudels, croissants, cream puffs, etc. There is a cozy warm feeling as people chat or work at their laptops on the wooden tables, lighted by small lamps scattered throughout the space.

At 527 W. 110th Street, between Broadway and Amsterdam, I find myself staring at no fewer than ten really large gargoyles, each about two feet high, jutting out at street level. They look like people from medieval times, with rather hideous but nonetheless impressive faces, full of expression. The building has French casement windows. The interior has a mosaic-tile floor, and the ceiling has a beautiful colorful frieze, with shields and grapevines surrounding it, plus gorgeous sconces around it.

(A) Manhattanville Coffee
(B) Dunbar Apartments
(C) Strivers Row
(D) Mysterious statue of man
(E) Medical mural on wall of Harlem Hospital
(F) Schomburg Center
(G) Aloft Harlem Hotel
(H) Flamekeepers Hat Club
(I) Harlem Tavern
(J) The Shrine
(K) Paris Blues
(L) Silvana
(M) Graham Court Apartments
(N) "Little Senegal"
(O) Malcolm Shabazz Market

(P) Kalahari Apartment Building
(Q) Former Theresa Hotel, where Fidel Castro once stayed
(R) Harlem Link Charter School
(S) Marcus Garvey Park
(T) Holcombe-Rucker Park, where famous NBA stars played

W 155 ST
W 153 ST
W 151 ST
W 148 ST
W 146 ST
W 144 ST
W 145 ST
W 142 ST
W 140 ST
W 136 ST
W 138 ST
W 134 ST
W 135 ST
W 132 ST
W 130 ST
W 128 ST
W 126 ST
W 124 ST
W 122 ST
W 120 ST
W 118 ST
W 116 ST
W 114 ST
W 112 ST

BRADHURST AVE
ADAM CLAYTON POWELL JR BLVD
HARLEM RIVER DR
EDGECOMBE AVE
ST NICHOLAS AVE
FREDERICK DOUGLASS BLVD
MALCOLM X BLVD
5TH AVE
MORNINGSIDE AVE
MANHATTAN AVE
ST NICHOLAS AVE
5TH AVE
CENTRAL PARK NORTH

Harlem River

Marcus Garvey Park

CENTRAL HARLEM

ONCE UPON A LONG TIME AGO, Harlem was home to poor whites, most of whom were Jewish but also included Italian, Irish, and German. They began coming in the late nineteenth century, and their numbers rose dramatically with the extension of the subway system to this part of town. With blacks migrating north to fill jobs made available by general industrial growth and the need to replace workers who went to fight in World War I—as well as overbuilding in the area, which forced developers to either accept black tenants or allow the apartments to remain vacant—the neighborhood became increasingly black. In the 1920s, Harlem experienced a great black renaissance, both culturally and politically, drawing thousands of visitors from elsewhere who flocked there to be entertained by its theater performers, singers, musicians, and writers. By the 1930s Harlem was about 70 percent black. Unfortunately, the Great Depression of the 1930s exacted a heavy toll on the black community, one that affected it for decades to follow. This was because they were often "the last hired and the first fired." From the 1940s until 2000, Harlem remained a generally poor neighborhood, becoming a symbol of neglect and hopelessness, notwithstanding the efforts of thousands of ordinary, hardworking residents to raise their families and somehow make ends meet. Today, if you include West Harlem, the area is perhaps 40 percent white, a trend that continues to grow as more and more white people are attracted to this gentrifying and centrally located part of town.[12]

Central Harlem's boundaries are both large and a bit complex, roughly accepted to be 155th Street on the north; Fifth Avenue and the Harlem River on the east; Central Park on the south; and Bradhurst, Edgecombe, St. Nicholas, Morningside, and Manhattan Avenues on the west. Spatially, Central Harlem is a study in contrasts. The main commercial thoroughfares, running from north to south, are Frederick Douglass Boulevard (formerly Eighth Avenue); Adam Clayton Powell Jr. Boulevard (formerly Seventh Avenue); Malcolm X Boulevard (formerly Lenox Avenue); and St. Nicholas Avenue, which below 125th Street becomes a diagonal street. The names of these avenues are emblematic of the fact that probably no community in the city has done as much to remember its history.

The avenues look pretty much the way they have since the 1940s— they are lined with faded, older apartment buildings, usually between five and seven stories, many of them once grand structures. But this is deceptive, as many of them have been upgraded inside and, in some cases, on the outside as well. The stores along these avenues, with some exceptions, are similarly unimpressive—fast-food outlets, many of them Chinese takeout joints, delis, groceries, bars, liquor stores, beauty parlors, nail salons, and laundromats. Then there's the New York City Housing Authority projects interspersed along the avenues, an unsettling reminder of the poverty that still retains a firm hold on Harlem's collective psyche. This reality is highlighted by the clusters of poor and often homeless men hanging out on the street corners and in front of the stores, their jacket collars turned up to fend off the winds that blow, unimpeded, through the wide streets, talking and laughing amongst themselves. There's a palpable feeling that these people have been left behind and their needs unmet, despite the efforts of public and private agencies to attend to them.

A notable exception to this pattern is Frederick Douglass Boulevard between 125th and 110th Streets, which has become gentrified, with sleek apartment buildings lining its streets and a plethora of upscale restaurants to suit every taste, shopping emporiums, boutiques, wine bars, taverns, and *biergartens* that would be equally at home in Chelsea or Tribeca. If the recent histories of Park Slope, Williamsburg, or Fort Greene are any barometer, then this area is a harbinger of what will eventually happen to much of Harlem. Let's remember that this part of Frederick Douglass, then known only as Eighth Avenue, was a notorious center for drug dealing and heavy drinking, during the 1970s, '80s, and '90s. I well recall seeing hundreds of folks gathering on this avenue back then, even in the daytime hours, the rowdy crowds spilling out beyond the sidewalks and into the street. To appreciate how far things have come, the new moniker for the entire area of Central Harlem south of 125th Street is now Soha (or SoHa, for *South Ha*rlem)! A creation of realtors, such designations give neighborhoods cachet and, according to agents with whom I've spoken, it seems to work with at least some buyers.

Support for this notion comes from the side streets, where gentrification has been under way for at least fifteen years. It's here where you'll find block after block of brownstones and row houses being refurbished or knocked down and rebuilt, along with small luxury apartment buildings (with affordable housing available too). Many of these urban newcomers are younger and white. More than a few have families and can be seen in the parks and playgrounds and even participating with the long-entrenched locals in the community gardens that dot the area. These people, who number in the thousands, will create demand for better shopping and other amenities, which will ultimately transform the main boulevards. Central Harlem is a large area and it will take time for this to happen, but barring unforeseen circumstances, like a significant rise in crime or a major economic collapse, it's quite likely to occur. Yet another harbinger of the future is Manhattan Avenue, a residential street with private residences and apartment buildings, running from 124th to 110th Street, which looks like any middle-class neighborhood in Manhattan. Ditto for Bradhurst Avenue from 145th to 151st Street, and Fifth Avenue below 120th Street.

Harlem has long been a national scene for music, dance, and art, and with the neighborhood's resurgence in recent years, its popularity in that regard has also gained. Famous cultural venues include the Apollo Theater, the Schomburg Center for Research in Black Culture, the Poet's Den Theater, City College's Aaron Davis Hall, the Dance Theatre of Harlem, the Harlem Repertory Theatre, the National Jazz Museum in Harlem, Jazzmobile, the Studio Museum, to name a few. These institutions attract both outsiders and insiders, unifying them through music and the arts. If you can, spend some time in one of the many individual clubs and see what it offers the community. New ones are constantly opening. The best approach is to walk the area and go in whenever you see something that interests you.

Of course, in the familiar version of New York that "everybody," as opposed to "nobody," knows, 125th Street—also named Martin Luther King Jr. Boulevard—is where former President Bill Clinton had his office for many years. It's still a brassy thoroughfare, with stores like Jimmy Jazz, Marshalls, Staples, and the like predominating. Regardless, if you visit Harlem, you have to go there, just for the vibe that comes from the throngs who shop and hang out there.

Finally, Harlem has many parks, some small, some large. The best-known one is Central Park, whose northern section along 110th Street borders the neighborhood. There's also Morningside Park, which runs along Morningside Ave from 110th to 124th Street; St. Nicholas Park, between St. Nicholas Terrace and St. Nicholas Avenue; and Marcus Garvey Park, between 124th and 120th Streets. All are heavily used by families, casual and serious walkers, sports enthusiasts, and bike riders.

I begin my journey through Central Harlem at 142 Edgecombe Avenue, and I immediately spot a telltale sign of gentrification, an Internet café called Manhattanville Coffee. Since Manhattanville is actually a neighborhood between 135th and 125th Streets, that's a bit of geographic license, but I doubt anyone minds. Fifteen years ago no one would have dreamed of this location for such an enterprise. What is it about these places that changes perception so much? More than anything, perhaps, it's the look—a gold-lettered black sign, subdued and dignified, sending a clear message that this area's on the move. Through the window, you can see serious-looking people, mostly white but black and Asian too: racial and spatial harmony. Most are pecking away on their laptops at wooden tables, beneath globes with soft lighting, sipping lattes, and eating croissants and sandwiches. There's an almost relaxed feeling. Those who serve in these places are young people with a touch of sophistication, which gives the impression that they're only passing through a stage in their lives that they will look back upon with fondness as they advance up the ladder on some professional track—unless, of course, they happen to be the boss, in which case they're already there. The subtler message is that this is a safe area, one to which upwardly mobile folks are moving and in which both prices and values are rising.

"What's in this sandwich you call the Italian Job?" I ask the young, upbeat-sounding fellow behind the gleaming, marble-top counter.

"Basically it's a caprese sandwich with a bit of zucchini."

"And the French Highway?"

"Brie, arugula, olives, and honey, and, today, with pears. Everything's really good here, like these chocolate croissants." And there are the loyalty cards, which I've seen elsewhere in these areas. You buy enough coffees, juices, or beers, and you get a discount.

"It seems this area's changing."

"Yes. I used to live on 155th, but I moved down here because it's where I work. It's great, like a melting pot. And people say, 'As soon as that coffee shop opened, things changed; it became safer and more "in."' Rents are going up now, as you might expect." This is a perfect instance of the gentrification process: embryonic at first, but sure to grow with time. The owners know what they're doing, as they have a similar place with the same name in more gentrified Crown Heights, on Rogers Avenue.

From here, I head east one block on 142nd Street and turn right on Frederick Douglas, stopping in at Londel's Restaurant near 140th Street. This place, which serves steaks, along with Cajun and Southern dishes, is a favorite hangout for politicians and power brokers looking for a quiet, low-key venue.

Walking another block east to Adam Clayton Powell Boulevard, I go left up to 149th Street and make a right. Here, between Adam Clayton Powell and Frederick Douglass Boulevards and running from 149th to 150th Street, I see some old red-brick buildings with long, grassy, inner courtyards, spanning the entire length of the block. There's a plaque in memory of Matthew Alexander Henson. He lived in the Dunbar Apartments, named after the African American poet Paul Laurence Dunbar. Henson sailed the world as a seaman, and he and Rear Admiral Peary made seven attempts to reach the North Pole, finally achieving success on April 6, 1909. He is a black hero, though not that well known to the public or the black community.

This complex was built in 1926 as housing for black people. It was designed by the architect Andrew Thomas, better known for his designs in the Jackson Heights area of Queens. People owned their units as co-ops rather than renting them. The Depression hit the residents hard though, and, as they defaulted, John D. Rockefeller, who created the complex, foreclosed and then repurchased the units at auction. This enabled him to turn the development into rental apartments. Now it's listed in the National Register of Historic Places and was probably the first garden-apartment complex in Manhattan.

Returning to Adam Clayton Powell, I walk south and pass 2321–39 Adam Clayton Powell Jr. Boulevard, between 136th and 137th Streets, where an unusual apartment house, built in 1928, is worth a look. The top three stories are red brick, but the bottom two floors have a facade of rough-hewn gray stone blocks. Some blocks are smooth and others have swirls or lumps. The entrance has several Corinthian columns on one side only.

In general, the area between 142nd and 136th Streets in Central Harlem has many gorgeous brownstones, including the historic area between Adam Clayton Powell Jr. and Frederick Douglass Boulevards, along 138th and 139th Streets, known as "Strivers Row." Built between 1891 and 1893, these magnificent row houses were constructed in various styles—Renaissance, Colonial, and Georgian. The name was meant to evoke the idea of regular folks trying to succeed. In truth, quite a few very successful African Americans lived there, including Scott Joplin, Adam Clayton Powell Jr., and Bill "Bojangles" Robinson. People understand the value of history here, so it's no surprise that a nice apartment building at 300 W. 135th Street, calls itself "300 Strivers Row" even though Strivers Row is really several blocks away.

At 226 W. 135th Street, a brownstone near Frederick Douglass Boulevard, there's a six-foot-high dark statue of a man, with an unidentifiable object on his head, featuring two straps across his chest, playing on an African djembe drum. No one seems to know anything about it and there's no one home. MOS, an architectural firm, has offices in the building, but a young man answering the door had no idea how the statue got there. He opines that it might be a Nigerian man but, when pressed on that, he admits that it's just speculation. A secretary who answered the phone several days later told me: "Yes, people sometimes stop in and ask me about the statue but I don't know the answer. We've only been here five years." The venerable Schomburg Center, a fount of knowledge about Harlem, had no information about it either. I spoke with their people and, as one of them said: "This is the kind of thing that drives people crazy. We cannot get any information about it. We've asked people on the block, including longtime residents, but no one knows who created it, who the person depicted is, and when it was constructed. But we are still trying to find out." Interestingly, people sometimes provide their own explanations when it suits their interests. A young white man with two small children passes by and I overhear him saying to them: "You want to see the Obama Man? Look, he's right here." Is it racism? Stereotyping? Possibly. Or perhaps this is his way of getting his children interested in either statues or President Obama!

Down 136th Street, near Malcolm X Boulevard, I come across a funeral parlor listing Sharon Pettey Taylor as the director. But what catches my eye is the sign, which reads: "Funerals by Design." Does that mean they design funerals? The place does have a nice blue/green/gold stained-glass window. A woman answering the phone explained: "What it means is we create a funeral that the family wants and that's in keeping with their financial needs." This makes sense and is essentially what everyone wants, but many funeral homes don't do that. Thus the sign is one that creates curiosity and is, therefore, an excellent way to attract business. Not so for the Great Wall, a hole-in-the-wall Chinese restaurant I pass farther down Adam Clayton Powell Jr. It's one of the most popular names in the city for a Chinese takeout place, but the name alone may not necessarily attract people. What's interesting is that no matter how modest the eatery, it will often try to capitalize on a great name. And why not?

At the corner, on Malcolm X Boulevard, I face a splendid mural on the wall of Harlem Hospital. It depicts black nurses at work, commemorating the fact that this was the first hospital to hire black women as nurses. There are excellent drawings of physicians treating patients and of former slaves coming up from the South.

One block down, on 135th Street, is the well-known Schomburg Center, part of the New York Public Library system and known as one of the premier research centers on black history and culture. I used it myself for a book I wrote about African Americans and Africa and found it to be truly outstanding. The curator, Ernest Kaiser, now deceased, spent many hours helping me, even inviting me to his home in East Elmhurst, Queens. This brilliant and dedicated man also helped many other researchers. Today, the Ernest D. Kaiser Index to Black Resources is one of the Schomburg Center's most unusual finding aids, providing more than 179,000 citations to articles in thousands of issues of black magazines and newspapers. This attitude remains a core part of the Schomburg's philosophy, as anybody who's ever been there knows.

As I stroll down Frederick Douglass Boulevard from 155th to 125th Street, it's clear that this section is in a pre-gentrification stage. That may or may not change. The stores are very basic and cater to those who are not at all well off, with quite a few NYCHA buildings lining the boulevard. The homes along these blocks aren't as nice as those below 125th. Frederick Douglass's appearance changes abruptly below 125th Street, where I pass the Magic Johnson Theater complex. A block farther down I come to the Aloft Harlem Hotel, 2296 Frederick Douglass between 123rd and 124th

Streets, a sleek new establishment with an enticing ambience. It has a contemporary bar, some art exhibits, a lobby with nice couches, comfortable easy chairs, and exquisite multicolored throw pillows to match. It bills itself as "The first hotel in Harlem in over 45 years," located two blocks from the famed Apollo Theater, and it offers tours of nearby Columbia University. But the staff is sensitive to stereotypes of old Harlem and urges people to "enjoy our *upper west side* hotel" (my emphasis). The fact is that Harlem must still contend with visitors who perceive it as an unsafe neighborhood. By contrast, the Upper West Side is seen more positively. There's nothing wrong with using this approach. Entrepreneurs always put their best foot forward, and one way is to associate the neighborhood with a familiar area that has a good image.

On the next block, a two-bedroom apartment in a nice, but not that special, building sells for $800,000. The building has affordable housing units too, and those tenants have the same apartments and equal access to its facilities. This can be a problem for some residents, who have told me that they resent the fact that they have paid full price for amenities that others can access while paying far less for their apartments. At the same time, others tell me that they "could care less about this."

On the corner of 121st Street and Frederick Douglass Boulevard, I discover a cool-looking shop, the Flamekeepers Hat Club. As you might expect, they sell dressy hats for men. I speak with an employee, Marc Williamson, whose business card identifies him as a "Flamekeeper and Hat Romanticist." It also features a drawing of a turtle whose shell is a bowler hat and holding a flame. Marc is elegantly dressed in an outfit that consists of trousers, jacket, shirt, vest, and scarf, in various shades of gray, topped by a dove-gray top hat, with a gold stick-pin. I walk along the tables and look at the items on the walls, which have great displays. There are bowler hats, trilbies, fedoras, derbies, Panamas, and flat, gaily patterned golf caps. The colors are a rainbow of blue, red, purple, yellow, white, black, and pink, accommodating every visual taste. The music is pleasant and soothing,

A hat for everyone with discerning taste.

with soft lighting illuminating the neatly arranged hats, resting on wooden shelves, awaiting their owners. Prices run from $75 to $380. Marc is friendly, even effusive, as are all the store employees. He explains that the shop's approach is very modern, trading in nostalgia for a forward-looking, ultra-cool twenty-first-century style.

The changes in this area are remarkable compared with even five years ago. The distribution of whites to blacks walking by, shopping, eating in bistros is about 50-50 along this stretch all the way down to 110th Street, where Harlem meets the Upper West Side. Restaurants on Sunday, around noon, are filled with patrons enjoying themselves and greeted by extremely friendly smiling people who give the impression that they will do anything to make you happy. For those who think that longtime Harlemites resent whites taking over their neighborhood, this may be true for some. This happens in any neighborhood that undergoes dramatic transition. Most locals, however, are proud that their community has become so desirable and recognize the economic value of extending a warm welcome to visitors and residents alike.

Attracted by the sight of so many people sitting at the outdoor tables, I enter Harlem Tavern, where the service is both prompt and friendly. If you're into sports they have many large screen TVs broadcasting a number of games all at once, with fans alternately screaming and groaning. But what's really worthwhile is their delicious food, especially the cornflake-crusted French toast, accompanied by dulce de leche and fresh fruit, or their banana spice pancakes with cinnamon, nutmeg, fruit, and whipped cream. Don't eat the day before or your diet will quickly descend into hell.

In terms of nightlife, restaurants, population shifts, and new housing, the changes in Harlem have been significant. But what about religion? The church has always been a vehicle both for religious expression and for displays of political power in the black community. Many national black leaders from Martin Luther King Jr. to Al Sharpton have successfully used it as a springboard for their ambitions. The storefront and larger churches are still a presence in gentrified Harlem. And now they are welcoming the young gentrifiers, just as they did the mostly white crowds that have always visited the churches in the past as tourists. I learn this anew as I enter a gospel church, on Frederick Douglass, near 120th Street. It's a small room but nicely decorated, with bright little chandeliers and attractive wall posters and paintings. It can hold perhaps twenty-five people who, in this case, represent a mix of what appear to be older regulars and young urban professionals. If you just look inside, they'll usher you to a seat, where you'll be entertained and perhaps even ennobled by gospel singing and music. In this case, a regular who had been away was invited to sing or, I should say, belt it out, for the assembled. She agreed and received a chorus of "Amens." First-time visitors were encouraged to stand and be welcomed by those in attendance. They also received a free CD of songs presumably performed by church members. For church officials, the new classes are an opportunity for outreach and donations. In short, the churches are embracing the newcomers and remain a vibrant part of the community; you can spot them on every commercial avenue in Harlem.

I can't resist touching on some really interesting places I've come across on this jaunt. One is the Shrine, on Adam Clayton Powell Jr. Boulevard between W. 133rd and W. 134th Streets. On any given night, a variety of bands play for an hour or two, then depart, with the offerings ranging from hard rock to contemporary jazz to rhythm and blues. So, for anyone looking for a musical sampling, this is a great place, especially for young people. No one will demand a steep cover price, but finding a place to sit will be a challenge.

Farther down the boulevard at 121st Street, I enter Paris Blues, which has been around for ages and has a loyal following. It's known for good jazz, but on the Saturday night I'm there, it's featuring '60s folk music, as in "The House of the Rising Sun." The singer is a young, talented Asian woman, but when I close my eyes I could swear I'm listening to Joan Baez, she's that good. There's a long bar with twinkling blue lights that reflect off the bottles of whisky on the shelves. In the back there's a romantic section with tables and red leatherette booths and wooden beams, where you're away from the noise but still close enough to be part of the scene. You feel like you're sitting on a veranda somewhere in nighttime New Orleans. Colored lanterns and balloons hang overhead, and the entire ceiling is covered with black-and-white photographs of musicians and bands. In short, it's an intimate, comfortable place to spend an evening. For the last forty-seven years it's been run by Sam Hargress, a large man who's wearing a straw hat and large sunglasses. He has a jovial face and demeanor to match.

"What would you say makes your place special?" I ask him.

"The main thing is how we treat the people. Harlem's had a lot of turnover, and we've been able to adapt in terms of how we deal with these changes. I own the property here and gentrification helps me. It's good for business. It's also important to make everybody feel welcome and show 'em a good time."

This racially mixed place is fertile ground for people to develop relationships, but it's important to remember that even when Harlem was almost completely black, there was contact between the races, albeit in different ways, and mostly in business areas. Looking back historically, there's the case of two white dentists, Drs. Benjamin Schneider and Victor Marcus, who served the community for many years. As one of them said in a *New York Daily News* interview: "Everybody in Harlem knows me. You see me walk down the street. . . . We've been up here for years. That's how we built up our practice."[13]

My next stop, shortly after midnight, is Silvana, on 116th Street, just west of Frederick Douglass Boulevard. I descend into a basement, where a seven-member band from Burkina Faso is playing on African musical instruments like the kora and the shekere. A racially mixed audience dances with abandon to the high-energy beat, their movements illuminated by the strobe lights. The club is owned by a Muslim-Jewish couple, he from Burkina Faso, she from Israel. The food is Israeli, the music—tonight—African. As I listen to them describe what they do here, I'm reminded that, even as conflict rages across the world between Muslims, Jews, and Christians, relationships can still flourish, at least on an individual level. And polyglot New York is the perfect venue for that. "What was your goal in setting up this place?" I ask. "When we started here there was very little African music being played in Harlem. We wanted to bring this form of entertainment to Harlem. And the fact that we are a mixed religious couple shows that people can live in harmony if they try hard enough."

A few days later, I continue my explorations, walking south on Malcolm X Boulevard from 125th Street. I remember being on this avenue with my students some years ago on a class tour when the Denzel Washington film *American Gangster* was being filmed in Harlem along Malcolm X Boulevard. No one—not the students or the nearby Harlemites—seemed to mind the disruption. To the contrary, they were thrilled by the fact that a major studio was using the area as a setting. In that sense, these neighborhoods have an advantage. They serve up authenticity galore. A reflection of how popular Harlem is becoming is the number of movies being filmed here. And Harlem, as opposed to some of the snootier parts of the city, welcomes the filmmakers. After all, it's good for business.

At 112th Street, two blocks from the Harlem border, I turn left and discover the Washington Irving, a Greek revival–style structure with Ionic columns and simulated, decorative wrought-iron balconies, all built in 1898. Located at #203, near Adam Clayton Powell Jr. Boulevard, the apartments are expensive and gorgeous with large rooms, some with four bedrooms. Many of the residents have been here for decades, and the prices, according to the concierge, are beyond the range of the typical young gentrifier. Overall, the blocks here, between 110th and 116th Streets, on either side of Adam Clayton Powell, are a mix of the expensive, the inexpensive, the well maintained, and the poorly maintained.

Continuing east one block, on 112th, I visit the Harlem Link Charter School, situated near Fifth Avenue. I take a tour, courtesy of John Reddick, a founding board member and director of its after-school program. Students here are selected by lottery, with many parents opting for Harlem Link because they feel that it's better than the regular public schools. Among the charter school's advantages are that the teachers get to choose and design their own curricula, private organizations provide additional financial support for programs, and the kids wear uniforms. The research on whether the uniform promotes discipline and esprit de corps is mixed, but it definitely reduces competitiveness in clothes among the students. The teachers' union and many city officials, including Mayor de Blasio, are not enthusiastic about these institutions, feeling that they undermine the other public schools. The evidence is mixed on this volatile issue. Some studies have shown that students do not do better academically and aren't necessarily better behaved, while others have shown the opposite. Ultimately, the government needs to provide more resources to help the public schools improve as well as hold them more accountable when they don't succeed. It's a very complex issue.

This particular school, which welcomes visitors by appointment, was certainly quite impressive. The children were attentive, respectful, and very interested in their studies. I walked into a classroom at random and began asking a group of second graders what values they were learning. They raised their hands and waited patiently to be called upon: "respect," "listening," "kindness," "patience," "knowledge," "courage," and "responsibility" were among the responses given. Predictably, recess was one of their favorite activities. Each classroom was named after a college—Sacred Heart, Brooklyn, Columbia, the idea being to give students the belief that they were climbing the proverbial ladder to eventual success. One sign on a classroom door was a textbook case in teaching tolerance and self-confidence: "We are each unique, but together we are a masterpiece." Humor was in evidence too, as a sign outside another classroom exclaimed "Nacho Average Class." Some fourth graders showed me the short fiction stories they were writing, which were quite good, as far as I could tell.

Here, I reverse course and return, via 112th, to Adam Clayton Powell, where I go right. At 116th Street and Adam Clayton Powell Boulevard, I stand in front of the Graham Court, a massive, landmarked, eight-story Italian Renaissance structure with eight elevators to match. Built in 1901, it has been called the Dakota of Harlem. Maybe so, but I can assure you it's a lot easier to gain access to the impressive inner courtyard here than at the Dakota. Just wait for someone to exit the building, smile, and murmur thank you as you enter beneath a molded arch with an elaborate keystone. The architecture of this limestone, brick, and terracotta building is first-rate and very special, with cornices, spandrels, pilasters, columns, tiles, and wrought iron. The distinctive aspect of the Graham Court isn't the building, but the courtyard itself. It's quite large and was one of the first sizable courtyards when built 117 years ago.

Next, I head east on 116th Street, and almost immediately feel as though I've come to another world, or continent, if you will. The African commercial area is here on 116th, mostly between Adam Clayton Powell Jr. Boulevard and Fifth Avenue. There are inexpensive restaurants, often catering to natives from one or another land—Guinea, Ivory Coast, Kenya, or Gambia. Inside, people eat rice and chicken on paper plates, staring intently as the TV beams the latest news from their homelands. Sometimes arguments and even fights break out as viewers take sides in what's being said, or not said. Clothing stores, barbershops, electronics outlets, and dry-cleaning establishments also crowd the street.[14]

The Senegalese Embassy is on 116th, near Malcolm X Boulevard, right next to Amy Ruth's soul food restaurant. While most embassies are located on the Upper East Side or farther down between the 60s and 30s, near the United Nations, its presence here isn't so surprising. From Malcolm X Boulevard west to Morningside, Senegalese businesses predominate. The street and the immediate area around it has been dubbed Little Senegal, with many Senegalese living in it as well. The embassy is therefore located where its constituents live and can better serve them as a result. Gentrification is affecting this population, but their presence here is still sizable.

Amy Ruth's is a worthy competitor to Sylvia's, the world-renowned eatery on Malcolm X Boulevard between 126th and 127th Streets. Both serve up yams, Southern fried chicken, ribs, black-eyed peas, pork chops, and the like. Across the street is the mosque where Malcolm X used to preach. The centerpiece of the area is the enclosed Malcolm Shabazz Market on 116th Street, between Malcolm X Boulevard and Fifth Avenue; it provides space for many artists and vendors selling African garb, jewelry, paintings, pocketbooks, and other items. Unfortunately, it's almost always rather empty. I guess 116th just isn't 125th Street, which has been Harlem's main thoroughfare for decades. The stately looking Kalahari apartment building stands next to the market. Its exterior designs resemble handwoven African textiles, with red, gray, yellowish, and brown bricks that form interesting geometrical patterns.

Returning to Adam Clayton Powell Jr. Boulevard, I make a right and continue north to the former Theresa Hotel, a thirteen-story structure with a white terracotta facade, located between 124th and

125th Streets. Today it's an office building, with nothing to indicate its rich and storied history except an old sign on the side of the building. Completed in 1913 as an apartment/hotel, it was known as "the Waldorf Astoria of Harlem" back in the day. It seems almost unbelievable from today's vantage point, but it was open only to whites until 1937, when a black buyer ended the policy. Perhaps its most famous guest was Fidel Castro, who stayed there while attending the opening session of the United Nations in 1960. His entourage was so large that eighty rooms were rented to accommodate them.

Among the numerous parks in Harlem, one special place is Marcus Garvey Park (formerly known as Mount Morris Park). Located between 124th and 120th Streets and bounded on the west by Mount Morris Park West and by Madison Avenue on the east, it's considered a gem by many locals. It has athletic fields, a giant pool, and an amphitheater, which has featured many marquee stars, including Aretha Franklin and Quincy Jones. It feels safe, as described by both white and black mothers pushing their kids back and forth on swings. Another different sort of place is Holcombe-Rucker Park on 155th Street and Frederick Douglass where there are great basketball games. Among the NBA stars who have played here are Wilt Chamberlain, Kareem Abdul-Jabbar, and Kevin Durant, who scored sixty-six points in the Entertainers Basketball Classic tournament held there in August 2011.

This is where I have chosen to end my walk. In a way, it's emblematic of the duality that characterizes this fascinating community. People watch these games where stars of the future, present, and past come to play. Often, they're hoping they'll be part of something memorable. At the same time, it's also a park for the residents of the Polo Grounds projects, a still-rough patch of the neighborhood where there's poverty and high unemployment. In short, it's a park for the famous and the not famous. And, in the end, it's what Harlem is all about.

(A) The Israelite Church of God in Jesus Christ

(B) Demolition Depot

(C) *Centro de la Paz* mural inside Dream Street Park

(D) Sisters Caribbean Cuisine

(E) East River Plaza Shopping Center

(F) Patsy's Pizzeria (the original one)

(G) Interesting Animal Mural

(H) Duffy's Hill

(I) Islamic Cultural Center

Harlem River

5TH AVE
E 135 ST
E 132 ST
E 130 ST
E 128 ST
E 126 ST
DR MARTIN LUTHER KING BLVD
E 124 ST
E 122 ST
E 120 ST
E 118 ST
E 116 ST
E 112 ST
E 110 ST
E 108 ST
E 106 ST
E 104 ST
E 102 ST
E 100 ST
E 98 ST
E 96 ST

5TH AVE
MADISON AVE
PARK AVE
LEXINGTON AVE
3RD AVE
2ND AVE
1ST AVE
PLEASANT AVE

Thomas Jefferson Park

Harlem River

EAST HARLEM

THE BOUNDARIES OF EAST HARLEM ARE ROUGHLY 142nd Street and the Harlem River on the north and east, 96th Street to the south, and Fifth Avenue on the west. The main commercial thoroughfares are Madison, Lexington, Third, Second, and First Avenues, plus 116th and 125th Streets, with Pleasant Avenue as yet another hub of activity.

During much of the nineteenth century, this was a rural area. Its urban development was spurred by the construction of an elevated rail line in 1880 and, in 1919, the Lexington Avenue subway. Originally Scandinavian, Irish, and German, the area became heavily Italian and Jewish by the 1920s. Today, it is mostly Hispanic, as well as African American. But there are a small number of mostly older Italian-Americans who still remain and are concentrated around Pleasant Avenue. It was also an early center for the Mafia, especially the Genovese family. The major influx of Hispanics occurred during the 1940s and 1950s.

East Harlem, also called, especially in the past, Spanish Harlem or El Barrio, is a largely Hispanic community. Most residents are Puerto Rican, but there are also substantial numbers of Dominicans and Mexicans, as well as smaller groups of Central American immigrants. Like Central Harlem, the neighborhood is gentrifying, though not as fast. One can see it here and there, especially closer to 96th Street and around Mount Sinai Hospital, along Fifth and Madison Avenues. The white population has increased in the older tenements between 97th and 124th Streets, and many of these structures have been upgraded, at least cosmetically. The number of new buildings in the area is not that high, and one can walk for blocks without seeing any. The pace of change will be slow due to the large number of NYCHA projects, where about 25 percent of the population lives, the elevated Metro North trains that run along Park Avenue from

125th to 97th Street, and the uncompleted state of the Second Avenue subway. Developers have, nevertheless, bought many properties, in anticipation of a surge of new residents when the subway tunnel, which will run from 125th Street to the Financial District, is finished. There are also two important museums on Fifth Avenue: the Museum of the City of New York and El Museo del Barrio, which celebrates Hispanic history and culture. Both are at 104th Street.

As I begin my trek eastward from Fifth Avenue down the main east-west thoroughfare of 125th Street, I notice that the blocks between Fifth and Second Avenues are kind of rundown, but there are signs everywhere that construction is beginning as gentrification spreads, albeit very unevenly, to the east, as well as south toward E. 96th Street. I turn right at Madison Avenue, attracted by a sign at #1941, a storefront establishment that calls itself the Israelite Church of God in Jesus Christ. There's a large Star of David in the window, and to the right there's a list that reads:

To the Twelve Tribes Which Are Scattered Abroad

GREETING

Judah—The Negroes
Benjamin—West Indians
Levi—Haitians
Simeon—Dominicans
Zebulon—Guatemala to Panama
Ephraim—Puerto Ricans
Manasseh—Cubans
Gad—North American Indians
Reuben—Seminole Indians
Naphtali—Argentina and Chile
Asher—Colombia to Uruguay
Issachar—Mexicans

This refers to the ancient Israelites who were exiled from Jerusalem and were resettled in other parts of the Babylonian Empire after Nebuchadnezzar II, a Babylonian king, destroyed the Jewish temple in 587 BC. According to legend, ten of the twelves tribes disappeared and were never found again. Among the peoples thought to have been descended from the "ten lost tribes" are the Japanese and the Irish; the Igbo (Ibo) and Lemba tribes of West Africa; the Pashtun tribes of Afghanistan and Pakistan; Native Americans; and Ethiopians. So these new selections have now joined the lost-tribe cavalcade in the minds of those who belong to this church.

What's a little different here is that each of these tribes has been matched to specific nationalities rather than just being called "the ten lost tribes." The church elders offer no evidence justifying these matchups that I know of. They believe that those Africans brought to the United States in 1619 emanated from the tribe of Judah. The Israelite Church, which has branches in other cities throughout the United States, holds strong anti-white opinions, believes that the uniting of the tribes has messianic implications, and adheres to the view that Hispanic and Indian peoples are descended, in part, from enslaved blacks.

At the corner of Madison, I turn left and walk down 124th Street. As I hit Lexington Avenue, on the southwest corner of the block, I see an intriguing and complex mural. It's multicolored, with numerous animals, people, and imaginary creatures, which I'll only partially describe. One depicts a white hulking dog with a twisted face. A man has wrapped his arm around its neck as he peers up at the sky. To the right, a red-handled dagger has been plunged into a green monster's neck. The inscription on the right reads, in part: "Many of us will continue down a path of destruction like chained slaves moving toward their grave. Be free my friends, be free." It's signed by James De la Vega, a Latino street muralist. Much of his work appears in East Harlem.

The block from 124th to 125th Street on Lexington is beautifully described in a photo essay by the world-famous street photographer

Camilo José Vergara that appeared in *Slate*. If you stand at that intersection, you will see the ghetto and much of its ugliness and liveliness all rolled into one. Along with plain old shoppers, there are recently released hospital patients with plastic ID bracelets still on their wrists; a few carry on intense conversations with themselves. This corner of New York is particularly attractive to street evangelists, who readily find people in need of salvation. There's a flourishing drug trade; "loosies," or single cigarettes, are available; men wearing sandwich boards advertise for nearby stores; and prostitutes advertise for themselves.

The intersection also makes for great free theater of a sort. Vergara explains: "Corner regulars tell me about the hustles they've witnessed, such as the wheelchair-bound man who suddenly stood up and started running from the police, wheelchair under his arm. Once I saw a street preacher instantly change his sermon when a recycling truck pulled up next to him. He began telling those around him that their souls were garbage and needed recycling—otherwise they were going to hell. The driver of the truck heard this and laughed loudly."[15]

I find myself questioning how many other wheelchair frauds are plying their trade around the city or whether such suspicions are uncharitable to the genuinely disabled. It's a tough call. I recall a story my friend from Brooklyn told me. She had always given money to a crippled woman on crutches who regularly rang her bell. She'd even invited her in for tea and cookies sometimes. The woman was not always appreciative. "You used to give me rainbow cookies," she complained once, not liking that day's offering. And then one day my friend was shocked when she saw the same lady walking in another neighborhood—but without crutches! Perhaps my friend should have known never to trust an ingrate.

Walking north on Lexington I turn left onto 125th Street and head toward Manna's, at #54. It's one of a chain of soul food cafeterias where delicious eats are sold by the pound. Most people don't realize it, but the Manna's chain was actually started by Betty Park, a Korean American woman who gained acceptance in the black community by donating food every week to local churches. Efforts like this can have a significant impact on changing or modifying how groups see each other.[16]

Turning around, I head east and at 216 E. 125th Street near Second Avenue, I go inside Demolition Depot and it's a truly special place. It is filled, and I mean *filled*, with all manner of artifacts, many of them vintage, ranging from lamps, shutters, fountains, and metal chairs made entirely of lug nuts to period pieces, blank-eyed stone lions, doors, and religious objects. Here I also discover the frosted glass door from former Board of Education Chancellor Joel Klein's office, available as a rental, and an old bright-red telephone booth straight from London, embossed at the top with a golden crown. To give an idea of the size of the place, these and hundreds of other items are spread out over three floors, plus a large outdoor area in the back.

I chat with Evan Blum, one of the owners, and ask him how he's doing. "Not great. Yes, we're selling stuff. I recently did a whole home for a celebrity, and the new, better-off people moving in [to the area] are starting to come in. So we're selling to people redoing their new places in Harlem. We'll also put fireplaces in people's homes, but I have a huge problem with parking for vehicles coming here. This new bus lane is killing us because no one can even stop here, and the police don't care. Neither does the Transportation Commissioner. I said to her [the commissioner], 'How would you like it if your salary was reduced by 80 percent?' I'm losing business, big-time." This is a common lament. Business owners frequently complain that the city doesn't care enough about them, and many times they're right. How can Evan get his trucks in if they can't even stop in front of the place?

I turn right on Second Avenue and go one block to 124th Street, where I turn right again. Here, on E. 124th, between Second and

The ultimate Manhattanite's museum with items for sale.

Bring the world's people together.

Third, change is very much a reality as most of the block now has luxury rentals, which was not the case five years ago. But one thing has remained, and it's a good thing. I'm referring to the "*Centro de la Paz*" mural inside Peace Place Park. Every day thousands of vehicles squeeze into the bottleneck on 124th between Third and Second Avenue that leads onto the Robert F. Kennedy (formerly Triborough) Bridge. Traveling eastward, they are unlikely to notice the remarkable mural that covers six stories of a tenement building wall, for you must face west to see it. It was sponsored by the Creative Arts Workshop and painted by more than 200 New Yorkers, many of them neighborhood youngsters, as well as some 100 artists from around the world—Argentina, Ecuador, Nigeria, England, and elsewhere. Their names are inscribed on a two-story-high scroll.

Moses Chaszar, an administrator at Teachers College, Columbia University, was fourteen years old back in 1995 when he volunteered for the project. He told me: "I grew up on E. 126th Street, and kids like me, we weren't always seeing the best things. So this mural represented our hopes and dreams. There's this one road through the earth, and all around it you have skyscrapers, igloos, pyramids, and the Grand Canyon. And on the side you have Mount Rushmore; only instead of presidents, you have Indians. Many of the artists donated money as well as time," Moses said. "It took us two summers working on scaffolds, and we used special paint from Germany that's supposed to last for eighty years." In a city with hundreds of murals, this one definitely stands out, in scope, design, quality, and size.

Adjacent to the mural is a small park surrounded by life-sized, gaily painted, aluminum figures of local ballplayers, NBA stars, and superheroes. And in the center of this urban tableau stands a huge weeping willow tree. It looks out of place, until you think of it as a real life example that fairly leaped out of the mural behind it. No one is sure when or even how it got there, but one botanical expert said he knew of no other willow tree this large anywhere in the city.

Farther west, between Park and Madison Avenues, on E. 124th Street, I pass the New York College of Podiatric Medicine. Tucked away in East Harlem, it has graduated more than 25 percent of this country's podiatrists. A bit farther up the block, I stop at Sisters Caribbean Cuisine. The Caribbean folks in the neighborhood love this place, and they seem especially fond of the roti dishes and of their signature offering, brown stewed chicken. I ask the chef how it's made. "It has a sweetness to it," he replies, in the lilting accent native to his homeland, St. Kitts. "It's not too spicy or smoky, and we use many ingredients, including brown sugar and onions. As all chefs will tell you, cooking's an art, not a science, and the trick is the amounts and the timing." "But is there a special ingredient?" I persist. "Well, yes," he says, with a soft chuckle. "It's called love."[17] I say hello to three students there from the podiatry school, and they agree when I ask if the food is good for the feet. "Absolutely!" says one with a smile. Who knows if it's true? But, regardless, it's been here for sixteen years.

From there I head down Madison Avenue to 118th Street and go left, all the way to the Harlem River. When we think about gentrification, it's not just boutiques and coffee houses that begin to appear in areas as they are changing. There's also an increase in major shopping centers that cater to people of greater socio-economic status. This is a key factor in making an area attractive. Enter the 117th Street shopping mall in East Harlem, next to the FDR Drive. It's a beautiful spanking-new shopping area, with a nice view of the river, called East River Plaza. This shopping area features a Costco, Bob's Furniture, Target, Best Buy, Marshalls, Old Navy, PetSmart—all discount places but apparently attractive to upscale folks—plus a Starbucks, etc. Not only do these stores attract people from the Upper East and West Sides, but they are also a real boon to those living in East Harlem, including the gentrifiers. The new arrivals can now walk to suburban-style outlet stores. If you don't want to carry your purchases home, then for $22, they will be delivered to your home or office anywhere in Manhattan.

From here I walk back up 118th Street to Patsy's Pizzeria on First Avenue and stop inside. Founded in 1933 by Pasquale "Patsy" Lancieri, it has delicious thin-crust pizza, made in a coal oven, and claims to have originated pizza sold by the slice. Whose pizza is closest to the original version is in dispute, but there's no doubt that this was one of the first in the city and that Patsy's pizza has remained faithful to what is seen as true New York-style pies.

Heading back down First Avenue, I turn west onto 116th Street and go up to Third Avenue, where I make a left. It's a commercial street, filled with cheap furniture outlets, cut-rate department stores, electronics shops, branches of large phone companies, bodegas, and clothing stores. In the midst of all this sits a co-op development, Franklin Plaza, between E. 108th and E. 106th Streets. For those who meet their lower-income requirement and are lucky enough to get into one of these apartments, they're a steal. Security is excellent, the apartments have large rooms, and the grounds include playgrounds, picnic areas, and lovely landscaped greenery. Shopping and transportation are nearby.

I turn right off Third Avenue at 108th Street and head over to Lexington, where I make a left. East Harlem is a major venue for street artists. There are murals, many of them outstanding, on almost every block, and it's a lot of fun to just cruise the streets on foot and find those you like. One of my favorites, because of its unique subject matter, is on E. 108th Street and Lexington Avenue. Drawn on the wall of the Lexington Gardens building and several stories high, it features excellent drawings of a squirrel, a muskrat, an armadillo, and an anteater meeting each other in what I presume is a fictional landscape of the artist's fertile imagination.

As I approach E. 96th Street and the beginning of the elegant Upper East Side, the slow but steady march of gentrification is evident, both along the side streets and the avenues. At 103rd Street, I hike up and down one of the steepest blocks in Manhattan, between E. 102nd and E. 103rd Streets. It was called Duffy's Hill, after a local builder named Michael James Duffy. In the old days, cable cars ran here, and accidents occurred because of the steep grade. Buses tended to avoid the hill altogether. Gentrification has made inroads, beginning at 103rd Street down to 96th Street where the tony Upper East Side begins. And so have colleges, buying up properties for both residences and classrooms.

At 97th Street, I go left one block to Third Avenue. Here, at #1711, somewhat out of place in an area that is predominantly Hispanic, is the Islamic Cultural Center. It was the first mosque built in the city (1991) and has both a mosque and a minaret, neither of them especially visible from the street. It's constructed on an angle so that it can face Mecca. Visitors are welcome and the interior is beautiful and serene, projecting an image sharply at odds with the turmoil going on today in some of the majority Muslim countries.

UPPER WEST SIDE

UPPER EAST SIDE

CENTRAL PARK

ROOSEVELT ISLAND

(A) Picturesque and gracious homes
(B) Smoke Jazz and Supper Club
(C) Henry's Restaurant
(D) Sal & Carmine Pizza
(E) Levain's Bakery
(F) Former site of Towers Nursing Home
(G) Pomander Walk
(H) Little Shop of Crafts
(I) Peace World mural
(J) Cleopatra's Needle
(K) Ballet Hispanico

(L) Jacob's Pickles
(M) Eagle Court
(N) Dead Poet Tavern
(O) Holocaust memorial
(P) Beautiful townhouses
(Q) Calhoun School Learning Center
(R) Westsider Rare and Used Books
(S) Ormonde, Dorilton, and Ansonia buildings
(T) Shalel Lounge

Hudson River

Riverside Park

RIVERSIDE DR

W 110 ST
W 108 ST
W 106 ST
W 104 ST
W 102 ST
W 100 ST
W 98 ST
W 96 ST
W 94 ST
W 92 ST
W 90 ST
W 88 ST
W 86 ST
W 84 ST
W 82 ST
W 80 ST
W 78 ST
W 76 ST
W 74 ST
W 72 ST
W 70 ST
W 68 ST
W 66 ST
W 64 ST
W 62 ST
W 60 ST

AMSTERDAM AVE
HENRY HUDSON PKWY
RIVERSIDE DR
BROADWAY
COLUMBUS AVE
CENTRAL PARK WEST
WEST END AVE
RIVERSIDE BLVD
FREEDOM PL
BROADWAY

Museum of Natural History

Lincoln Center

UPPER WEST SIDE

THE BOUNDARIES OF THIS SPRAWLING, LARGELY RESIDENTIAL AREA,
also referred to as the West Side, are 110th Street on the north, Central Park West on the east, 59th Street on the south, and the Hudson River on the west. Some call the section east of Broadway and north of W. 96th Street Manhattan Valley, but for most residents it's just seen as the West Side.[18] Below 72nd Street, the neighborhood changes because Lincoln Center is there. It has a more commercial feel, yet it's still mostly residential, and includes Riverside South, a $3 billion apartment development between 72nd and 59th Streets, along the Hudson River, which removed Donald Trump's name from its exterior shortly after he was elected president. Broadway, Amsterdam, and Columbus Avenues are all commercial thoroughfares from beginning to end, but they contain mostly small shops, along with an increasingly greater number of large chain stores. This gives the area the feel of a more intimate community, notwithstanding the many tall apartment buildings that line these avenues, as well as Riverside Drive, West End Avenue, and Central Park West.

The area between 59th Street and 67th Street underwent significant development in the late nineteenth and early twentieth centuries, especially after the IRT subway line was completed in 1904. In 1932, the IND line opened along Central Park West. Among those who moved there were poor African Americans who migrated to the city from the Deep South in the '40s and '50s and were placed in low-income projects. In addition, large numbers of impoverished people came to New York from Puerto Rico. As opposed to today, when all sorts of social programs are available, almost none existed then. As a result there was high unemployment, desperation, and a high crime rate. The area around what became Lincoln Center had a general reputation for being unsafe until it was developed in the 1960s for use as a center for the arts.

From the early 1930s and onward, the area north of 72nd Street was largely Jewish and, to a lesser but still significant extent, Irish and Italian, along with other white ethnic groups, and white Protestants of various backgrounds. By the 1950s, the area between Broadway and Central Park West had become more Puerto Rican and black, with an uneven distribution along the side streets where the cheaper tenement housing was located. Tabloid newspapers talked about "terrible blocks" from W. 80th Street between Amsterdam and Central Park West, and said the same about all the side streets north of 96th Street. The picture wasn't so clear on the ground, as I know from having grown up here. One block could be safe and the next two dangerous, followed by four safe streets.

In the 1970s and 1980s, people were afraid to walk the streets at night, as was the case in many other parts of the city. There were rooming houses, filled with unemployed younger people who often preyed on the defenseless elderly who had lived there for decades. Gradually, however, the neighborhood changed for the better, and developers began to build. Gentrification came to pass, and today it's a very safe community, with current apartment prices outstripping those of the Upper East Side, an area that never really went through a decline. The many bars and eateries along the avenues attest to the fact that large numbers of singles and young couples of all backgrounds reside here. The Jewish population remains large, with a substantial number of younger, Modern Orthodox Jews. In fact, for them it's the number-one singles scene in the city. And Hispanics and African Americans and West Indians still live here as well.

Of course, the Upper West Side has two of the city's premier parks, Central Park and Riverside Park. But there are also smaller parks and oases of peace worth looking at, such as the West Side Community Garden, on W. 89th Street between Columbus and Amsterdam Avenues. It's really a mini-park with beautiful tulips in season and a walking path around an oval filled with greenery.

There are more than a few gracious homes and townhouses on Riverside Drive. I take a long walk along the Drive from 110th Street south to 72nd Street, and find it to be an aesthetic and architecturally rich experience. Consulting the *American Institute of Architects Guide to New York City* is also very helpful. Here are some examples of what this glorious part of Manhattan looks like: On Riverside Drive, at the corner of 108th Street, #353 was built in 1899. It's a five-story red-brick and limestone structure that has intricately carved leaves, flowers, and fruits on each side of the entrance, with French balconies made of wrought iron on the second floor. Inside, there's a beautiful wooden staircase and a lavishly designed red, black, and beige runner going up the stairs. There's also an elaborate oriental rug in front of the fireplace, and a picturesque mahogany hat rack. One block south, on the corner of 107th Street, you'll find a freestanding mansion made of white marble. In 1907, when it was built, the Drive had many freestanding homes. Now there are only a few left. The blocks between 107th and 105th Streets are equally outstanding and include #331–332, home to the New York Buddhist Church.

I head east to Broadway and begin walking downtown. For really good jazz, there's the Smoke Jazz and Supper Club at 2751 Broadway, near 106th Street. It features a different group almost every night, but this isn't just a place where people eat and continue talking with their dates while jazz musicians play in the background. The patrons listen attentively because they take their jazz seriously and expect everyone else to do so as well. It's a small, intimate place, and so no matter where you sit, it's a good seat.

A half block down on the corner of 105th Street, Henry's Restaurant has a very different vibe. An American bistro, it has a great bar with super-friendly bartenders, large tables for comfortable dining, and a spacious outdoor area, surrounded by a white picket fence. Inside, it has a warm, inviting feel, with checkered tablecloths, wood paneling, and mahogany wainscoting. Is it a hidden gem? Not if you're from the neighborhood; probably yes if you're not.

A Riverside Drive beauty.

From here on down to 59th Street, it's one huge restaurant food-fest, with one place after another on both sides of the street. I spot Sal & Carmine Pizza, which I remember from my childhood days, then at 95th Street, now at 2671 Broadway, between 102nd and 101st Streets. Sal died seven years ago and, as the new owner says, "Everything's the same, from the attitude [gruff!] to the cheese and sauce!" Most of the locals seem to think it's decent but not great. They continue to dine here, though, because it's been around forever and it's convenient.

In fact, the Upper West Side has many establishments that have been in business for a long time. This may be because it has the population density that can support such enterprises even as different groups of people move in and then out after a number of years. In addition, it has a stable resident base that hasn't changed as much as other neighborhoods. Examples are Albee Baby, a baby-care shop on 95th and Amsterdam that's been there since 1933 and Acker, Merrall, and Condit on W. 72nd Street, the oldest wine shop in the United States, established in 1820. There's also Zingone Brothers Grocery on Columbus, near 83rd Street, which has been there since 1935. Make no mistake: These are not relics of another era. They're busy places with robust customer bases.

But you don't have to have been around forever to be famous. Levain's Bakery, on W. 74th Street just off Amsterdam, has already achieved rock-star status even though it was founded as recently as 1995. The lines outside the tiny store are often a block long, and even as they wait up to 45 minutes, people say it's well worth it. Its walnut chocolate chip and oatmeal raisin cookies are legendary across the country, especially since it opened a mail-order business.

I head east from Broadway on W. 105th Street and come to a beautiful building on Central Park West that has a history. The combination of new construction and the passage of time has a way of erasing history for many people. This is especially true when the building itself is significantly altered. Who remembers the Towers Nursing Home, infamous as a place where old folks were allegedly abused? Today, the site, at 455 Central Park West, between 106th and 105th Streets, is home to high-end condo apartments. The building is landmarked, and some of the original bricks and mortar survive, but what dominates is the new twenty-five-story residential structure.

On the south side of 95th Street between Broadway and West End Avenue there's an entrance to a unique little walkway. It's private, but easily visible by peering through an iron-grated doorway. As I look, I see a beautiful group of eight Tudor-style homes with a similar gated entrance on 94th Street. This is Pomander Walk, one of the city's private blocks, built in 1921. There are such private blocks elsewhere in the city, in Bayside, Queens, for example. And I might say "Nice homes" upon seeing them. But this one feels particularly special because it's located in the midst of tall buildings and because a locked wrought-iron door renders it inaccessible, makes it seem more enticing. It also has a history, having been named after a 1910 play, *Pomander Walk,* an imagined street near London, England. If you wait long enough for a resident to approach, he or she might actually let you in.

Interested in something a little different, especially for kids? I was, so I walked east on 95th Street and turned right on Amsterdam, where I found the Little Shop of Crafts between 95th and 94th. I'd seen it before, but only from the outside. While there are lots of hands-on places like this in the city, this one is unusual in that it lets people, mainly kids, stay for as long as they like to paint whatever they select off their shelves. If they don't finish, they can return the next day. There's a lot to choose from—bowls, trivets, mosaics, stuffed animals. Is it, as their business card proclaims, "New York City's Largest Do it Yourself Craft Studio"? Hard to say, but it is spacious. The staff is pretty helpful too. A young and friendly employee who's there on a Tuesday afternoon explains: "We have pottery that takes a week to get back because it's fired in the kiln. Other items take a day. We've been here about ten years. We also do birthday parties. We also do parties in the back room." Why not simply buy and paint at home? Some people do that, but others need "a working atmosphere," especially if their apartment is too crowded. In a way, this is similar in concept to places that charge a membership fee and let people write in peace and quiet, like The Writers Room in the East Village. In both cases people feel a sense of purpose when they do what they love with other folks doing the same. It's also a chance to meet people with whom they share a common, even passionate, interest.

Across the street, I discover, hidden inside the middle of the block, between 94th and 95th Streets, a long wall mural that's unusual by the fact that it's so easy to miss. It runs east to west from Amsterdam to Broadway. It's a colorful, jaunty affair, filled with life, and children have created it, with the help of adults. There are happy scenes of kids playing, holiday themes, igloos, pumpkins, trees, a witch sailing off to nowhere on a broom, flowers, birds, bumblebees, etc. It's called "Peace World—Love, Hope" and is sponsored by CITYarts, which was founded in 1968 with the goal of uplifting communities in New York through murals. The organization is supported by Bill Clinton and ambassadors from Yemen, Israel, Jordan, Korea, and India. The space presents a sharp contrast to the mayhem in the world that's reported daily on the airwaves and in the newspapers. As you walk along it, seeing the entire mural is a challenge because the cars parked along the wall partially block the view.

Cleopatra's Needle, at 2485 Broadway, near 92nd Street, is, like Smoke, another good local spot for jazz. Named after a genuine ancient Egyptian obelisk, reconstructed and placed in Central Park just behind the Metropolitan Museum of Art, it serves up tasty Mediterranean-style food. It features a different group almost every night, offers jam sessions, open mike nights, and has no cover charge. Unlike Smoke it's not intimate, and there is a large-screen TV for sports fans.

Continuing down Broadway, I turn left at W. 89th Street and stop in at #167, the Ballet Hispanico, between Amsterdam and Columbus. It's not exactly unknown, as the dancers here have performed before audiences around the country, but then again, most New Yorkers are unfamiliar with it, to say nothing of the millions of tourists who visit here annually. It bills itself as "the foremost representative of Hispanic culture in the US" and it might well be, judging from what I've read about it. The company was founded in 1970 by Tina Ramirez, a nationally recognized dancer who happened to be the daughter of a Mexican bullfighter. The people there are friendly and helpful, as I discovered upon entering. Classes are offered for adults, preschoolers, and everyone in between. The site was once home to the Claremont Riding Academy. So we go through time, from equestrian arts to ballet and Flamenco dancing. A meaningless coincidence? Perhaps, but it exemplifies how understanding the city involves appreciating the layers of history and different ethnic groups that have gone into making it the great urban center that it is.

It should come as no surprise to denizens of New York that restaurants are a fulcrum of its existence. On any given night, hundreds of thousands of people are eating out. This brings tax revenues to the city and provides material benefits to untold numbers of individuals from suppliers of food, builders of eateries, and tablecloth and cutlery manufacturers to the taxicab industry, and, most important, it provides tens of thousands of jobs at all levels. And who knows how many tempers were soothed, disagreements patched up, events commemorated, and bonds strengthened by this idea of communal activity?

Some places fare better than others. I walk down Amsterdam Avenue on a Sunday afternoon and observe a long line of people waiting outside Good Enough to Eat, between 86th and 85th Streets on a weekend. It must *really* be "good enough," I say to myself. I ask the waitress inside to explain the interest in this New England home cookin' place. Her riposte? "It's me. That's why they're here"— meaning "it's *not* me." Ask a New Yorker a question that sounds like a challenge and you're going to get an "in your face" retort. I laugh and move on.

Long lines to get into restaurants are so common in the city. People stand outside and meet each other, owners walk by with their dogs, which serve as icebreakers. I stop in at Jacob's Pickles, at 509 Amsterdam Avenue between 85th and 84th Streets, a place that offers a lot more than just varieties of pickles. It also sells sour cukes, kosher cukes, candied red beets, and pickled carrots, but that's just the hook to draw patrons in. It has a nice bar with a good selection of beers, biscuits, and regular food too. One Yelp wag described the smothered gravy sausage chicken biscuit sandwich as "True comfort food and, oh, so decadent!" I chat with the owner, who explains the origins of the name: "I always loved pickles. It was my passion. That and beer. I see pickles, beer, and biscuits as the ultimate comfort food. I lived in Queens—not the Lower East Side, where Guss' Pickles and Ba-Tampte Pickles were—but we brought that stuff home all the time." This is a very New York thing, the right to indulge your fantasy and to expect others to buy into it. I doubt this enterprise would have the same appeal in Wichita, Kansas, but in New York there's a craving for the offbeat. It's an element of the city's collective psyche, that instead of saying: "I'm not going to a pickle restaurant. It sounds weird," New Yorkers look at it with curiosity and wonder: "What's this all about?" Once that happens, they have you, or at least some of you.

My attention is drawn to a most unusual rental building, at 215 W. 84th Street between Broadway and Amsterdam Avenues, called the Eagle Court. In fact, two lifelike concrete statues of eagles stand guard on each side of the entrance, like the lions you see in front of thousands of New York buildings, large and small. There's also a large, gold-painted eagle protruding from the center of the building, under a second-floor window. There's a history to this site, as it sits on part of the farm where Edgar Allan Poe lived in 1844 while he wrote his classic poem, *The Raven*. I chat with a middle-aged resident who tells me about the building and what it's like to live here.

"It used to be a milk factory and it's where Edgar Allan Poe lived. As to being here, the realtors will tell you all the apartments are the

Edgar Allan Poe wrote *The Raven* here in 1844.

same but they're not. I live in this huge studio that's like a loft in Soho. In fact, every apartment's different and they're all really cool. It's really New York's little secret."

"Why do you call it a secret?"

"Because nobody knows it's here. I grew up in Manhattan and these places are amazing. One's a four-room duplex and you don't know it until you walk in. And the prices are pretty competitive too."

She's right on certain counts, but not necessarily on all. First, it was formerly home to the Borden Milk Company, and the decorative gold-leaf eagle is what the factory left behind when it moved. Then, for a while it was a garage, before morphing into an apartment building—a typical example of New York's varied architectural history. It does, in fact, have different types of apartments, and surely there are many people, even those hunting for apartments in the area, who don't know about it, but several other residents with whom I spoke did. Perhaps making it into a story gives the place a mysterious aura, both to the woman and to others who hear it, that helps it stand out from the rest. Indeed, she presented it in a lowered voice, in keeping with her calling it a secret.

Until it moved to another location because of a rent increase, 255 W. 84th was the location of a coffee house called Edgar's Café. When I visited the original location, I saw that some of Poe's poems adorned the walls, as well as a drawing of him. Looking around at the young crowd, I asked the waitress, "Do the people here know who Poe was?" "Not really, hardly any," she replied. "In fact, people call up here, asking to speak to Edgar. They think he owns the café." I gave her a skeptical look. "I swear it! I swear it!" she exclaimed, almost gleefully. "So what do you tell them?" "I tell them he's not in," she says, laughing. "And then I ask if I can help them." And so we see how a Ukrainian waitress, in the United States for but three years, can outdo native-born Americans in the knowledge game! Edgar's is now on Amsterdam and 92nd Street and the Edgar Allan Poe theme, with photos on the wall remains the same.

The restaurants on the Upper West Side have character, as do the bars, like the Dead Poet tavern at 82nd and Amsterdam. It turns out not to have much to do with nearby Edgar Allan Poe Street (84th Street). "Who's the dead poet?" I ask, as blues music plays in the background. "All of them who aren't around anymore," replies a patron sipping his Seven and Seven. He tells me that the owner, who was a teacher, decided to open up this literary joint and thought of the name. It does, in any case, express the intellectual tone of the area. In that way "space" becomes an advertisement for cultural expression.

From here I head west on 82nd Street. Just inside Riverside Park, by 83rd Street, at the southern base of the Promenade, there's a most unusual Holocaust memorial. Most of these memorials, in New York and elsewhere, are large and prominently displayed. This one is stark in its understated simplicity and almost impossible to find. It consists of a small granite slab, perhaps three feet by three feet, set into the ground and surrounded by some landscaped shrubbery. At first sight it seems to contradict the belief by those who erect memorials of this sort that the Holocaust should never be forgotten. Placed there in 1947 shortly after the Holocaust ended and approved by William O'Dwyer, then New York City's mayor, it reads: "This is the site for the American memorial to the Heroes of the Warsaw Ghetto Battle, April–May 1943 and to the six million Jews of Europe martyred in the cause of human liberty." But there's more, as a nearby sign by the Parks Department/Riverside Park Conservancy explains. Buried beneath the slab lie two boxes of soil from two Czechoslovakian concentration camp sites—Terezin and Sered—as well as a scroll in both Hebrew and English describing the uprising in the Warsaw Ghetto. From looking at it, you'd never know. It's believed to be the first Holocaust memorial erected in the United States.

Why is it so modest? It was originally intended to serve as a cornerstone for a larger memorial. Proposals were submitted by prominent architects, but none ever received funding, and today the area has been spruced up by volunteers but not expanded. Perhaps the memorial wasn't funded because at that time what happened to the Jews wasn't well publicized. Survivors were disinclined to talk in those early days about their experiences. They felt that no one was really interested in their stories—not even American Jews, many of whom felt guilty that they didn't do more to advocate for their European brethren. There was no established State of Israel in 1947, and Jews felt less secure in the United States.

At the same time, the ceremony marking the memorial's creation was well attended. More than 15,000 people came, including 100 known survivors. Because of the large Jewish population, the Upper West Side became a preferred destination for survivors, many of whom were sent to the old Marseilles Hotel, on W. 103rd Street just west of Broadway, between 1946 and 1952, to be resettled in both New York City and elsewhere in the country.[19] Thus, the memorial's location on the Upper West Side, in light of this, made a lot of sense. Every April, a small ceremony is held to commemorate what happened.

As I leave the memorial, I take a peek at 109 Riverside Drive, on the corner of 83rd Street, and three other connected five-story townhouses on the right. They are crowned with peaked roofs and have brick and limestone trim and shields, along with a ziggurat-like chimney. The entranceway has diamond shapes with circles inside them, and it's flanked by two urns. Farther down, at #86 on the corner of 81st Street, there's another five-story beauty, made of textured blocks of stone and curved at the edges to provide a bow effect. The outdoor stone vestibule is in a Romanesque style, and there's an iron fence inside in front of the entrance door.

I walk one block east to West End Avenue and 81st Street and come to what some think is a monstrosity totally out of character with the neighborhood—the Calhoun School Learning Center. Its appearance strikes me as resembling a TV for a giant. Others think it's an innovative building, and it has, in fact, won several awards for its architecture. Notable too is what the school calls its "Green Roof Learning Center," the first eco-friendly roof devoted to education. It has gardens that include vegetables and fruits; and it cuts stormwater runoff by almost half the normal amount, filters the air, and provides food for wildlife, in short, it is a model of sustainability. Students study there and gain an appreciation of their obligations as humans to improve the environment.

I must admit that I sometimes crave the look, feel, smell, and contents of one of those used-book stores with the ladders for the high shelves that were once common to the New York scene. So I head to Westsider Rare and Used Books, at 2246 Broadway between 80th and 81st Streets. Apparently Woody Allen agrees, as it was a setting for his film *Fading Gigolo,* chosen by a location scout. It's a small place, almost cozy, but it has tons of used books, a rare-book section, and signed first editions, and even some pretty new books.

One can get lost here for a whole day and night, since they stay open late. I trip up the wooden stairs to the second floor, watching out for the books piled precariously on the right. The service isn't very good, as they lack the ability to even find a specific book. For that, there's the Barnes & Noble on Broadway near 82nd Street.

At 452 Amsterdam Avenue, between 81st and 82nd Streets, there's a rather innovative creation, the Treat House. What's special about it? They have delicious gourmet treats, many of them gluten-free, nut-free, and dairy-free. There's a whole line of Rice Krispies treats and they also customize items, putting your face or another image of your choice on it. I ask Chris, the owner, if there's anything unique about what he sells. "Yes, the cookies and cream and marshmallow treat. Where have you ever heard of that combination? And have you seen an eggnog Rice Krispies treat before?" I guess not. Regardless, the stuff's pretty good.

As I pass by the Jewish Community Center (JCC), on W. 76th Street at 334 Amsterdam Avenue, I see a crowd of people waving signs and shouting. Led by a man with a bullhorn, they are protesting the JCC's support for organizations that indirectly encourage the boycotting of cultural performances in Israel's West Bank. The JCC proclaims its fealty to Israel and its hard work for the Jewish community. The protesters say it is pushing an extreme liberal agenda and is hurting the Jewish State. People walk by but generally don't stop unless the issues engage their interest. No one questions the right of people to vociferously express themselves, but such protests also have meaning for those who live here. They illustrate the crosscurrents of opinion that prevail within a community and, in so doing, reveal its complexity. And there are demonstrations about everything in this city—crime, unemployment, bicycle lanes, construction, filming, surveillance, loud noise, health issues, politics, etc.

There's a trio of buildings in this area that can best be appreciated by viewing them in ascending order of beauty. First, at 154 W. 70th Street, on the southeastern corner of Broadway, there's the Ormonde. A twelve-story brick and limestone structure, it was built in 1900. It is elaborately designed, and its rounded corner with single windows facing diagonally out to Broadway reminds me of the famous Flatiron Building on 23rd Street. One block up, again on the eastern side of Broadway, at 171 W. 71st Street, on the northeast corner, there's the gorgeous Dorilton, in the French Beaux-Arts style, a landmarked brick and limestone creation with lots of exquisite terracotta, dating back to 1898. Architectural historian Andrew Dolkart thinks it may be "the most flamboyant apartment house in New York," with its striking French-influenced sculptures and a large iron gate resembling those outside French palaces. As I approach the building, I feel as if I'm entering one of these palaces. Grand and screaming for attention is probably the best way to describe this work of art. And then, there's one that's even more impressive, the Ansonia, at 73rd Street on the northwestern corner of Broadway. It's both enchanting and overwhelming in its design: seventeen floors of French architecture, a dormered mansard roof, turrets, towers, filigreed balustrades, and more.

These brief descriptions are meant merely to whet the appetite of those seeking architectural treasures. Some of the greatest masterpieces are very near the Dorilton. These include the famed Dakota on 72nd and Central Park West, the Apthorp on Broadway and 79th Street, the Belnord on 86th Street and Broadway, and the San Remo on Central Park West between 74th and 75th Streets. The San Remo's famed temple-like towers on top of the building neatly conceal its water tanks!

At the end of my walk, I descend the narrow stairs at 65½ W. 70th Street to the Shalel Lounge. There isn't a sign to attract tourists, but West Side insiders know this place, and once I'm seated I feel certain that no one could find me in the dim light. It strikes me as a romantic dive spot—there are dark corners to sit in, flowers scattered throughout, and a tiny waterfall toward the back to gaze upon. The walls are exposed brick, the decor sort of Mediterranean/Middle Eastern/North African, as is the food. All in all, I can't think of a more private place on the West Side than the Shalel.

(A) Russian Orthodox Church Outside of Russia
(B) Art Farm in the City
(C) R. C. Church of St. Thomas More
(D) Liederkranz Club
(E) Comic Strip Live of NYC
(F) Orwasher's
(G) Tiny Doll House
(H) The Cherokee
(I) The Impala
(J) Park East Synagogue
(K) The Elder Statesman

A
C
D
E 84 ST
E 82 ST
E 80 ST
FIFTH AVE
MADISON AVE
PARK AVE
LEXINGTON AVE
3RD AVE
E 78 ST
F
G
I
E 74 ST
E 72 ST
E 70 ST
J
E 68 ST
E 66 ST
K
E 64 ST
E 62 ST
E 60 ST
ED KOCH QUEENSBORO BRIDGE

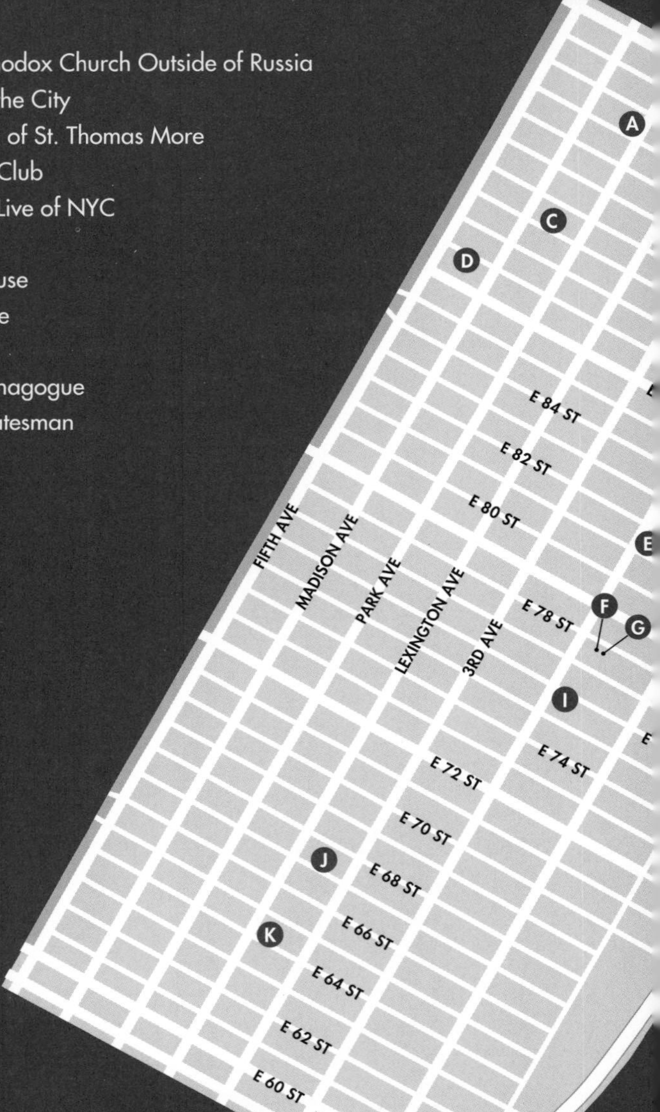

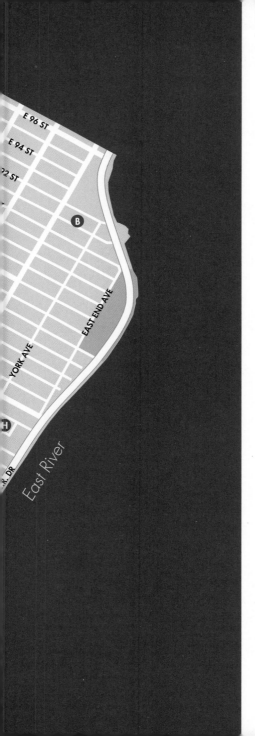

UPPER EAST SIDE

THE UPPER EAST SIDE is one of Manhattan's most famous neighborhoods. Its boundaries are 96th Street on the north, the East River on the east, 59th Street on the south, and Fifth Avenue on the west, which runs along Central Park. Within its borders you will find the world-famous Metropolitan Museum of Art and the Guggenheim, Cooper-Hewitt, and Whitney Museums. There are major houses of worship for all faiths, diplomatic missions, some of the world's most prestigious art galleries, important universities like CUNY's Hunter College and Rockefeller University, and an array of exclusive private schools. Some of the leading hospitals in the world are here, too, including Memorial Sloan-Kettering, Columbia Presbyterian, New York Hospital, and the Hospital for Special Surgery. The area is, however, primarily residential, with Park and Fifth Avenues and most of its side streets comprising some of this country's most expensive real estate. The Upper East Side has a decidedly upper-class feel to it, and it is home to many of the rich and powerful, like Michael Bloomberg, Woody Allen, conservative political donor David Koch, Eliot Spitzer, and many others.

Initially, in the mid-nineteenth century, the Upper East Side was farmland. In the mid-1870s houses began to be built there, and by the turn of the century, it had become much more urban. Park Avenue was avoided by the wealthy because of the smoke that poured out from the railroad that ran beneath it. Instead, they built and bought lots along Fifth Avenue and the side streets, opting for Park Avenue only after the railroad was covered in 1910. The large luxury apartment buildings that define the Upper East Side in the public mind were first constructed around 1916, and they have dominated the landscape since the 1920s—a trend that accelerated as time went on. There is very little public housing here.

The main commercial thoroughfares are Madison, Lexington, Third, Second, and First Avenues. While avenues like Fifth, Park, and East End are almost exclusively residential, all of the commercial avenues are also lined with apartment buildings for their entire length The major east-west, two-way arteries are 96th, 86th, 79th, and 72nd Streets.

While residents consider some of the areas to be distinct subcommunities—Carnegie Hill, Yorkville (home, in the past, to a large German population), and Lenox Hill—the vast majority of both residents and New Yorkers know it simply as the Upper East Side.

While the Upper East Side clearly has a reputation as a tony neighborhood, this isn't universally the case, as a walk in the lower 90s east of Second Avenue reveals. The side streets contain many five-story walk-ups that are perhaps a century old, with the old-style fire escapes and faded brick exteriors. Young people who can't afford better, or older residents from decades ago, find this a good deal, as it's a safe area and they can even tell people they live on the Upper East Side. There are also two low-income NYCHA projects in this area near the East River: the Isaacs Houses and the Holmes Towers.

I begin my explorations at 8 E. 93rd Street, where I see on the wall of a brownstone and slightly below the ground floor several embossed white terracotta images. From left to right, there are three fish, one on top of the other, followed by a winged, bare-breasted angel, followed by a seahorse, Neptune holding his trident and riding on a mythological creature, and another figure holding a giant fish over his shoulders. It's just one example of the hundreds of interesting townhouses to be found and enjoyed on the neighborhood's side streets.

This street is also home to the Russian Orthodox Church Outside of Russia, at 75 E. 93rd Street. It's a large five-story red-brick building with white marble and a copper roof. You simply can't miss it. I speak with an elderly woman who lives on the block, who tells me that Billy Rose, the Broadway impresario, once lived here, at #56 on 93rd Street. Many New Yorkers, especially Manhattanites, love playing the deferred status game, namely that they live near or have met someone famous, etc. This takes an unusual turn, however, as she continues:

"I remember years ago I went down the block to the Russian Orthodox church to say a prayer and light a candle for this Jewish woman. I went in, it's empty, I'm lighting a candle, and all of a sudden, you know how you can tell when somebody's behind you? You know how it is. And a man says to me, 'Excuse me, ma'am, would you please leave?' As soon as I heard that statement I knew I was talking to a military. So I did my Agatha Christie, you know, Miss Marple. I turned around and I saw the pin, Secret Service. And then I saw the bishop. He pulls my arm down and says, 'Stay.' And suddenly I see the helicopters and I'm wondering: 'What have I got myself in for?' And what comes up the steps, guys with rifles. One was speaking Russian, the other English. And then, what comes up the steps, but Vladimir Putin. You know he's a very shrewd guy. Don't put too much past him; a short guy though. The church never wanted to talk to Moscow. They're outside Russia."

"Why was he interested in coming here?"

"Are you kidding? A lot of Russians come over here and he doesn't want to lose them."

The idea that Putin showed up at the church on her corner is very important to this woman. It gives her something to talk about that's of interest, and it gives her status. She lives in an interesting place, where world leaders come to discuss important matters. And she was there—a part of history, as it were. And the bishop allowed her to witness his arrival. In a way, it's a story that could only happen in a place like New York City. Putin doesn't go to Dubuque, Cincinnati, or any one of a thousand places in the United States. Did the visit really happen? It's hard to say, but it is a fact that Putin met with Metropolitan Laurus, the church's leader in New York, on September 24, 2003, at the Russian Consulate General on E. 91st Street. It wouldn't be hard to imagine a private visit to the church, a two-minute ride away.

As I talk with this woman, I come to see that she's also a community character. She knows everyone on the block and what's going on—who bought a house, who's having trouble. These are generally people who give the block a certain flavor, but they are also persons who can be counted on when someone needs advice or a favor, or just wants to know what's really happening on the block.

At 1185 Park Avenue, spanning 93rd to 94th Street, there's an impressive building with an imposing Gothic triple-arched entrance. Built in 1929, it's the only building left on Park Avenue that has an interior courtyard. There are six lobbies, each one with an elevator that opens to two apartments per floor. I look toward downtown, taking in the canyon-like view of the famous building-lined avenue. Quite a distance down the avenue, I am struck by the pencil-thin super-tall structure that appears to be in the middle of the avenue, but which is really 432 Park Avenue, situated between E. 56th and E. 57th Streets. I chat with a woman walking her dog who suddenly says to me, "You see that tall building down there. I call it the middle-finger building, like it's giving me and everyone else the finger." I laugh and say, "That's a pretty strong statement." "Well, I think it's hideous. You can see it from New Jersey, from anywhere in the area." She's talking about what in 2016 was the tallest residential building in the country, topping out at 1,396 feet. It's interesting that it has evoked such a strong reaction from someone who sees it from two miles away. Who knows what others are thinking about it? Changing a view by constructing a building or blocking someone's view can be seen as a violation of private space even if the skyline is really public space, and even if what was built is miles away from a person's home. People whose view of the Hudson River is blocked feel that way, but here it's not blocked; it's just that the building is *intruding* on a view, and that's bad enough for some people.

Around the corner, on 93rd, between Park and Lexington Avenue, I walk by a freestanding ten-room, lone clapboard house at #128 from a much earlier era, 1866, that recently sold for a reported $12 million. The house reportedly also has a fourteen-foot treehouse in the backyard. A resident who knew the seller informs me: "[The previous owner was] from the Boston area and was married to Geraldo Rivera. As you know, the marriage went on the rocks and eventually she sold the house and returned to Boston with her children. She had a golden retriever, she was nice, she was fun. Everyone misses the lady."

As I'm crossing Lexington against the light, there being no cars in sight, it occurs to me that New Yorkers have a peculiar advantage over residents of many other American cities, like Los Angeles. They believe they have a right to cross even when the light is red. Since enforcement of this law is minimal, if not nonexistent, they get to do something illegal about twenty times a day and get away with it! In how many cities can people make that boast? Naturally, anyone who does this needs to look every way, especially for bicyclists, before crossing.

Continuing east, I see an unusual-looking bust of Elvis Presley in the window of a brownstone at 184 E. 93rd Street. The doorman tells me people often take note of it. A little farther east is the Gaga Center. It has nothing to do with Lady Gaga. It's actually the name for an updated version of dodgeball, and there is a bunch of kids inside playing the game.

A few blocks south, at Ruppert Towers on E. 91st Street between Second and Third Avenues, there's a plaque dedicated in memory of the actor Jimmy Cagney. When he was the mayor, David Dinkins renamed the entire block James Cagney Place. Cagney actually grew up on E. 96th Street, and Ruppert Towers is on the site of the Ruppert Brewery, originally located between 90th and 94th Streets and owned by Jacob Ruppert, who also owned the New York Yankees. There's overlap here, as the brewery was founded in the nineteenth century and closed in 1965. Cagney was born at the dawn of the twentieth century and died in 1986. In Manhattan, virtually every street has a rich history. For example, the Marx brothers were raised at 179 E. 93rd Street, and the building still stands.

At 419 E. 91st Street, between First and York Avenues, my attention is drawn to the Art Farm in the City, an arts center with an array of programs for children. It bills itself as "New York City's only indoor farm" and includes a petting zoo. The "animals" are a fairly conventional collection of hamsters, bunnies, and birds. But it is the old red-brick and terracotta building that it occupies that catches my eye because it's covered with a labyrinth of vines that bloom in the spring, sprouting purple blossoms. This is the best time to view it, in all its glory. In the summer, the entire structure, first built in 1886, is obscured by the vines.

I head east on 91st Street, one more block, to East End Avenue. Turning right, I soon come to Gracie Mansion, on 88th Street. This is where Mayor de Blasio makes his home, but for me the real attraction is glorious Carl Schurz Park, which surrounds the mansion and runs from 89th to 84th Street between East End Avenue and the East River. It's a public park but is amply endowed by private donors. The walkways are well maintained, with fieldstone walls and little stone-lined bridges, and the landscaping is beautiful, with many varieties of flowers and trees. Heidi, my dog, was especially appreciative of the dog run, which has a nice view of the river. The East River Greenway, or Esplanade, runs along the park and the rest of the Upper East Side and is used daily by thousands of walkers, runners, and those who simply want to look at the bridges and islands.

Continuing south on East End, I pause between 86th and 87th Streets. Starting with #140 on 86th Street is a row of townhouses made from brownish-gray fieldstone and red brick, with arched doorways and windows as well as roof gardens. Sergei, a Ukrainian immigrant wheeling an elderly lady down the street, tells me about their history: "Many years ago a Jewish woman tried to rent a house here but was turned down because of her religion. Later, when she became famous in the cosmetics business she bought it. Maybe you heard of her. Her name was Helena Rubinstein." Rubinstein has been described in books and articles as the first self-made female millionaire. The story told by Sergei is true, but the location is wrong. Here's the scoop: Denied an apartment at 625 Park Avenue near E. 65th Street, Rubinstein bought the entire building and moved into a stupendous twenty-seven-room penthouse triplex. This story once again illustrates the importance of doing research and establishing the facts. When passed from mouth to mouth, something can quickly become a fact when it isn't, transforming into an urban legend, if you will.

Heading back two blocks to 89th Street, I turn left and walk west. There's a truly impressive-looking church on E. 89th Street, between Park and Madison Avenues, the R. C. Church of St. Thomas More. Made of Nova Scotia sandstone and built in 1870 in the Gothic Revival style, it's a real standout. It's modeled after Edward B. Lamb's Church of St. Martin's, Gospel Oak, London, built in 1865. Inside, there are outstanding stained-glass windows, a wide basilica, intricately carved pews, and a high white ceiling embossed with golden sunbursts from which intricately designed lamps hang.

Continuing to Madison Avenue, I go left to 87th Street, where I make a right. Halfway up the block I arrive at #6, the Liederkranz Club. Established in 1847, it's a group dedicated to preserving German cultural life. Outside, on the left-hand side of the building, there's a statue of Polyhymnia, the Greek goddess of poetry and

R.C. Church of St. Thomas More. A real Nova Scotia sandstone standout.

hymns, with a child next to her, singing, perhaps. It was created by Giuseppe Moretti, a renowned sculptor who also worked on the base of the Statue of Liberty. Here, the names of famous German composers are inscribed, encircling the statue's base. I enter the building and ask a German-accented man what the club does. "Partly it's a singing group which sponsors competition among singers. Can you sing?" he asks. "Yes," I say. "What do you sing?" "A little of everything." "Are you a tenor?" "As a matter of fact, yes." "Good We need tenors. We absolutely need tenors. There's only one. You have to come and sing with us. Can you learn German a little bit?" "*Ich kann Deutsch sprechen.*" "Then you absolutely must join us. Our group is getting small. Stay here. We start our rehearsal in an hour. Once a week. Every Thursday. You come in the right time. We need you desperately." His approach is a combination of desperation and an expectation that, if I have the credentials there's no excuse not to join his club, almost as though it's an obligation.

Mr. Donat is a kind gentleman in his 80s and turns out to be completely immersed in German culture. He came to the United States in 1948. I don't ask why because I worry it might be too intrusive. He shows me the bar and proclaims German beer to be "the best beer in the world." Perhaps it is. "What really killed the German language in this country is World War I." "Because Germany went to war with America?" "No," he corrects me. "Because America went to war with Germany. Woodrow Wilson was a prime idiot. He had good intentions but not the wherewithal to make them work. He just set the situation up for World War II." He gives me a tour of the building, including the basement, which features a stern-looking statue of a helmeted man clad in heavy armor. "If you join the club, the entertainment consists of making puns and they give you a fancy title, but it's all just a put-on."

For this man and his small choir, the club is a mainstay of their social life. Music is what holds the group together. And even though hardly anything remains of the Yorkville German community, save for a few churches, restaurants, and small organizations, Donat is fiercely loyal to it. Yet, probably because he is aware of its precarious position, he will welcome anyone, including me, no questions asked. In fact, Donat's club is similar to a German/Slovenian musical group I came across in Ridgewood, Queens. These communities were once very vital. Today, all that's left are a few individuals who enjoy re-living the past—singing, belonging to clubs, and frequenting the few German eateries that remain in the city. For the newer groups of Albanians, Cambodians, and Nepalese, it's a window into their futures, should they follow the seemingly inevitable cycle of accul-turation and then finally, assimilation.

Next, I head east on 87th down to Third Avenue and turn right. On E. 82nd Street I swing left. Hungarians are another, though smaller, ethnic group that once had a presence on the Upper East Side. They tended to live between 75th and 83rd Streets, and 79th Street was their grand boulevard, so to speak. To see what's left and what once was, I stop at the still functioning Hungarian or Magyar House, at #213. It's a small Federal-style red-brick building accom-modating several Hungarian-oriented organizations, and it includes a small library and a center for meetings, concerts, and talks. On the day that I am exploring the neighborhood, there's a commemoration of the Hungarian Revolution of 1848 scheduled for 7:00 p.m. at Hungarian House. An excursion like this is a perfect example of how walking New York often becomes a three-dimensional histor-ical lesson about its different eras.

At Second Avenue I turn right, where I see a line of about 150 people on the east side of the street. Young folks are waiting for a once-a-year audition opportunity with Comic Strip Live of NYC. They'll get a ticket and a time to show up for their big chance. Since New York is a center for this sort of thing—with eight comedy clubs in Manhattan alone—I decide to find out more by striking up a conversation with Don, a thirtyish man with a black beard, dressed in a black tee shirt to match. He's from Midwood, Brooklyn, and graduated Brooklyn College with a degree in communication.

"You only have this opportunity today?"

"Yes, you should try it yourself."

"Well, I'm not that outgoing, I guess. What kind of crowd do you get?"

"Well, there are 'bringer shows,' where you get a chance to perform if you can guarantee paying customers, namely your friends and relatives. But this place doesn't work that way. Here, if they like you, you can get a show for a week, even a month."

"Have you done this before?" I ask.

"Yes, but it's my first time here. I have a full-time job in TV production, but this is what I love doing."

"Isn't it a brutal profession? I mean, what if you tell jokes and nobody laughs. How do you deal with the humiliation?"

"I haven't experienced that, but I know others who have. It's an awful feeling because you're trying to sell your brand of humor and people don't want it. And when that happens, you just have to go back and polish and keep trying."

"Are good comics born or made?"

"You have to have that inclination to be funny, and then you have to practice and perfect your delivery, tempo, how to control a crowd. There are places to try out your material, but a lot of times most of the people who show up are comedians, and they don't laugh because they're analyzing your material. I've done okay though. My biggest crowd was 200 people and it went well."

This conversation makes me realize how there are many people for whom their day job isn't necessarily what they love and that it's these kinds of opportunities that make life interesting for them. A number of people whom I spoke with on the line were from elsewhere—in one case, Arizona; in another, Michigan; in a third, France. They come here because there are so many comedy clubs, but that's also why the number of people applying is much larger.

When you walk a neighborhood in its entirety, patterns become apparent. One that struck me was the presence of many tall buildings with white-glazed-brick exteriors, many of them dating back to the 1950s and earlier. This is a phenomenon not seen elsewhere in the city. It was, in large part, a snobbish response by an upper-class neighborhood to the proliferation of red-brick public housing projects and tenement buildings, including some on the Upper East Side. The architectural trendsetters were unimpressed, however, viewing them as lacking in creativity, and in a short time they became unpopular. Nonetheless, today they are seen as an important part of the area's history.

On E. 78th Street, I make a left off Second Avenue and soon come across two stores next to each other, each of them unusual in a totally different way. One is Orwasher's, at #308, a terrific bakery specializing in creative bread products. How many bakeries, even in New York, have been around for 100 years? They're not on a main shopping artery; they don't have to be since they have legions of fans. During the summer months, limos heading toward the Hamptons line up to purchase their breads, which include Spelt Bread, Pumpernickel Raisin, New York Rye, Irish Soda Bread, and Cabernet Rustica. The breads look really interesting and there's a line even on a weekday at 11:00 a.m. The new owner, Keith Cohen, has introduced new offerings while keeping the old favorites. I speak with an older Hungarian woman, who's worked here for many years. She has sparkling eyes and steel gray hair, and she loves what she's doing. "What's special about your breads?" "We use no preservatives, and we never sell day-old bread. Instead we give it away to charities." Next door is the Tiny Doll House. "To me they're not tiny at all," I say to the owner. "Why did you name the store 'Tiny'?" "Because they're tiny compared to regular houses," she responds with a laugh. Every single house contains intricately designed furniture—settees, dining room tables, chess tables, bedroom sets. I learn that this is not a cheap hobby. One really small couch can cost $400. A furnished home is at least several thousand dollars. As far as I can tell, their claim to be the only store devoted exclusively to doll houses is correct. It's worth seeing as a museum even if one doesn't wish to buy one.

RUSSIAN PUMPERNICKEL
$4.50 // HALF
$7.75 // WHOLE

SWISS HEALTH
$5.75

MORNING SPELT
$7

RAISIN PUMPERNICKEL
$5.25

NEW YORK PLAIN RYE LONG
$4.75

NEW YORK PLAIN RYE ROUND
$4.75

CINNAMON RAISIN
$5.25

NEW YORK SEEDED RYE LONG
$4.75

NEW YORK S...
RO...

Bet you can't eat just one!

Cherokee Place runs from E. 78th to E. 77th Street, a block east of York Avenue. To get there I walk east on 78th past York and turn right. It's not a street anyone except locals are likely to know about. Indeed, I asked a longtime resident of 78th and Third about it, and he was unfamiliar with the street. It is, nonetheless, not an undistinguished place, since John Jay Park, known for its great large public swimming pool, is there. Unsurprisingly, it's packed with visitors during the summer.

But the real point of interest for me is a large, attractive, and unusual six-story walkup called the Cherokee, extending from 77th to 78th Street. It is divided into four separate buildings that can be accessed by crossing over a footbridge from one of the roofs to the other. It has several locked entrances that lead into the apartments and an inner courtyard. The exterior features Juliet balconies with railings on all floors, so named after the scene in Shakespeare's play where Romeo courts Juliet as she appears on the balcony, or patio. They are usually a half-foot to a foot wide, thus making it just possible to stand on, with ironwork railings and a small tiled roof for protection from the rain. Built in 1912 as lower-income housing, the buildings had several innovations, including high radiators that could be easily swept clean, high and triple-hung windows, glazed terracotta and tile in various parts of the buildings, especially on the ground floor and near the top. And those balconies were designed to provide fresh air, with TB sufferers in mind. Apartments facing the east had pretty views of the East River. As I stared at this imposing structure, I wondered why there were no fire escapes. That question was answered when I entered through a gate and discovered circular exterior stairwells with a separate entrance for each apartment. It is regarded as probably one of the finest complexes ever constructed for the poor.

At this point I head west on 77th Street to First Avenue, where I make a left and then go left again on 76th Street. A few yards away I come to the Impala, a building that immediately captures my attention. "Captures" is an apt description because what made me notice it was a great, life-size bronze, shiny, golden-colored statue of an impala, an antelope that ranges across the savannahs of Africa. As it is known to be an adaptable creature, it's no surprise, perhaps, that it should end up in New York City! It's actually standing on its hind legs, looking like it's about to take off—and why not, as it's famous for its ability to leap up to ten feet. It's one of fourteen impalas, the remainder of which are to be found in the back garden, behind the lobby, in various poses. The building, designed by the acclaimed architect Michael Graves, is mostly red and white brick with interesting patterns and unusually large windows. While it looks like a seven-story structure, it's actually a thirty-one-floor high-rise, the two buildings being connected by a passageway.

The elegantly dressed doorman, Renold, a friendly and gregarious fellow originally from Haiti, is standing outside the entrance. Pleased by my interest in the building, he invites me inside for a tour. The lobby, also by Graves, has wall panels with drawings of African motifs of zebras, giraffes, and woodlands and is surrounded by highly polished blonde-colored wood imported from Italy. Renold explains why: "The main owner, Trevor Davis, is from South Africa, and he wanted to retain aspects of his native culture. And the impala is native to his region. Way back, around 2001, I saw a man taking photos of the building and asked him what he was doing, and he said he was taking photos for a newspaper article. And at the same time, he said, laughing: 'The newest building on the block, but the one with the biggest you-know-whats!'" As I look again at the impala standing upright, fully exposed, I get the joke, as Renold adds: "You will notice that the antelope is missing an essential part of his anatomy, which was removed. We left nature as nature had intended. Later on we had to cut and remove parts of the statue." "I see. The impala had an operation." "Yes!"

I speak with a couple in the lobby, Morris and Sondra Silver, who tell me about the building's amenities, which include a sauna, steam room, business center, cinema room, and even a wine cellar. In truth, placing a shiny, exquisitely sculpted, and unique statue outside the building draws attention to what is only one of many high-rises searching for buyers who can afford to live in them.

Leaving this building, I head west on 76th and turn left on Third Avenue, strolling down to 67th Street, where I make a right. The Upper East Side has a large Jewish population, and its numerous synagogues reflect that. Here, about 200 yards up the street, is where the Park East Synagogue is located, just a few doors down. Built in the late nineteenth century (1889), when Moorish-style synagogues were popular, it is a national landmark. It's magnificently preserved and has a rose window, more commonly associated with churches. It violates the symmetry found in most buildings in that one of its twin towers is asymmetrical; yet it still seems to harmonize nicely with the rest of its structure and is fun to explore inside as well.

I return to Third Avenue and walk down to 64th Street. I turn right and see a sign above a shop that reads, "The Elder Statesman," a name that definitely sounds unusual for a store. In fact, Manhattan has thousands of retail shops trying to attract customers by distinguishing themselves from others. These stores deserve mention in any book describing the borough, so I decide to focus on this one. Was this shop pitching clothing for older men by referring to them as statesmen? Curious to learn more, I ventured inside and discovered the error of my ways. The Elder Statesman, which first started in Los Angeles, sells high-end luxury items made of cashmere and is well known in the fashion industry. It's on the ground floor of a townhouse that also is owned by the proprietor of the shop, and its sweaters, hats, and other cashmere items lie neatly on tables made in a small woodworking shop in Greenpoint, Brooklyn. They are flanked by whitewashed walls in an appealing combination of elegance and simplicity. For me, the goal was to find out what went into such an effort and why it stood out. The store opened in December and was empty when I entered on a Friday afternoon in March.

"This is a really neat-looking place," I began, and then asked, "I was just wondering about something—why did you call it The Elder Statesman?"

"It's a sort of homage to the founder's older brother," says Jake, a young, nattily attired salesman. "But what we sell is for anyone, young or old. We're all about great cashmere." This is an accurate description. The owner, Greg Chait, has made pillows and stuffed animals from cashmere, and even a sleeping bag, simply because he was going camping in his backyard with his daughter. He also created a huge cashmere quilt, just for the hell of it.

"How are you doing?"

"Fine. We didn't want to be downtown, where we might get lost in all the foot traffic. We make one or two appointments a day, and that's really all we need. And, of course, people just walk in. Today, a woman came in and picked out a bunch of sweaters and bought them. Our sweaters generally go from $600 up to $3,000 off the table. So that was easily enough business for an entire day. And we also will do a lot of custom creations where you can pick any color and design and we'll make it to order in our factory. Of course, that's expensive. It could be up to $10,000, depending on what you want. What's somewhat unique is the custom work we do even while we're a retail shop. Our founder, Greg Chait, is from California, a surfer. He wanted to use the best yarns from the best sources, and make the best cashmere."

"Is there something unique about this cashmere?"

"Besides the best quality, Greg found a way to wash and tumble it that gave it a relaxed look and feel, emphasizing the LA culture, a sweater that's fluffy and light, not flat, actually to make it look like you live in the sweater and have had it for a long time. Also, we had to make them in darker colors for our New York line. It's a real winter city. And we have this really neat garden behind us." I look and see a backyard garden that's indoors, with palm trees, or what looks like palm trees.

"Does this garden actually make a difference?"

"Yes, because when people see it, they say 'I feel like I'm in Santa Barbara.' You have to pay attention to the details."

That's one important takeaway here. Shops that cater to a discerning clientele must pay attention to detail. It has to have a certain look. Left unsaid but surely intentional is the laid-back feeling associated with California. The salespeople are relaxed, in no hurry to make a sale, unintrusive, dressed very informally, and as friendly as you want them to be. They're proud of their product and knowledgeable. Most shops want to be on the avenues and pay a premium for it. But for these types of boutique stores, being on a side street is part of the cachet. It tells you they don't necessarily need your business, though they certainly want it. In a way, this epitomizes what the Upper East Side is all about to its many well-heeled residents. They're self-confident in who they are—not showy, but satisfied in a deeper sense with the lifestyle they've created and subscribe to.

Yet it's also important to remember that while this demographic constitutes a large slice of this neighborhood, many other types live here too—working-class white, young people in the fast lane, poor people living in public housing—in short, a microcosm of the city. These groups may not pay much attention to The Elder Statesman, but they are surely aware of the lifestyle it represents. The fact that so many different groups live so closely together is what makes Manhattan such a special place. You can't wall off your space completely.

As I walk around the Upper East Side, especially along Park Avenue, I notice the gold brass signs of the physicians and dentists. There's a general perception that offices here are better than others. I find myself wondering: Are these doctors and dentists really that much better than those elsewhere? Or is it that they're not better but are thought of as such because they're able to afford offices here? Well, certainly they make more money in this locale, given their upper-crust clientele. The answer, it turns out, as gleaned from conversations with several doctors, is that most of them received their training in the prestigious, largely local hospitals—Columbia,

Rockefeller, Sloan-Kettering, Cornell, and Mount Sinai. Thus, they established offices in the communities surrounding them. Also, those interning and doing their residencies here develop relationships with the senior medical staff and, if they're good and/or well liked, are invited to join the practices. This is just one example of how educational/professional choices and location can determine destiny.

A Strawberry Fields
B Ladies Pavilion
C Blockhouse
D Conservatory Garden
E Sisters of Charity of St. Vincent De Paul
F Seneca Village
G The Ravine and Huddlestone Arch
H Chess and checkers area

CENTRAL PARK NORTH (110 ST)

Harlem Meer

The Pool

WEST DR

97 ST TRANSVERSE

EAST DR

CENTRAL PARK WEST

The Reservoir

86 ST TRANSVERSE

FIFTH AVE

Turtle Pond

79 ST TRANSVERSE

The Lake

WEST DR

TERRACE DR

65 ST TRANSVERSE

EAST DR

CENTER DR

CENTRAL PARK SOUTH (59 ST)

The Pond

CENTRAL PARK

CENTRAL PARK ISN'T A NEIGHBORHOOD with streets and buildings. So why include it here? It's the size and the quality of what it has to offer that make it such an essential part of the immediate residential neighborhoods it borders—Central Harlem, the Upper East Side, and the Upper West Side. In fact, it's a large part of what makes these communities so much more attractive to live in. It's remarkable when you consider the value of this 843-acre piece of land. Just think how many residential and commercial towers could have been erected here. That it's a worldwide destination simply adds to the allure and further justifies its inclusion. And the public has spoken. With over 40 million visitors a year, it's easily the most visited park in the nation. One fact that the majority of people, perhaps even native New Yorkers, are unaware of is that Central Park is manmade. Its lakes were created and its trees were planted. It was not a natural forest tamed by those who came upon it.

The park was established in 1857 and designed by famed architects Frederick Law Olmsted and Calvert Vaux. Its boundaries are 110th Street on the north, Fifth Avenue on the east, 59th Street on the south, and Central Park West on the west. There's really nothing that's totally unknown in the park, at least as far as I know! And yet, no book on walking Manhattan would be complete without a brief discussion of this oasis of sheer pleasure and tranquility. People vary in what their favorites are—the reservoir, the Ramble, the fountain at Bethesda Terrace, the Sheep Meadow. There are, however, places that are less well known than others, which we'll note here.

Locals treat Central Park in a similar manner to how suburban dwellers treat their backyard. People have frequently said to me that they didn't miss their home in rural New Jersey or Roslyn, Long Island, because they now had an entire park at their disposal. For others, myself included, it's the memories it evokes that make it special. As a child living two blocks from the park, I remember playing cops and robbers at W. 105th Street on the rocky formations, with their many hiding places and lookout points. Others will recall going to playgrounds when they were children, or ice skating at Wollman Rink—a great place for a romantic date.[20]

At 72nd Street and Central Park West, I take a quick look at the Dakota, where John Lennon had lived. Even if I hadn't, the park entrance with the sign "Strawberry Fields" would have reminded me of both his life and murder. Halfway up the walkway to the fields, a man is selling buttons with Lennon's name on them, but what impresses me is his detailed knowledge of the park in terms of places and trails. I guess if you stand in such a strategic location, you have to be ready to answer visitors' questions.

Walking north on a path to my left, I pass a lake. I ask a park worker what it's called. His answer is almost apologetic: "It's called the Lake. I wish I had something more poetic to tell you." On this cloudy August day, it's nevertheless quite pretty. The reflection of trees, which are very close to the water, cause the lake to appear very green. I soon come to the Ladies Pavilion. "Why is it called that?" I ask a young woman. "Because it's a very pretty place," she responds, laughing. "But I'm sure there are other reasons too, that I don't know." She's right. The beautiful wrought-iron, filigreed gazebo there was originally a shelter for people, and ladies in particular, to stand under while they waited for the trolley that once went by here.

One important historical site in the park is the Blockhouse, one of the oldest forts in the city, with some of the ruins dating back to the Revolutionary Era. It's rarely visited, in part because it's hard to climb up to where it is. The location is best accessed by entering the park from the north at Adam Clayton Powell Jr. Boulevard and walking along the road that once allowed cars to enter there.

Central Park—man-made but forever wild. Can you locate the spot?

A visit to the Conservatory Garden on Fifth Avenue and 105th Street makes it amply clear why the park is such a special place. Looking out from the gateway entrance onto the perfectly manicured lawn and gardens, I'm reminded of the gardens at Versailles, France, and in Ravello on Italy's Amalfi Coast.

Of course, the park has its problems too. In northeastern Central Park, the lake known as the Harlem Meer is almost completely covered with toxic algae bloom. A woman sitting on a bench nearby comments: "It's nature's way of rebelling." Against what, she didn't say. It's sad, but algae bloom is a common problem in many parts of the country.

The park has lots of history and a few yards away, I see a sign on the grass that reads: "Somewhere along this road was the site of the first motherhouse of the Sisters of Charity of St. Vincent De Paul and the Academy of Mount St. Vincent, a convent school, which lasted from 1847 to 1881." This was probably the only convent that was once a tavern and then became a tavern again. History buffs might also want to view the site of Seneca Village. As evidence of how little is known about it, when I asked a number of New Yorkers familiar with the park, all except one said they believed it was an Indian village. It was actually a community of predominantly black property owners that existed from 1825 to 1857, when it was razed to make way for Central Park. The location was from about 82nd to 89th Street along the western edge of the park. About fifty yards east of the 85th Street entrance to the park, there's a rocky area on the left. Although I saw no commemorative marking, it was reportedly the site of the Methodist Episcopal Zion Church that was part of this community.[21]

North from here, equal to about 104th Street and to the east, is a charming section called the Ravine, seldom visited. Not so long ago, the northern section of the park, from 100th to 110th Streets, especially on the west side, was considered somewhat dangerous, and the Ravine is in this area. Today, that's no longer the case. Reputations of this sort die hard, but walking along there I was impressed by the large number of park personnel active in the area. It's worth the trip because when I walk through the Ravine, especially the Loch part at the bottom, it feels like I'm not in a city, but in the lower Adirondacks or the Catskills. Of particular interest is the Huddlestone Arch, a pretty stone arch held together by sheer gravity.

The southern portion of the park, from 86th through 59th Street scarcely requires mention here, as it is quite well known. For chess and checkers aficionados, there is such a center near the Wollman skating rink, at roughly 64th Street. The chess players there are quite skilled, and it's a very relaxing setting. I sit and watch two teenagers, who seem to be really good, playing a timed match. As I sit there, hoping to play the winner, I remember the day when, as a teenager, I played against Bobby Fischer. I was one of thirty contestants. When he came to you, if you didn't have your move ready, you forfeited the game. Who won? That's a story for another section of this book.

A Main Street Dance/Theatre Alliance
B Riverwalk Bar and Grill
C Tom Otterness sculptures
D The Octagon
E FDR Four Freedoms Park

Lighthouse Park

WEST RD

EAST RD

C D

MAIN ST

RIVER RD

MAIN ST

ROOSEVELT ISLAND BRIDGE

East River

A

East River

WEST RD MAIN ST

B

ED KOCH QUEENSBORO BRIDGE

WEST LOOP RD

EAST LOOP RD

E

ROOSEVELT ISLAND

GEOGRAPHICALLY, ROOSEVELT ISLAND IS A REALLY UNUSUAL PLACE.
Situated between Manhattan Island and Queens, it's considered
part of Manhattan. Its boundaries are the East River on all four
sides. And its north-south equivalents are roughly from 85th to
46th Street. It can be reached by tram from Manhattan on Second
Avenue between 59th and 60th Streets. There's also a stop for the
F train, and cars and buses can get there from Queens via 36th
Avenue. As a result, Manhattan and Queens are only minutes away.
It has but one major artery, Main Street, which runs the length of
this narrow strip of land. The island is owned by the city and leased
to the state. Like nearby Hunters Point in Queens, this part of the
city has stunning views of the Manhattan skyline.

From 1666 until 1828, when the island was purchased by the
city, it was privately owned and known as Blackwell's Island. During
the nineteenth century, it was home to several hospitals, a prison,
and an insane asylum. In 1921, it was renamed Welfare Island in
recognition of the City Hospital, which was located there. The
prison remained until 1935, when Rikers Island was established.
Its final naming occurred in 1971 when it became Roosevelt Island
in memory of former president Franklin Delano Roosevelt. Today
big changes are afoot, as a huge technology center, created jointly
by Cornell University and Technion-Israel Institute of Technology,
goes up. Roosevelt Island comprises a mix of various ethnic, racial,
and religious groups. Shopping is enough to cover basic needs, with
a Gristedes supermarket, a Starbucks, a pizza shop, and other stores,
but the options are limited. The crime rate is quite low.

I begin walking from the northernmost part of the island, on the
west side and near the equivalent of 79th Street, where there are
some sculptures by Tom Otterness that are critical of money's

corrupting influence. Called "The Marriage of Money and Real Estate," they're in the water and appear or disappear according to the tides. I also notice some high-quality community gardens in this area. The people who have plots tend to be quite sophisticated in their tastes and it shows. They're members of the Roosevelt Island Garden Club, and they grow an incredible variety of plants, including lemon balm, portulaca, great blue lobelia, and morning glory, to name just a few.

Housing here is mostly for middle-class folks. Many of the people have been here for decades. There's a mix of condos and housing that's rent-stabilized, but there is luxurious housing too, like Southtown, Manhattan Park, and the aptly named Octagon, which features nicely sculptured blue-gray stone; there are apartments for middle-class residents here too. No one seems the least bit deterred by the fact that the Octagon was once an insane asylum. Of far greater interest to them, no doubt, is that it has the largest number of solar panels of any building in the city. In what may become a pattern, these high-end apartments are especially attractive to those who cannot afford Manhattan or Brooklyn prices. Until now Roosevelt Island has been home to mostly families and older people, many of whom have been here for a long time, dating back to the 1970s and '80s. A new trend is the arrival of many young men and women who are students at various schools and find the lower rents quite enticing.

As I continue south on Main Street, I see some cultural activity at #548 in the form of the Main Street Dance/Theatre Alliance, which has been here for many years. They attract a mix of established performers and new stars seen as having potential. Tickets to these shows are cheap, and there's talk about expanding the offerings to include more evening entertainment. Other than that, there isn't that much to do by way of nightlife except for the Riverwalk Bar and Grill, at 425 Main, whose menu includes a little bit of everything, from fish and chips to pierogies. Service is slow but very friendly.

The Octagon—a former insane asylum, now rehabilitated.

Families like the feeling of safety that their kids have on the island as well as the weekly farmer's market. While there's no movie theater or nightclub, the residents with whom I spoke don't seem to mind much, though their teenaged children often do. The older people like the quieter life, and they know they can be in Manhattan proper within fifteen minutes if they have a yen for a more entertaining evening. They also fret about the new technology center, worrying that it will bring too many people to the island. "I like the fact that there's really nothing to do here because then people don't come here to do anything," one woman said, laughing. In other words, boredom is a good trade-off if it also results in peace and tranquility. It's worth mentioning, in this vein, that some less-than-tranquil people who have lived here include Sarah Jessica Parker, at the beginning of her career; Kofi Annan, while he was UN Secretary General; Al "Grampa Munster" Lewis, at the end of his career; and Buddy Hackett, sometime in midcareer (probably a pied-à-terre, since his main residence was in Malibu, California). Grampa was sort of an unofficial mayor here and could easily be found at one of his favorite hangouts, the senior citizens center on Main Street.

A half-mile farther down, I reach the FDR Four Freedoms State Park, which is situated on the island's southern tip. The path along the river that leads to the park is lined with many cherry trees that are beautiful when they blossom sometime in May. The park is only four acres in size, but the vistas of the city are first rate. Ascending a number of steps, I look southward over a large lawn flanked on each side by trees. Off in the distance you can see a large bust of FDR, in which he looks like he's staring intently at me or anyone else who happens to be standing here. Behind the bust are the water and the deep blue sky. All in all, it's a well-designed and dignified memorial tribute to the man. Still, there are those who yearn for the old days, as one longtime resident told me: "I loved it when it was wild, not planned, and the geese came here. It just felt really rural. We could also watch the [Macy's Fourth of July] fireworks for free, and now you need a ticket to see them." It's a theme I've encountered over and over again. People become accustomed to something, find they like it, and disapprove when things change. Sometimes they remember their own youth and vigor as they reflect on what once was and can never be again. Over time, the good parts are remembered, while the bad fades into obscurity. What can be certain is that just as there are those recalling the "good old days" of the '70s, young people today are apt to see the 2016–17 period as very nice in 2040.

CLINTON
(HELL'S KITCHEN)

CHELSEA

CENTRAL MIDTOWN

MIDTOWN EAST

(A) Odd display in front of tenement at 424 W. 56th St.
(B) Centro Maria
(C) Nation's first community court
(D) DeWitt Clinton Park
(E) Clinton Park Stables
(F) Chateau Stables
(G) Mother Ad Agency
(H) Ryan Community Center of Chelsea Clinton
(I) Orchid Man
(J) Alice's Garden

Hudson River

LINCOLN
TUNNEL

J.K. Javits
Convention
Center

12TH AVE
11TH AVE
10TH AVE
9TH AVE

W 5
W 52 ST
W 50 ST
W 48 ST
W 46 ST
W 44 ST
W 42 ST
W 40 ST
W 38 ST
W 36 ST
W 34 ST
W 33 ST
W 31 ST
W 30 ST

D
E
B
F
G
H
J

CLINTON (HELL'S KITCHEN)

THE BORDERS OF CLINTON (MOST OFTEN REFERRED TO AS HELL'S KITCHEN) ARE, roughly speaking, 59th Street on the north, Eighth Avenue on the east, 30th Street on the south and the Hudson River on the west. Some prefer to designate 34th Street as the southern border, but in terms of its commercial and residential characteristics and its look and feel, 30th Street makes more sense. It's also the designation adopted by Community Board 4, which covers Clinton and Chelsea.

Hell's Kitchen was the original name for this area, one that dates back to the 1870s and 1880s, and it might have been the name of a local gang or was just a term that caught on because the area was a slum and had an unsavory reputation. It has also been attributed to a London slum of the same name and even to a comment made by the frontiersman Davy Crockett about Irish slums in Manhattan. It was changed to Clinton after several gang-related murders took place there in 1959. The most famous gang there was the Westies, and the play and film *West Side Story* was based on the neighborhood's history of violence. The name "Hell's Kitchen" does make the neighborhood sound more exciting, and so many commercial establishments have adopted it. Two of many examples are the American Retro Bar and Grill, on Eleventh Avenue and 51st Street, whose sign proudly says it's in Hell's Kitchen, and a Korean eatery at 641 Tenth Avenue called Hell's Chicken. Today, the area is actually quite safe.

In the past, Clinton was populated largely by poor working-class whites, the majority of whom were Irish. It has also been home at various times to Eastern and Southern Europeans, African Americans, and Puerto Ricans. It's been gentrifying since the 1990s, a process that is accelerating today, although there are still many low-income people living in it, generally on the side streets. The area is also home to the Jacob K. Javits Convention Center, CBS headquarters, smaller TV studios, off-Broadway theaters, the Time-Warner Center at Columbus Circle, piers along the Hudson, the Long Island Rail Road Yards, and some very large residential, commercial, and hotel construction projects, both completed and well under way. Although these well-known places are not our focus, it's important to know they're here. Parks include a portion of Hudson River Park as well as the local but full-service DeWitt Clinton Park. The major commercial thoroughfares are Eighth, Ninth, Tenth, and Eleventh Avenues, plus 34th, 42nd, and 57th Streets. Most of the establishments on these avenues serve the local residents—nail salons, delis, restaurants, and the like. Eleventh Avenue also has a number of auto dealerships.

The blocks between Ninth and Tenth Avenues in the mid-50s through the upper 40s are where many of the five-story walk-up tenements that made up Hell's Kitchen a century ago are located. Once cheap, unwanted structures, they have become desirable digs for those unable to afford better who nevertheless want to be somewhere in Manhattan. These include students, aspiring actors and actresses, artists, and immigrants who share these spaces with old-timers who have lived here affordably for decades. Although these buildings are old, the crime rate here today is pretty low, especially compared to earlier days. As I'm walking, I spy a man in a white tee shirt, with steel-gray hair, looking out from a window that opens out to a metal fire escape. It's an unusual a sight these days, whereas looking out the window to take in the passing scene was a staple activity for New Yorkers up until the 1960s, when the ever-increasing popularity of TV watching sent many people indoors. While only 9 percent of Americans had TVs in 1950, 90 percent did in 1960.

At 424 W. 56th Street, I pass such a tenement. On the ground in front of it is an odd display consisting largely of cheap items behind an iron railing, ranging from ceramic ducks flanking a couple of plastic tulips, and broken window screens, to useless pieces of tubing, a couple of white seashells, and a birdcage with a tiny one-winged plastic bird perched on it. The items are carefully arranged in an orderly fashion, leading me to believe their owner sees value in them. And therein lies its appeal—a statement of sorts is being made: "I may not have much, but I take care of it and do my best." Perhaps the "curator" has seen hard times. A placard on the right reads: "Life is not about waiting for the storm to pass. It's about learning to dance in the rain." And it does not appear to have been disturbed despite being only a few doors down from the High School for the Environment, one of the city's roughest high schools. I watch as several large groups of rowdy teenagers pass by this exhibit, paying it no mind.

Just east of Eleventh Avenue, on 54th Street, is the Centro Maria, a four-story, red-brick, Gothic-style residence for young women from all over the world, ages 16–27, with welcome signs in French, Swedish, Tagalog, Korean, and other languages. The organization was founded in Spain more than a century ago by Santa Vicenta Maria and has 129 locations worldwide. A pleasant-faced woman in a pale-blue habit explains to me: "We give the women a home, with two meals a day, for $187 a week. Most are studying in dancing schools around the area. Where else could they get a safe place in Manhattan for this price? That's our mission—to prevent them from getting into trouble, especially drugs." Applicants must be recommended and they must also come from "good families." I comment on how quiet it is inside, as opposed to the noise of traffic on the street. She responds: "I know. It's a characteristic of our houses everywhere. I think it comes from God, because He knows we care. We pray every day for the girls and their families. We know that many of them don't believe in God."

Farther down, between Ninth and Eighth Avenues, on the south side of 54th Street, directly opposite a Romanesque Revival–style Greek Orthodox church, is an exquisitely designed courthouse, dating back to 1894, with four terracotta Corinthian columns framing the windows on the second floor. But it's what's inside that's significant. It's home to the nation's first community court. These courts, which have gained in popularity since this one was launched in 1993, address "quality of life" crimes like shoplifting and prostitution and offer community-based solutions instead of the usual revolving-door prison terms, by getting at the underlying issues. Inside the building, I spoke with Betsy, a well-dressed woman with deep, dark eyes framed by wire-rimmed glasses, who "graduated" from the program and is now a full-time employee there. She had a thirty-year history of alcohol and drug abuse, and this place saved her life, literally. How? "I spent most of my twenty-eight years in New York in jail, but people here had faith in me and told me I could do it, and that changed my life." No doubt, plenty of folks could and perhaps did convey this to Betsy over the years, but the people here apparently got her to believe it. As Betsy put it, "It's trite, but I got 'tough love.'"

I walk around DeWitt Clinton Park on Eleventh Avenue, from 52nd to 54th Street. Inside the playground, alongside the area in front of the benches, there's a long slate-blue ribbon painted over the concrete. The words "Hudson River" are on it, and I realize it is part of a 100-yard-or-so long, gaily colored map of New York State with the major cities identified, as well as points of interest. One of them is the Erie Canal, built by DeWitt Clinton, who had been the governor of New York and, before that, mayor of New York City.[22]

I approach an elderly woman sitting in a padded wheelchair. Barbara welcomes my questions about the park. Born here and of Irish descent, it turns out she has lived in the area her entire life, suffering a moderate stroke only recently. "This is Hell's Kitchen, you know," she tells me. "It's what *West Side Story* was about. I never did see it, though. Didn't need to. I lived it. I've been coming here my whole life. Took my four kids here every day, and now my great-grandchildren play here. And a bunch of us still get together here regularly."

"What do you remember most about this park?" I ask her.

"There used to be a long, white house here, in the '40s and '50s, where we had games of checkers and whatnot. Oh, it was great when we were young." As she speaks, there is a faraway look in her eyes, as if she is remembering what once was. "We stayed in the neighborhood," she continues, "because my husband, he died in 2002, worked right on the docks by 53nd Street."

"What would you say is the most interesting thing you ever did in your life?" I asked Barbara. "I had *them*," she replies, beaming.

"Who?" I ask.

"Who do you think?" she replies. "The kids."

As I leave the park, I approach a middle-aged, balding, heavy-set Hispanic man lying on a piece of cardboard, his head resting on a blue backpack, a large bottle of water standing next to his new-looking Nike sneakers. Clad in faded jeans and a black T-shirt with the words, "San Francisco" emblazoned on it, he is deeply engrossed in a book and hardly pays any attention to me as I stand next to his head. "What are you reading?" I ask. "It's about how to teach yourself Italian," he answers, holding up the slim volume for me to see. I had expected the book to be a novel or popular nonfiction work of the self-help variety. Seeing the surprised look on my face, Manuel continues: "I visited Italy when I was in the service in Europe, and I want so much to go back there again. So I'm waiting to win the lottery to pay for my trip, and this time, when I go, I'll be ready." His tone and expression are dead serious, and I believe him.

This part of town is also where the carriage horses of Central Park fame go to sleep after a hard day's (or night's) work. There are four such stables in the city, all of them on the far West Side. I stop in at the largest one, the Clinton Park Stables, on 52nd Street between Eleventh and Twelfth Avenues, and chat with a driver. He's from Turkey and came to the United States twelve years ago. "At night the horses sleep upstairs and come in through this entrance. The carriages are cleaned and prepared for the next day. The pay is okay especially because at night I also work in a gas station. De Blasio make a lot of trouble for us, but I think we gonna stay. I hope so." The man was referring to Mayor de Blasio's efforts to ban horses from Central Park. There's also the Chateau Stables at 608 W. 48th Street, the smallest of the four stables. It bills itself as providing "theatrical animals." I learn that this means animals for performances, proms and parties in general, TV shows, even funerals. There's an old photo of the Beatles riding in one of their carriages, reportedly on their way to an appearance on the *Ed Sullivan Show*.

I head east on 52nd Street to Tenth Avenue and see, near the corner, a place called Orchid Man, at 762 Tenth Avenue. It claims to be the only place in the city devoted exclusively to orchids and it certainly has an excellent range of choices. They are pricey, but they're likely to last longer. These places cannot compete in terms of price with outfits like Whole Foods, so they must make it on quality and service. If this were not the case, then there would only be large chains in this, or any other business. On the next block, 53rd Street, are two murals of a tree with exquisitely painted leaves, one mural in sunlight and the other in the shadows, both visible from

Tenth Avenue, looking east on 53rd Street. They are on the side of a six-story modern residential building and were the winning entry in a competition for a $20,000 prize, garnered by Corinne Ulmann, a Brooklyn artist.

Heading back down Tenth Avenue, I turn right on 44th Street. On Eleventh Avenue and 44th, I discover the headquarters of the avant-garde full-service ad agency Mother. I walk in with a young Asian man named Seth who works there. He's originally from California's Apple Valley, situated in the Inland Empire east of Los Angeles. It's a typical millennial-style layout, with a bar in the middle of a large open space selling drinks, and a small area off to the side for those who want a cup of coffee, open staircases, plus a recreational area. There's a large realistic-looking bear hovering over the foyer, and inside, off to the left, an exhibit of models of clipper ships behind a glass-enclosed breakfront. There's also a classic red British telephone booth. Hanging above the bar, affixed to a wallboard, are a bunch of gleaming pots and pans of various sizes and shapes. I ask Seth about them, and he tells me: "It's really from the partners who were working in London, from their kitchen, though I'm not sure whose it was. And you can see ahead of you there's a whole wall behind that couch with photos of mothers whose children work here, including one of my mom. It's as in: 'Your mother's always watching,' or 'Don't do anything your mother wouldn't do.' A lot of people walking by look in and mistake us for a large café. We have some large accounts you might have heard of, like Bailey's, Stella Artois, Microsoft, and Calvin Klein." Certainly an interesting place to see if you can get inside, which is something of a challenge. But once you're in, no one will ask any questions.

The far West Side in the 40s is a center of construction for very tall shiny apartment buildings and hotels. I'm especially struck by an old gray classic-looking Gothic church that's on 41st Street and Tenth Avenue. I see it off to the right as I'm walking east from Eleventh Avenue on the north side of 42nd Street. From this angle, the church, surely built over a century ago, is dwarfed by the blue-glass skyscraper immediately behind it. There was a time when church spires of this variety were considered towering, but not in the world of twenty-first-century towers. What does this portend for the landscapes of the future? Will almost everything be homogenized?

Clinton and Chelsea are adjacent to each other, but it's here on Tenth Avenue that I discover a new, more current meaning when they are brought together that demonstrates the power of word associations within, in this case, a political context. The sign above a brick building entrance, located between 45th and 46th Streets, reads:

RYAN COMMUNITY CENTER
OF
CHELSEA-CLINTON

This is probably the only public space where the names Ryan (as in House Speaker Paul Ryan) and Chelsea Clinton coexist in harmony! At least, that's the connection my brain made when I saw it. Of course, as with Ryan, the placement of Chelsea-Clinton together is a coincidence and refers only to the neighborhoods.

Clinton-Chelsea also has a historical resonance that is, in fact, quite real. Bill and Hillary Clinton reportedly named their daughter, Chelsea, after the Joni Mitchell song "Chelsea Morning," recorded for her 1969 album *Clouds*, whose opening lines about the New York City neighborhood are: "It was a Chelsea morning, and the first thing that I heard was a song outside my window, and the traffic wrote the words. . . ." Others, however, have written that she was named after London's Chelsea section while the Clintons were walking through it. Which version is correct? The answer comes from a great source, Bill Clinton's autobiography, *My Life*: "One day [in 1978], as we window-shopped down King's Road in Chelsea [London], the loudspeaker of a store blared out Judy's [Judy

Collins] version of Joni Mitchell's 'Chelsea Morning.' We agreed on the spot that if we ever had a daughter we'd call her Chelsea."[23] And so, we see that Chelsea's name refers to both locations.

I meander down to 33rd Street and Tenth and turn left. Clinton is certainly expanding on its southern end, as evidenced by the cranes, bulldozers, and other machinery in use to help launch a huge project called Manhattan West. It's a mixed-use residential/commercial undertaking, between Ninth and Tenth Avenues and running from 33rd to 30th Street. It will feature a sixty-two-story luxury residential tower with many amenities, as well as millions of feet of office space. This site is a key anchor in a larger area running from 34th to 30th Street and from Tenth to Twelfth Avenue, called Hudson Yards, which will eventually have sixteen skyscrapers. The site is controlled by both the city and the state of New York and by the Metropolitan Transit Authority. These plans and their realization will change the landscape of Clinton, of which it is a part, as well as adjacent Chelsea.

A brief walk through the area makes it abundantly clear that construction is well under way here, and perhaps the best place to view it with perspective is the High Line (more on the High Line later) extension, which runs along Twelfth Avenue, from 34th to 30th Street. I head up there, walking west along 33rd Street. Viewed from a height equivalent to the third floor of a building and looking eastward, the magnitude of what's being created here seems overwhelming. As I look down at the Long Island Rail Road cars beneath me, I realize that they will soon be invisible, hidden under new office buildings that will reduce the options for those walking on these blocks. As a result, foot traffic into the areas below 30th Street where row houses and brownstones are much in evidence, will mushroom, making these residential blocks much more crowded than they are now.

One of the busiest arteries in Clinton is 34th Street. Here, between Twelfth and Eleventh Avenue, thousands of travelers gather every day to wait for buses carrying them to Baltimore, Washington,

Boston, Dallas, Little Rock, Toronto, and many other locations. They do not appear to consist of the well-to-do, just ordinary folks of all ages, trying to get somewhere on a limited budget. Here, there, and everywhere are food trucks serving those waiting in long lines, eating while they're standing, almost as if it were a pastime, a way of keeping boredom at bay with food.

On the south side of 34th Street between Dyer Street and Tenth Avenue I peek through a gate leading to a remarkable place called Alice's Garden. It's named after Alice Parsekian, a woman of Armenian ancestry who immigrated here from Turkey many years ago and dedicated much of her life to the public spaces of her neighborhood. Her most famous project was creating a garden in a small space between a commercial building and the incredibly busy Dyer Avenue entrance to the Lincoln Tunnel, which it overlooks, but one to which tens of thousands of drivers below are totally oblivious. Even passersby along crowded 34th Street are likely to give it only a passing glance since it's behind a locked gate. On a blustery March day, I noticed it only because I've become accustomed to searching for the unknown and the unusual.

Alice's Garden is in a long and narrow space, with the outlines of individual plots framing a winding, dull-brick, weathered walkway with cute lamps along the path that stretches beyond what the eye can see from the street. A small sign briefly tells the story of Alice, who fought valiantly and relentlessly to make this an oasis in a sea of commercial buildings and 24/7 traffic. As I learned, it took decades for approval to be granted in 2011 from the Port Authority, working in coordination with various Clinton community groups. Over the years, permission was granted, only to be rescinded, during which, time and again, the garden area was closed down, yielding to neglect, which made it look like so many overgrown lots in this city. I wanted desperately to gain entrance, but it was locked. Lady Fortune smiled on me, however, and a man came up, seemingly out of nowhere and said, "Excuse me." David Howard, a salesman,

A tiny community garden clings for dear life to the Lincoln Tunnel.

introduced himself, told me he owned one of the plots in the garden, and invited me inside.

"What's remarkable to me is how you made use of such a small space to the fullest extent possible," I say. "Is that a rat trap I'm looking at?"

"Yes, that's a major problem here. The rats eat *everything*. It's a mess, with papers floating around because we haven't done our spring cleaning yet. Most of our plot-holders are local. We used Belgian blocks to build the path." There's a poem in the back, on a handmade sign, that beautifully expresses the sentiments of these hardy volunteers:

The kiss of the sun for pardon
The song of the birds for mirth
One is nearer God's heart in a garden
Than anywhere else on earth

Dorothy Frances Gurney

I ask David about a plaque on a wall and he responds: "That's one of our awards. That's fine. We have enough awards. Let me show you these barrels, which we use for water so we can irrigate our plots where we grow both vegetables and flowers. And we have hoses stretched out along the plots. When this project began, the whole lot was garbage. And Alice was disgusted by all this. She was seen as an authoritarian by some, but she persevered and got it done."

David is not interested in recognition. He's much more focused on how to make nature prosper in this inhospitable environment. His family hails from Utah, a place where his grandfather was a farmer, so maybe there's a green thumb gene here. And I must agree that his priority is what matters because I've never seen a garden in New York located in such an unlikely place, clinging to the tunnel entrance wall next to it. There's a question here: Why is it that in this city, as demonstrated by its hundreds of gardens, people are so committed to the concept of making things grow, be it a garden or even a flowerbox outside an apartment window? Is it an urge to remain in touch with nature? Is it a way of affirming life itself?

Visitors can obtain a key to Alice's Garden for just $2 by calling Community Board 4. With all the new hotels and residential projects going up here, perhaps recognition and financial support will, one day, turn this into a veritable Garden of Eden. In fact, David believes that the Manhattan West people and a Marriott Hotel have shown some interest in having the garden listed as an amenity. And why not?

As I'm walking on 33rd Street, a piece of my candy bar wrapper floats to the ground. I bend down and pick it up and am surprised when a black-haired man in his twenties, listening to music on his smart phone and walking past me, suddenly says to me, "Good man!" He repeats it for emphasis two seconds later. It strikes me as an expression of solidarity and appreciation, as if to say: "We're all in this together, and you and I share the same values." These fleeting interactions are a validation of something I did, almost by instinct, with no expectation of praise. It's also an intimate moment in the metropolis, almost like a shared secret that makes one's day worthwhile in a personal and meaningful sense.

A Rubin Museum of Art
B Joyce Theater
C French Hospital
D Division of Traffic Control
E B & D Halal Cafeteria

12TH AVE

W 29 ST

W 27 ST

Chelsea
Park

C

11TH AVE

Chelsea
Waterside
Park

Hudson River

10TH AVE

9TH AVE

8TH AVE

W 26 S

J

I

W 23 ST

W 24 ST

11TH AVE

M

H

W 22 ST

B

W 20 ST

K

L

W 18 ST

N

W 16 ST

A

W 14 ST

CHELSEA

THE BOUNDARIES OF CHELSEA ARE, approximately, 30th Street on the north, Sixth Avenue on the east, 14th Street on the south, and the Hudson River on the west. For much of the nineteenth century, it was a quiet residential area that was also home to the Episcopalian General Theological Seminary, founded in 1825. The area along the Hudson River was industrial during this period, with factories, warehouses, and lumberyards in which thousands of immigrants, many of them Irish, labored. There was also a theater district along 23rd Street, as well as an opera house. In the early twentieth century, several motion picture companies were established nearby.

Today, most of this is gone. Nevertheless, it is still a mixed residential and commercial neighborhood, with the charming old homes remaining, and the commerce part having evolved into service-based industry. This is unsurprising since it is right next to Manhattan's Midtown section, the city's most commercial area. There are hundreds of beautiful row houses and brownstones in Chelsea, many of which date back to the nineteenth century, that can be found on the side streets. One excellent section for viewing them runs from 22nd to 17th Street and from Tenth to Seventh Avenue. The twentieth century saw the construction of apartment buildings, the most prominent of which was the London Terrace complex. Penn South, a large co-op development, was built by the International Ladies' Garment Workers' Union and remains vibrant to this day.

The major commercial thoroughfares are Sixth, Seventh, Eighth, and Ninth Avenues, as well as 14th Street. The side streets between Sixth and Seventh are much more commercial than those to the west. There are many fine eateries and boutiques in Chelsea, and it is a major center for art galleries. In addition, the Rubin Museum of Art is located at 150 W. 17th Street and focuses on artistic works from the Himalayan countries, especially Tibet. Chelsea is also home to Google's New York headquarters, which occupies a square block bounded by Eighth and Ninth Avenues and by 15th and 16th Streets.

Ethnically, the area is a polyglot of white cultures and ethnicities, together with a substantial number of African-Americans and Hispanics. In short, it's representative of most of the groups that populate the city. Added to this mix is a large LGBT population. Economically, Chelsea is quite upscale, but it also has some low-income public housing. It is a low-crime area, very safe to walk in, day or night.

Chelsea was a quiet neighborhood until the 1980s. The key event that marked the change in Chelsea from a quiet neighborhood to a real "scene," was probably the renovation of the Elgin Theater, located on 19th Street and Eighth Avenue. Once a mecca for experimental film, it reopened in 1982 as the Joyce Theater and has been dedicated to showcasing the best in dance performance. In the 1990s, art galleries relocated there in large numbers. By 2000, there were well over 100 such galleries there. These were followed by boutiques, restaurants, and many other high-end retail establishments. Once this commercial draw existed, developers came in and a massive building boom began that continues unabated, marked by luxurious new hotels and residential towers, many of them between Sixth and Seventh Avenues.

In addition, the opening in 1995 of Chelsea Piers, a full-service entertainment complex situated on thirty acres, featuring golf, ice skating, and a jogging track, along with restaurants and catering for large parties, made the area even more appealing to residents of the city and those beyond it. People from the outer boroughs and the suburbs flocked there for parties, especially child-oriented ones.

Added to all this was the creation of the High Line, perhaps the greatest draw of all. Once a railway for freight serving the needs of industrial Chelsea for many years, the High Line has been transformed into a park for walkers, joggers, and nature lovers. The first portion reopened for public use in 2009. Today, it runs through all of Chelsea and a bit below and above it.[24] Finally, a portion of Hudson River Park, along the river, also serves as a scenic recreation site, with playgrounds, bike paths, and walkways.

Chelsea begins on W. 30th Street, with small houses interspersed with five- or six-story apartment buildings. Between Eighth and Ninth Avenues on 30th, I pass by an older twelve-story building that, from 1929 to 1978, was known as French Hospital. You can still see a sign etched into its wall on the left: "Clinic Entrance." Among its most famous patients was Babe Ruth, who was treated there for cancer. An equally famous but fictitious patient from Mario Puzo's *The Godfather*, Don Corleone, was rushed to the hospital after being shot. In the building's current state, it's a Section 8 assistance apartment complex stretching south to 29th Street, with a beautiful garden between its two buildings.

There are plenty of police buildings in New York City, but few have as grandiose a headquarters as the Division of Traffic Control, at 138 W. 30th Street. Located between Sixth and Seventh Avenues, its cornerstone was dedicated in 1907. The first two stories, made of granite blocks, are in the shape of a castle, with four turrets, on top of which are gaps for the imaginary firing of arrows. The upper floors are a light-red brick. The interior, with its high ceiling and other decorative elements, is also worth seeing.

Thirtieth Street between Sixth and Seventh is the place to go for a cheap pocketbook that looks expensive. Owned by Koreans, the stores here are more reliable than sidewalk vendors where, if there's a problem with a purchase, it's harder to get a refund or exchange. The pocketbooks are colorful and the selection is broad. Don't be deterred by the "wholesale only" signs. I smile and say: "I may be interested in a pocketbook for my wife," and the woman replies, "Okay, we give you special deal for $25. But if you want real Gucci you have to go to Macy's." The sellers readily admit that their fancy-looking handbags are made of plastic, not leather.

I enter the B & D Halal Cafeteria on 29th Street, between Sixth and Seventh Avenues. A simple place, it has tables and chairs for customers, and the food is priced by weight. It specializes in West African foods, an assortment of meat stews, chicken, lamb, goat, rice, and vegetables. Each item has a West African name and a brief English description. A quick perusal of the restaurant's Google reviews suggests that it has more than a few non-African aficionados, namely Americans interested in trying something new, who don't much care what they're eating as long as it's cheap and tastes good. As one put it: "Just tell yourself you're eating a brown or any other color stew and that's what you're eating. For $10 or less you'll get a big mess of hearty gut-busters. It's also a great place for white dudes like me to feel cool and exotic."

The location is convenient for the West Africans who work in the area in the garment industry and for the vendors who buy their handbags to sell on the streets. I talk to a B & D worker I'll call Ali. Wearing a black sweatshirt and a matching black cap with the letter A on it, he's from Nigeria and has been here about a year and a half. Ali is thin and wiry, has sparkling black eyes, and is very friendly. He gestures with his hands, speaking in rapid-fire English as he describes the dishes offered, asserting that it's one of "the best such places in Manhattan." Most of those eating here seem to be from

French-speaking lands, but the TV is tuned to news from Africa rendered in English.

"How did you learn to speak English so well?" I ask him.

"It's the main language in my country, though I also speak Arabic. I'm from the Yoruba tribe. What do you do?"

"I'm a professor at City College and I'm writing a book about New York."

"Oh, you teach at a university? I would like to go to school here, maybe study political science, so I can get a good job. I passed my levels exams with distinction."

"Why don't you?"

"Because I'm here illegally. Instead, I'm a peace activist."

"But can you make any money doing that?"

"No," he says, laughing. "But I hustle. You know what I mean?" I say I do and decide not to press the matter as it can mean something illegal. Besides, the evidence we have suggests that most of the undocumented immigrants work hard at regular, if low-paying, jobs. What's interesting is that he doesn't hesitate to acknowledge his undocumented status with a complete stranger who's writing a book. He's even told me his first and last names. It suggests that many people in his situation do not feel it's dangerous to reveal such sensitive information. And indeed, in a way, it's not, because people like him are generally not bothered by immigration authorities unless they're caught doing something wrong. On the other hand, after the Trump administration took a much harder line on the undocumented, he might have been unwilling to be so open. This interview took place before the 2016 election.[25]

I head south on Sixth Avenue and make a right onto 28th Street, the heart of the Flower District. It's not as large as it used to be when it stretched from 26th to 29th Street but this block, between Sixth and Seventh, still bustles with activity. The best time to see it is in season, namely late spring and summer, when walking through it is like a trip through a jungle. Small trees and high flowerpots stand proudly on both sides of the sidewalks, fairly beckoning you to make a purchase. I step into the stores, where foliage is everywhere and it feels moist and humid, like the tropics. Some have tiled walls with interesting designs. But hurry if you want to visit them, because as real estate developers continue to encroach on the blocks, the district is becoming even smaller.

Not much remains of the Fur District because of changing tastes and opposition to killing animals for their furs. Nevertheless, I pass by a number of survivors on W. 30th and W. 29th Streets, between Sixth and Seventh Avenues. Seeing these places, with only an occasional customer inside, feels like a journey to another time period.

Heading south on Seventh Avenue, I turn left at 25th Street and stop in at Johny's Luncheonette at #124, on the right side of the block. It's a small, very old-school place with the grills in front of me on the other side of the counter, so I can see how the food is made. I'm sitting on a plastic-covered round stool with people who are here for a quick bite. They don't dilly-dally, paying as soon as they've finished, and I must follow suit because the pace is very fast. One minute after sitting down I'm asked to order. In about five minutes, my meal has arrived along with the check. Johny's feeds into all the stereotypes of fast-talking, in-a-hurry, no-nonsense New Yorkers.

Next, on the same street, I check out New York Vintage at #117. There are other such places in the city, like Williamsburg's Stella Dallas, but this shop is very high end. In fact, there are photos of Michelle Obama wearing their items—a '50s wrap, for example—at White House events. She doesn't personally shop here, but her stylist does. Lady Gaga is another famous client. Prices range from $300 to $10,000. This is far from the ordinary used clothing, which is sometimes also advertised as "vintage." There are some very exquisite dresses for $900, a genuine Hermès bomber jacket for $1,200. A young, pretty salesperson with blue eyes and dark hair, wearing a knit hat, provides further details about the merchandise: "A new bomber jacket would cost a lot more. Here's a hand-painted red-black couture dress. It shines. It *really* shines. That one's my favorite. Here's Yves St. Laurent, and there's a Givenchy for $4,900. You won't see another one like it. There are other high-end stores, but we have our own special niche in that we span over 100 years. We have things from the Victorian Era. These laces are really special, from the 1930s; you'll never see these anymore. Or like the lamé on this dress; you won't even find lamé today. Here are some lawn dresses from the 1920s. This one's only $400. We also have great jewelry."

The status game is clearly in play here, big time. Some customers will want to shop in a place where Michelle Obama gets clothing. And then, perhaps, at a party, the wearer is asked where her shawl came from, which opens up the story line: "I got it at New York Vintage, a Chelsea place where Lady Gaga (or Michelle Obama) shops." Nothing wrong with that. It's a conversation piece that's enjoyable for the teller and entertaining for the listener. It's also a very New York thing to do because there are so many celebrities who shop and even live here and now the shopper is part of that scene in some way. Every store that sells high-end products emphasizes what is special about what they offer, so you have phrases like "You won't even find lamé today" or a comment about the fact that the goods being sold span a century. Price will also be part of the picture, dispensed almost casually in a one-two punch. The buyer will hear that there's a Givenchy for about five grand, but also that other items can be purchased for $400 in the same shop that has much pricier things for sale.

Everyone has heard of the Chelsea Hotel on W. 23rd Street between Seventh and Eighth Avenues. Since its opening in 1884, a parade of famous people in the arts have lived here—Mark Twain, Brendan Behan, Thomas Wolfe, O. Henry, Jack Kerouac, and Jimi Hendrix, to name but a few. Today, it's under renovation. Far less well known, in fact, almost unknown, is the Carteret, an apartment building next to it, that is quite unusual in appearance. At first it looks like many other residential buildings of the 1930s, except that the third and fourth stories have arched windows, with shields between the windows. As I glance upward, I'm struck by its design, most notable on the highest floors. There are geometric shapes of different colors, with Romanesque arched windows near the top of the structure as well as what looks like a rose window. I can also see two statues on either side of the rose window and crenellations at the very top. With a zoom lens, one could take some beautiful photographs.

The block between Ninth and Tenth Avenues on 23rd Street is especially beautiful. On the north side is the London Terrace Gardens apartment complex, which has both co-ops and rentals. When completed in 1930, it was the largest apartment complex in the world and boasted a pool, gym, and restaurants. One famous Christmas party there in 1932 featured Babe Ruth as Santa Claus, who obligingly signed autographs and mingled with the excited and surprised crowd.

Interestingly, the previous owner of the property was Clement Clarke Moore, who wrote, "A Visit from St. Nicholas." It's a huge place, running about a square block, from 23rd to 24th Street and from Eighth to Ninth Avenue. With about 1,700 apartments and fourteen buildings, it even has its own post office, located on Eighth Avenue. The style is Romanesque and Spanish Revival, with lots of terracotta, yellowish bricks, and all kinds of motifs, including clinker bricks and fluted columns running the height of the structure.

The south side of the street, known since the nineteenth century as "Millionaire's Row," has well-maintained Anglo-Italianate town-houses, where today a two- to three-bedroom duplex apartment can fetch upwards of $5 million. And this is true throughout Chelsea, especially between 23rd and 14th Streets from Seventh Avenue to the Hudson River. As I walk these quiet blocks, the hubbub of Manhattan feels very far away indeed.

Just west of Tenth Avenue is the High Line, a nicely landscaped park that runs through the neighborhood. Opened in 2009, it's so popular that it's almost always filled with walkers in warm weather during the daytime hours. The elevated park provides a third-floor view and gives walkers a unique perspective, almost as if they're looking through the streets, devoid of sidewalks. A perfect example of the new architecture is the modernistic, curved, shiny, glass and metallic high-rise with sleek white diagonal lines at 515 W. 23rd Street. It looks as though it's partially hanging over the High Line. Inside, the apartments are stunning creations with all the amenities the heart can desire. The asking price for a four-bedroom, four-bathroom, penthouse apartment in April 2016 was about $20 million; a two-bedroom, about $4 million.

Around the corner on 22nd Street, between Eleventh and Tenth Avenues, I pass by what has become a very commonplace scene in Manhattan, the filming of a TV show. In this case, it's *Law and Order* playing out in front of #525. One person says to me, "It's my favorite show. I *have* to watch what's going on." A man walks by with his dog, looking straight ahead, paying no heed. Production assistants keep things flowing, with the crowd of about forty extras who are part of the shot. A knot of curious onlookers stares down at what's going on from the vantage point of the High Line, about 100 feet away. A woman with a distinctive hairdo is in the director's chair, barking out instructions. As I stand there, I find myself thinking: "So this is what a show looks like as it's being created and before it's perfected for public viewing."

Across the street is the New York flagship store of the Japanese fashion label Comme des Garçons. The entranceway is made of cast aluminum, which came from an English ship in Cornwall. The door resembles the shape of an egg with a flattened bottom. Inside, there's a sculpture made of many hardened, gold-colored Styrofoam pieces. It looks like a giant Christmas tree. An employee elaborates on the store: "We were one of the first stores to locate in this western part of Chelsea. The art galleries you see now came much later. We're also part of the Dover Street Market department store, located on Lexington Avenue and 30th Street. Our brand has been around since the '70s, and we have many followers. We kept the auto repair sign 'Heavenly Body Works' above the store when we bought the place in 1999 in order to give it the authentic neighborhood feel." Again, we see this desire on the part of people to retain an organic connection to the city's history and to respect it.

So many of the blocks in Chelsea are pretty that one can spend days just wandering through them. One of them, 22nd Street, between Seventh and Eighth Avenues, has some really neat details. Most keystones atop windows are just that, plain keystones. But the one at #246 has carved faces on both sides of the entrance that seem to be contemplating each other with expressions that are at once wistful and serious. The male figure on the left, with a curling mustache and a beard, is wearing a helmet, while the female on the right has soft curls held together by a headband. In addition, on both sides of the entrance, two fierce-looking lions with buckteeth stand guard ready to pounce on any intruders! At #244 there's what appears to be a gunmetal colored, cast-iron face of a bearded and mustachioed man with a wise, peaceful, and somehow, droll expression. The next house, #238, has balconies on which are wrought-iron ships' steering wheels. Farther down are #236 and #234, two strikingly red sandstone four-story structures. The windows are tall and the wooden arched entrances are well made. The window guard on the left is very ornate, with beautiful curlicues. Such discoveries await those interested on many a block in this charming neighborhood.

An Italian bistro at 191 Seventh Avenue, just north of W. 21st Street catches my attention because its name is Il Bastardo, Italian for "the bastard." Thinking it an odd name for a restaurant I ask an employee why it's called that. "It's just a name, no special reason." The owner, however, Tareq Alam, overhears this and introduces himself to me. "Can I help you?" he says. I decide to tell him why I asked: "I teach at City College and I'm writing a book about Manhattan, the unknown things about the borough." "Really," he responds. "I know about City College. I have relatives who studied there." Hearing an accent that I think I recognize, I ask, "Where are you from originally?" "Bangladesh." "Aha. That's what I thought. I have had many students from your country." He smiles broadly, and as I look at him I can see he's a handsome man, dressed well, wearing an expensive-looking white linen shirt, open at the top, neatly pressed gray slacks, and impeccably combed hair. "And you, if I may say so, look like the picture of success." He smiles in appreciation, thanking me for the compliment.

Having established some rapport, I pop the question: "So tell me, since you probably heard what I said before, why is your place called Il Bastardo?" His answer is both surprising and quite honest: "Simple. One of my partners had a, the way you call it, a bastard, an illegitimate child, and he decided to name the restaurant after him." "Do you mind if I put that in my book?" "Not at all. It's the truth. It's sort of a joke we have." Perhaps this says something about the decline in the institution of marriage and the rising acceptance of children being born out of wedlock. He assures me it's not a sensitive issue, and I tell him that, regardless, it's certainly an attention grabber.

"Well, this looks like a really nice place. I guess you made it in America." Suddenly his face lights up and he exclaims: "God bless America! I came here in 1992, with twenty dollars in my pocket. I was a busboy in a restaurant called Zucchero e Pomodori, and today I'm a wealthy man, thanks to this land where everyone can make it if they really want to. I made it in real estate and owning restaurants. In fact, because that's where I started I went back and also bought that building." Il Bastardo is definitely a happening place if you're young and like to party. As for Tareq, this is the true rags-to-riches tale, but it's also a reminder that America has always been and continues to be a magnet for those who have dreams and want to realize them.

A few doors down is the Kove Brothers hardware store. It looks like a true original from the old days. That turns out to be the case, as they've been here for close to a century, having been founded in 1920 and operated by the same family through all these years. In a retail business, if you don't treat the customers right, you're gone sooner or later, probably sooner. I walk inside, and the past comes to life as I look down at the old, weathered wooden floorboards. I'm told they're the originals, save for occasional repairs. "In the old days, things were built to last," a clerk observes. On the wall outside, along the side of the store, there's a colorful mural with various tools displayed—different kinds of saws, a lock with MASTER on the bottom of it. These places are disappearing, so it's great to see one of them still alive. From here I go a block south to 20th Street and turn right.

As I reach Tenth Avenue and 20th Street, I see a sign on my right advertising the High Line Hotel. The hotel purchased the structure from the General Theological Seminary. The hotel, as I discover upon entering, has interior gardens and courtyards. The rooms, with modern amenities, also have the feel, in terms of decor—original wallpaper and old-style furniture, like wooden bedposts and rustic-looking dressers—of being in a B & B in the country rather than in the heart of the city and minutes from the High Line. Actually, the property was an apple orchard before the seminary purchased it.

Heading east, I notice a sign on the second floor of a very old red-brick building at 109 W. 17th Street, near Seventh Avenue, reading "Carriages, Coupes, and Hansoms," and if I hadn't been looking at the Serenata Mexican restaurant on the left and da Umberto's, a famous Northern Italian classic on the right, I would have missed it. Chelsea, like Clinton, had numerous places like this that once offered such services, but it's rare to see one of these signs in their original, if faded, lettering. It marks the location where these vehicles were kept in the nineteenth century, and in those days there were hundreds of ads like this. This sign is one of only three that have survived in the city.

Coupes, carriages, and hansoms to let.

(A) Alwyn Court
(B) 130 W. 57th St.—a building with very special tenants
(C) City Center theater
(D) University Club
(E) Chartwell Booksellers
(F) Chabad Center
(G) Center for Fiction
(H) Kabbalah Centre

CENTRAL PARK SOUTH
BROADWAY
W 57 ST
E 59 ST
E 57 ST
W 55 ST
E 55 ST
W 53 ST
E 53 ST
W 51 ST
E 51 ST
PARK AVE
LEXINGTON AVE
3RD AVE
W 49 ST
E 49 ST
W 47 ST
E 47 ST
W 45 ST
E 45 ST
8TH AVE
W 43 ST
E 43 ST
7TH AVE
W 42 ST
E 42 ST
BROADWAY
W 40 ST
6TH AVE
W 38 ST
5TH AVE
W 36 ST
W 34 ST
PARK AVE
W 32 ST
Murray Hill
W 30 ST
MADISON AVE
W 28 ST
PARK AVE SOUTH
E 32 ST
W 26 ST
E 30 ST
W 24 ST
E 28 ST
W 23 ST
E 26 ST
LEXINGTON AVE
W 22 ST
E 24 ST
W 20 ST
E 23 ST
BROADWAY
E 22 ST
W 18 ST
E 18 ST
Gramercy Park
W 16 ST
E 16 ST
W 14 ST
E 14 ST
IRVING PL

(I) New York Public Library
(J) Scandinavia House
(K) Society for Jewish Science/Center for Applied Judaism
(L) Modern Pinball NYC, arcade, party place and museum
(M) The Cannibal restaurant

CENTRAL MIDTOWN

CENTRAL, OR MIDTOWN, MANHATTAN IS KNOWN AS THE BOROUGH'S commercial center and has been so since the 1920s, in part because so many subway lines ran through the area. But it is much more than that, as it includes the theater district (whose beginnings date back to the late nineteenth century), Times Square, and many other tourist sites; transportation hubs like Penn Station and Grand Central Terminal; several residential communities; museums; colleges; diplomatic missions; and sports arenas. Some of the city's most famous and tallest hotels and residential towers are located here. In terms of the "nobody knows" theme of this book, there are many additional points of interest as well.

There are varied interpretations of where Midtown begins and ends. The one used here is based on how what's in a neighborhood fits together and how it works for people walking it. The northern boundary is 59th Street; the eastern, Third Avenue; the southern, 14th Street; and the western, Eighth Avenue down to 30th Street, and then Sixth Avenue from 30th to 14th Street. The main commercial thoroughfares are all of the north-south avenues and most of the side streets, except for those in residential areas, where there is some business activity. Murray Hill and Gramercy Park, both discussed here, are very residential communities that overlap into neighboring Midtown East. Their exact boundaries can be found on the Central Midtown map. The rest of Central Midtown is much more commercial than residential. The residents of Midtown are mostly white and well-to-do, and it is a low-crime district.

One of the most gorgeous buildings in the city is the Alwyn Court, on Seventh Avenue and W. 58th Street, built in 1909. While it is well known, I'm fairly certain, based on personal experience, that a majority of New Yorkers, not to mention tourists, have never seen or noticed it. It is a unique architectural marvel, with nearly every inch of its twelve-story exterior encrusted with crowns, fire-breathing salamanders, dragons, flowers, urns, and statues, all done in exquisite stone-carved, glazed terracotta. In keeping with the building's French Renaissance facade, the salamander was the symbol for the reign of French monarch François I. The interior courtyard also has inspiring architecture, including an atrium and intricate carvings on its walls. In truth, it must be seen to be fully appreciated.

Walking east on 58th Street from Sixth to Fifth Avenue, I spy on my right a forty-nine-story gleaming glass tower, vertically concave, whose address is actually 9 W. 57th Street. Immediately to the left is a seven-story structure, fairly ordinary looking except for the fact that the well-known Paris movie theater is on the first floor. What is visually remarkable is that the curvature of 9 West makes 8 West 58th Street, reflected inside the curve, look like half of it is falling down! I haven't seen such an image to this extent anywhere else in Manhattan, one so striking that I posted it on Instagram as well. Interestingly, security guards in the two buildings were completely unaware of this optical illusion. Since both of these buildings extend all the way through the block to 57th Street, I walk down 57th from the same starting point at Sixth Avenue and am treated to the same image—curved tower, second building falling down, this time on the left side of the street.

Making an about-face, I head west on 57th Street, which has quite a few famous buildings. There's the Osborne, at 57th and Seventh Avenue, a dark, brooding apartment-co-op built in 1883, with a brick and brownstone exterior and a marvelous stucco and marble lobby with mosaic tiles and multicolored glazed terracotta walls and ceiling. Catty-corner from it is Carnegie Hall, and farther east on the north side is One57 (as in #157), one of the city's tallest and most expensive residential towers. It has a wavy blue facade that most find unappealing, to say the least.

For a proper perspective of the area's richness, it's better to focus on a much less familiar building, 130 W. 57th Street, between

Seventh and Sixth Avenues, one you could pass by in ten seconds and not notice it. It's a pretty, though not especially striking, place that belies its rich history. It was built in 1907–1908 in an area that was already a center for art and music, and it immediately attracted artists who loved its exposure to the northern light. It had high, projecting bay windows with cast-iron frames, which gave these spacious studios even more appeal. A walk through the lobby and the building in general reveals many original details—the offices themselves, floor tiles, and the like. But a building's essence is also shaped and preserved by those who have made it their home. The owner of Terry Steiner International, a film distribution company and a tenant here, tells me more about this aspect: "First, the building has been owned by a woman, Mira Jedwabnik Van Doren, the daughter-in-law of the famous intellectual Mark Van Doren, an English professor at Columbia. Many well-known people lived and worked here. Part of our office complex on the tenth floor was once a pied-à-terre for the actor José Ferrer, who, in 1951, was the first Hispanic and Puerto Rican actor to win an Oscar for *Cyrano de Bergerac*. Look at this bathroom [in our offices], for example, which has been preserved and looks like it always has [been]. Where will you see this kind of richly colored blue and white tile on the walls? There are many other famous people who were in this building at one time or another."

As a person who regularly attends meetings, dinners, and other events for show business people, Steiner has a solid grasp of this world. Besides Ferrer, Joseph Heller, Ray Charles, the Rolling Stones, Woody Allen, and Tony Bennett (Terry Steiner's next-door neighbor for a while) all had offices here. Going back even further, there are records showing that the filmmaker D. W. Griffith and the writer William Dean Howells spent time here. Scenes from the first season of *Mad Men* were also filmed here. This little description is not like the status game of "I saw him in a restaurant" or "She came in and bought something in my boutique." This is evidence of how the city's buildings are intertwined with those who became leading figures in what made New York a world capital for the arts and more. With a little bit of digging, one could easily build an impressive geographic map of New York intellectuals, political figures, or corporate titans and where they lived and worked.

In this architecturally rich part of Manhattan, it might not attract that much attention, but the New York City Center theater, built in 1923 and located on W. 55th Street between Sixth and Seventh Avenues, certainly caught my eye because of the glazed multicolored tiles on the outside. It has a neo-Moorish design outside and inside the building, including some desert-scene murals on the mezzanine level. This is in keeping with the center's history, since it was once home to the Ancient Arabic Order of the Nobles of the Mystic Shrine or, as they are better known, the fraternal order of the Shriners. Above it is a large dome featuring 28,000 individual tiles.

At 55th and Seventh Avenue, I approach the famous eighty-year-old Carnegie Deli, now closed. It's shortly before 5:00 p.m. on a weekday, yet the line to get in stretches out the door and beyond. I also take notice of a deli right next door, the Premier Deli Café. I begin to wonder, how does a seemingly ordinary deli survive next to one with an exceptional reputation? Do they get the overflow? Do people go in there because a pastrami sandwich costs $4 less? So I walk into the Carnegie and ask one of the hostesses, a tall black woman. She responds: "I don't know how they survive. Who cares? They're no competition. People come in here and have to wait on line. Some people will say, 'I'm going to Katz's.' I never heard of Katz's. We're the best. Next door, they're just trying to live off our name." Generally true, I'd say, but in terms of Katz's (located on East Houston Street) this is certainly untrue, since Katz's pastrami sandwiches are widely considered the best of the best, with the Second Avenue Deli in the mix as well. But she has an excuse—she's from Chicago and, as I learn, also thinks Chicago pizza is far superior to New York's.

Most folks will stand outside, even braving the cold because this is where they want to be. I ask a man from Atlanta, shivering in his light jacket, why he and his family don't go next door to the Premier Deli. His response: "Are you kidding? I'm here visiting all the way from Atlanta. I've heard about the Carnegie, and I didn't come here to go to some no-name place. Besides, what will I tell my mother-in-law when she asks me how it was?" I begin feeling sorry for the Premier, which has almost no customers. So I go in and ask them: "How are you doing?" "We're doing just fine," says the portly Hispanic man. "Do you get the overflow from the Carnegie?" "Sometimes, on theater nights. But we are doing very well on our own. We have our customers and they have theirs. Try our great chocolate cheesecake."

I'm sure the Premier benefits a little from the "halo effect." But let's face it. People who care enough to go to a famous deli will not be easily dissuaded once they've made the trek. First, there's the taste and quality that made it famous; and second, there's the fact that they want to say to others that they ate there. To them Premier Deli is like where they could eat in their hometown. What we see here is that visiting and even living in Manhattan means partaking of a smorgasbord of events—the theater, nightclubs, sights, museums, hotels, restaurants, and shopping. And this means no substitutes.

At 54th Street and Seventh Avenue, I head east and in two blocks, near Fifth Avenue, I'm face-to-face with the University Club. Founded by alumni from Yale, Harvard, and Columbia Universities, it is dedicated to serious intellectual discussions and meetings. It is probably the finest Italian Renaissance palazzo-style building in the city and includes unusual features such as elephants as keystones and graduation cap mortarboards by the entrance doors. The receding, sloped, three-story-high grand facade, made of exquisitely designed pink granite from Maine, cleverly conceals the fact that the structure is actually seven stories high. One block over, on 53rd Street between Fifth and Madison Avenues, Paley Park, privately owned but open to the public, has a nice area with tables and a soothing, twenty-foot-high artificial waterfall for anyone desiring a brief rest, and that includes me.

Those who care about the artistic and social cachet of 54th Street may be interested to know that it also contained quite a few speakeasies during the days of Prohibition, such as the Texas Guinan Club Intime at 203 W. 54th Street, and, on the East Side, at #131, Jimmy Westin's club. The latter is today the site of a fine eatery, Bobby Van's Steakhouse. I spoke with a knowledgeable regular of Bobby Van's, who pointed to the long bar and explained: "Sinatra and the rest of the pack would be playing over here, the cops on the other end, and the hookers in the middle."

Midtown Manhattan isn't often thought of as a real community, but it can be. I stroll into St. Peter's Evangelical Catholic Church on E. 54th Street and Lexington. The interior is modern with comfortable benches in warm colors. It bills itself as welcoming to people of all faiths and of no faith. I ask the minister, Pastor Amandus "Mandy" Derr, what's unique about it. His answer: "We are well known for our longstanding jazz concert series. Most important, we welcome all religions. When there was a fire in the nearby Central Synagogue, they used our building. There are other churches that welcome different faiths, but ours is remarkable in how *it moves.* Just like a stage set, it can become a mosque, with all the symbols, or a synagogue in a very short time, with all traces of Christianity removed." For the pastor, it's very important that New York, a truly international city, be open to all residents and visitors whatever their creed.

I walk into 55 E. 52nd Street, also known as the Park Avenue Plaza. Inside is something truly unusual, a perfect fit for a "nobody knows" book. It's a bookstore called Chartwell Booksellers, the only store in the entire world devoted almost exclusively to the writings of Sir Winston Churchill. Chartwell, located in Kent County, England, is the house where Churchill lived on a refurbished old estate. He loved it and once said, "A day away from Chartwell is a day wasted." The store has a very luxurious feel to it, with expensive wooden bookcases lining its walls. The owner, Barry Singer, grew up in New York City. Middle-aged with sky-blue eyes, he's trim and fit—not surprising, since he walks the streets of the city every day,

The only bookstore anywhere devoted entirely to Winston Churchill's works.

at random, as a hobby. Friendly, highly intelligent, and with a quick sense of humor, he tells me about the shop.

"Everyone who studies Churchill, and countless people do, comes here. There's greater interest about Churchill in the US than in England. There's no store dedicated to him, even in the UK, and so I decided to open one here."

"Was it your idea to do this?"

"Not really. The fellow who owns this building was an enlightened English literature major and a graduate of Penn who wanted to put a bookstore into this building. He met me and he loved Churchill. And he thought about naming the store after his [Churchill's] home, Chartwell. He didn't envision it to be a store focused on Churchill. I didn't either at first, but gradually it became one."

"What are these coffee mugs?"

"These are called Toby jugs. They're character mugs with the character seated and this, one of their most famous, is a likeness of Churchill. They were produced until 1991. The ones you're looking at are originals from 1940, which makes them very valuable. Let me show you some of our books, which are either about, or by Churchill. He's so complex, and I learn something new about him every day."

"Who are your typical customers?"

"There isn't one type, but many of them are rich. Here's a book signed by him that is offered at $15,000."

"What's the most expensive book you've ever sold about Churchill?"

"Well, I'm offering for sale one book of speeches by Winston Churchill, a rare first edition, for $185,000."

"Wow! What was that?"

"It's a 136-page softcover book called *For Free Trade*. We sold the other rare edition, *Mr. Brodrick's Army*, for $75,000."[26]

"If you had to sum up people's fascination with him in a few sentences, what would you say?"

"He was so protean, so versatile and able to change so easily. No matter how you approach him, you can turn him into what you want him to be. For example, he was a liberal for so long. Yet he led the Conservative Party for many years. He was a war leader and had the foresight after World War I to see what was coming, along with the ramrod backbone to save the world, to say we would stand up to fascism and 'never, never give in, never, never, never.'" He was a painter, and he also won the Nobel Prize for literature. There was so much to him that you could learn about him endlessly. And also, he was truly decent. His decency was tremendous, and here's something I've only recently realized. I've sold to so many people and several of them are actually scoundrels. And yet whatever is decent in them is brought out by Churchill."

I find myself intrigued by Barry's passion for Churchill at the same time as I can easily understand it. He has beautifully displayed posters, letters by Churchill, rare books, all of his speeches collected in a first edition, and more. Barry has also penned a book about the man, called *Churchill Style,* an illustrated volume that focuses on Churchill's private life at home—his preferences in fashion, cigars, books, dining, choice of friends, and the like.[27] Many people have "passions." I have a friend who collects owls; another who amasses Mickey Mouse items. The difference here is that Churchill was a hugely important figure in history, and so many people in addition to Barry have a passion for the man as well. Barry found a way to translate his area of interest into a successful business venture, one that's been in existence for thirty years. In a city where retail stores go out of business every day, that's quite an achievement.

From here I head west on 52nd to Fifth Avenue and make a left, turning right on 47th Street. As many people know, this block, between Sixth and Fifth Avenues, is the heart of New York's diamond district, and it has been so for decades. The previous generation consisted mostly of European Jews, many of them Holocaust survivors, and a good number of them had learned their trade in Antwerp, Belgium, a major center for the diamond trade. It has a bazaar-like feel to it, as young men, most of them Bukharian Jews, stand outside the shops trying to entice you inside with offers of "really special, once-in-a-lifetime deals." But I was curious to find out if anything had changed over time, so I spoke with a middle-aged woman I'll call "Susan," who has been very active in the business for many years.

"How have things changed here?"

"Well, the business is very hard, there are bankruptcies, but this has always been the case. The big change is you can't charge exorbitant prices because of the Rapaport price list, which is published every Thursday and available to all on the Internet. So everyone pretty much knows the price of a diamond. The only thing the seller can do is reduce or not reduce their profit margin."

"Well, if that's the case, then why come here? They can go to Zales or Jared."

"Because the people here are more willing to *handel* (Yiddish for negotiate). But the real reason is psychological. Here the people feel they've come to the source of the diamonds, the place where people also buy and sell wholesale. It has a certain aura of being the place where you'll get the best deal. And maybe you will, depending on how good you can bargain and how desperate the seller is." To really feel the vibe of this line of work, it's necessary to walk the streets, observing how the people look and and listening to how they talk to each other.

At 17 E. 47th Street, a block away in the other direction, across Fifth Avenue, is the Center for Fiction, essentially a place that features presentations by authors—when I visited, Lee Child had just spoken there—and rooms upstairs for writers, some of them published, to rent so that they can write in peace and quiet, away from children and/or tiny apartments. The first floor sells books at steep discounts, but they're not new works by any means. I speak with Soili from northern Canada, who, like her colleague, Patrick, is an intern. Why do they do this? "Because we like to be around writers. I actually adjunct teach at Rutgers University in Newark."

A few blocks east, on Lexington Avenue and 47th Street, I see a woman holding a big placard for a Subway restaurant. These people are on every corner in mid- and lower Manhattan. Who are they and why do they do it? Is this a career?

"Hey," I say to the youngish woman holding the sign. "This doesn't look a barrel of laughs. Where are you from?"

"Nigeria. I'm a Yoruba." As I know about the Yoruba, the Hausa, and the Ibo, and have Nigerian friends, we establish a common ground.

"Why do you do this kind of work?"

"I have no choice. In Abuja I was a banker."

"What do you mean by 'banker'?

"I was an officer in a bank, but here I'm just an immigrant who doesn't know the system. And nobody believes me anyway when I tell them. There are these Nigerians who do fraud on the Internet. They scam and tell people to invest their life savings in things that don't exist. So they give my people a bad name. It's a shame what they do." I genuinely feel sorry for her. It's a perennial problem. People in an identifiable group do wrong things, and others are smeared. As my mother used to say, "When it rains, everybody gets wet." But when one is already at a disadvantage as an immigrant, it's worse.

I turn left on Lexington and then right on 48th Street. Halfway down the block on the left is the Kabbalah Centre, located at #155. The sign outside declares: "You Deserve Great Things." I walk in and notice that most of the people there are young. It's well known that these days quite a few young Jews are becoming interested in religion, but not necessarily the established denominations. Off to the side of the welcome center, featuring piles of leaflets and videos of the group's goals and activities, are several shelves of books for sale. I glance at a display of bottles of "Kabbalah Water" for sale. Beneath the display is a book by a Japanese author, Masaru Emoto, detailing how his research found that water that has positive thoughts directed at it changes its composition. Called *The Hidden Messages in Water*, it is claimed to have sold over 400,000 copies. A young worker with a slight Russian accent tells me, "We have a meditation on the water, and it becomes infused with holiness. Actually, if you drink Poland Spring water and have the right consciousness, it can change also."

"So there's no difference between Poland Spring and Kabbalah Water?" I ask, sounding a bit skeptical about the whole thing.

She eyes me warily and says, "I don't say it's gonna be exactly the same, but it can work either way." I also meet Adi Bar, a graphic designer, who's into kabbalah and has written a self-published book called *Madonna's Tattoos*. Originally from Tel Aviv, Israel, she's been in the States seventeen years and is very open in her views. She is fascinated by Madonna and by kabbalah and has a tattoo featuring words from a Madonna song.

Chabad, or the Lubavitcher Hasidic sect, has six centers in the area, one of them on Fifth Avenue, between 42nd and 43rd Streets. To get there, I walk down Third Avenue to 42nd and head west to Fifth Avenue. I enter the building and walk upstairs to the second floor. Inside, there's a large carpeted room with chairs for worshipers—it's a synagogue, open to all. There are tables around the perimeter for those wishing to drop in and study with members of the Chabad *kollel*, a postgraduate institution made up of married scholars engaged in full-time religious study. That is, in fact, their full-time subsidized job for a few years until they find work outside the *kollel*. A member of the group explains the center's purpose: "We cater largely to businessmen and tourists. On Shabbes we have maybe 200 people, mostly from out of town, who come for a Friday night meal. Businessmen come in to pray and learn. If people need advice from a rabbi or just want a cup of coffee, we're here for them."

"What's the most exciting thing that happened to you in the year that you've been here?" I ask.

"Well, I'd say it was probably the time a Holocaust survivor came in from Connecticut. We talked for a while and then I asked him if he'd like to put on tefillin. He hesitated and then said yes. And then, suddenly, as he did so, he collapsed into a chair and began crying uncontrollably. 'I was supposed to be bar mitzvahed just as the Holocaust started,' he explained, 'and because I never had my bar mitzvah I never put on tefillin. So this is very emotional for me.' Imagine, he lived sixty years without putting on tefillin, and then he came in and on the spur of the moment he did it! I felt so fulfilled."

"Do you still have contact with him?"

"Well, he hasn't come in again, but on Pesach we send him matzos. His name is Frankel and he lives on his farm."

"Did you get a nice donation from him?"

"No, and we didn't do it for that, we just want to help Jews out, and if they give, that's nice, but it's not the main reason."

The New York Public Library clearly doesn't fall into the "nobody knows" category. With over 53 million items, it's the biggest public library in the United States after the Library of Congress. It has branches throughout the city, but the most famous building is the one on Fifth Avenue between 40th and 42nd Streets, and because of its importance, no book on Manhattan worth its salt can fail to at least briefly talk about it. So, since I'm passing by anyway, I decide to make it part of my journey.

While most people think the marble found in various parts of the library comes from Vermont, that's only partially true. It's also from Pennsylvania, Tennessee, Massachusetts, New York, and Connecticut. There's also marble from Italy, Greece, Germany, France, and Belgium. The cloudy white marble from Greece has true historical cachet because it's taken from the same quarry used in the construction of the ancient Parthenon.[28] It can be seen, for instance, in the area where remnants of the Croton Reservoir that lay under the library site are displayed.

The library is an institution with great respect for tradition. One of the ways in which this is demonstrated is in the way books are requested. Even in the computer age, the call slips for books must still be filled out by putting pen to paper. And harking back to its founding, the walls of the library lobby prominently display the names of its founders: John Jacob Astor, Samuel Tilden, Simon Guggenheim, Andrew Carnegie, and others. Few people, however, are familiar with the name Martin Radtke. Radtke arrived in New

York in 1913 at the age of thirty, a penniless and illiterate immigrant from Lithuania. He made a fortune on the stock market, a million dollars, by carefully reading books and magazines about finance in the New York Public Library. He died in 1973 and left his entire estate, $368,000, to the library. Some people will say that's not a lot of money compared to the millions donated by people like the Astors, but it is when you consider that this amount in 1973 was worth about $1.5 million in today's terms. And proportionately, it's even more since he left *all of his money* to the library. And why? Because it changed his life. There's a small floor plaque in the lobby with Radtke's name on it, the only one of its kind. But how many people ever notice it? I almost didn't, and I was standing on it!

The DeWitt Wallace Periodical Reading Room is one of the nicest—and quietest—in the library. Its carved wooden ceilings are magnificent, and so are the golden lampshades and polished wooden tables that give the room a warm cozy feeling. Wallace was the founder of *Reader's Digest*. The library was his workplace and he spent countless hours here, selecting and condensing articles for publication in his magazine. Adding greatly to the allure are the striking and colorful paintings by the architectural muralist Richard Haas that grace the walls here. They depict the original buildings in Manhattan that were occupied by the city's leading publishers— the Hearst Building, the former New York Times Tower, the Look Building, the Puck and Tribune Buildings, and others. Sitting there, I feel like I am actually in old New York.

Another unadvertised but great pleasure of the library's interior is something outside that one can see from the inside. There are three large windows facing south in the Bill Blass Public Catalog Room. Stand in front of the middle one and you will see the Empire State Building, six blocks away and framed perfectly between two other buildings, 8 W. 40th Street on the left and a new building that went up in the last few years. The presence of these two structures on either side as it rises to its soaring height makes it look even taller than it is and, in my opinion, even more beautiful. As

I teach at the Graduate Center on 34th Street and Fifth Avenue, I've seen the Empire State Building many times from different perspectives—along 34th, southward and northward on Fifth, but never quite like this.

While Midtown is a largely commercial area, there are significant exceptions, such as the Murray Hill neighborhood, which extends from 40th to 34th Street and from Madison to Third Avenue. The side streets feature many row houses and brownstones, some of which serve as consulates or embassies for smaller countries like Benin, Chad, and Armenia. Even Park Avenue, which is dominated by office towers, turns into a small enclave of luxury apartment buildings from 39th to 34th Street. Among the few exceptions to that rule are a co-op apartment structure at #23 that is landmarked, a church, a private club, the Consulate of El Salvador at 46 Park Avenue, and Scandinavia House, a sleek six-story modern glass building at #58, between 37th and 38th Streets.

It is this last entity, with its bright colors outside representing the flags of Norway, Sweden, and other countries in the region, that catches my eye. Leaving the library, I turn left on 38th Street, make a right at Park Avenue, and enter a multipurpose building devoted to Scandinavian life and culture. There's a restaurant called Smörgås Chef, offering authentic Scandinavian fare like Swedish meatballs, gravlax, and lingonberries at reasonable prices. The small, hard-back chairs—a lot more comfortable than they look—are also painted in bright colors, giving the space a clean, modern, and inviting appearance. The gift shop has many unique items made by Scandinavian artists. I ask a pleasant young woman, studying at Hunter College, why she chose this job. Ashley's response is interesting: "Well, it's extra money, but I also like it because my grandmother was Swedish, and this way I get back to my traditions." There are also art galleries here emphasizing Scandinavian art and spaces for cultural events.

At 109 E. 39th Street, between Park and Lexington, I pass by the Society for Jewish Science Center for Applied Judaism. It's an elegant townhouse with an interior to match. The first floor contains a nice room with comfortable chairs, and the prayer shawls in the back indicate that it is also used for services. I meet Terry Katz, the group's executive director, a silver-haired, good-looking former accountant from central Long Island, who started here as a volunteer before assuming his current position, and ask him which denomination his group is affiliated with. "We're actually not affiliated with any of them. Everyone's welcome and we have all types. By examining and studying the works of the prophets and other Jewish books, we try to show how Jewish principles help people gain health, peace of mind, and success. We call this Jewish Science, and it was founded in 1922 because, in part, Jews in those days who were not observant were attracted to Christian Science. Our beliefs, however, are rooted in biblical and rabbinic traditions, and we strongly believe in the importance of prayer."

Terry admits the organization is small, with only 150 members, and that they are trying to grow it, but it's tough because Judaism has more-established and better-endowed denominations. There's also a congregation in Los Angeles and some small study groups in other cities. Their members are mostly older, and they are solvent because of a trust fund set up by generous donors. What this demonstrates is that even a group without significant membership numbers can exist and function if it has wealthy individuals who believe in it. In my walks I came across such groups periodically, cults and sects of all kinds, and they are part of the fabric of this city, which seems to have something for everybody.

I turn around and head east to Lexington Avenue, where I make a right and at #150, near 29th Street, I peer into a display window and see beautiful old prints of mountains, forests, and rivers, as well as nineteenth-century street scenes in American towns, harbor views, and urban tenements with laundry lines stretched out across them. Called the Old Print Shop, it's an art gallery with a different twist. It's definitely old, having been founded in 1898, and its focus is on American printmakers from the 1700s to the mid-twentieth century. It has the air of a place that has not in the least been affected by current trends in the art world. Rather, it draws you in to an earlier period that is often overlooked.

The next establishment I visit is also unique, but in a totally different way. The Cannibal, a restaurant at 113 E. 29th Street, between Lexington and Park Avenues is, to my knowledge, the only such establishment with that name. It's an appealing-looking place, emphasizing a meaty menu, with lots and lots of different beers. The crowd is young, and the outdoor dining garden in the back is most attractive. On the back wall, I see large hooks where people can hang their bicycles while they're dining. As I enter, a friendly trio of greeters offer a cheery hello.

"Wow, what a name for a restaurant," I say. "The only problem with what you're offering is my wife is allergic to human food, or food made from humans."

"We have other things on the menu too!" a young woman says, with mock seriousness.

"Like what?"

"Well, our specialty is a pig's head. It's special because we split it in half so it fits on a plate and is easy to eat."

"Well," I respond, laughing, "you know, your next-door neighbor is a women's residence hall for Yeshiva University, which is an Orthodox Jewish institution. Given their dietary restrictions, I'll bet *they're* not coming in here."

"No they're not," a waiter chimes in. "It's a shame, being that college students really dig this place, but what can you do? I have seen some women who dress like they're from the school, long skirts and whatnot, come in here once in a while for a glass of wine or a beer, but never any food." In an ideal world, the school would be cloistered away from such unholy enterprises that could tempt someone. But, as I've seen many times, you can't easily pick your neighbors in a crowded city, especially in Midtown.

I head back down 29th Street to Third Avenue and make a right. As I pass an open doorway on my right between 27th and 26th Streets, I hear a familiar sound. It's the noise of pinball machines emanating from a place called Modern Pinball NYC Arcade, Party Place and Museum. Inside are about twenty-five such machines, and it's pretty crowded for 3:00 p.m. on a weekday. A young man wearing a Ghostbusters tee shirt greets me with a smile.

"Is there anything special about your place? Are you a one-of-a-kind?"

"Generally speaking, yes. There are a few other places, but we charge by the hour and the others by the game. This means you pay $12 and you can play for an hour. The other system favors excellent players who can keep a game going for a while, but ours favors the casual, fun-oriented type, who isn't a pro but just wants to have fun. We do, however, have leagues for more serious types too."

"How do you keep the excitement going?"

"Well, we're always upgrading, getting in new stuff. Our newest machines are Thrones and Ghostbusters. We're open from morning until 12:00 a.m." I think back to a time when pinball machines were much more popular in the city. One would find them in bars and in arcades, along with Skee-Ball, a game popular at carnivals and amusement parks.[29] It seems that at the same time as technology grows more complex and people play all sorts of video games on their phones, like Candy Crush Saga, the old-timey games maintain a tenacious hold among young people who find them quaint but also relevant and fun. I think of the young pigeon flyers of Bushwick, Brooklyn, who have revived a dying sport; or the young shuffleboard players in Gowanus, Brooklyn. Perhaps it's a quest for rootedness in personal history, a desire for things that don't change so fast and that anchor them, in a sense. They're not major trends, but they have a following, albeit somewhat under the radar.

I head down Third Avenue to Gramercy Park, an enchanting part of Midtown that runs here from 23rd to 18th Street and from Park Avenue South to Third Avenue. Its crown jewel is the private two-acre Gramercy Park, between E. 21st and E. 20th Streets and I turn right on 20th Street to see it. It's one of the most beautiful in the city, complete with aesthetically pleasing gardens and flowers along winding paths, and even birdhouses. Alas, a key is needed to enter the grounds and only those living near Gramercy Park can use it. Of course, the gardens that exist in the interior grounds of many city apartment buildings are also off-limits to the public, but they are not on the street itself, where those walking by are apt to feel particularly frustrated at being denied access to what is easily mistaken for a public park.

Leaving Gramercy Park, I turn left onto Park Avenue South and head south. At 17th Street, Park Avenue becomes Union Square East and I find myself looking upward at four huge Corinthian stone columns on my left. There aren't many of these buildings left. This one was once home to the Union Square Savings Bank. Today, it houses an off-Broadway theater. Built in 1905, it is a lonely monument to a triumphant era of American capitalism. Its massive size is a reminder that the roots of this country's admiration for materialistic success are both deep and enduring, notwithstanding the equally strong and rich history of radicalism and populism that are also a part of our nation's history and culture and its concern for the downtrodden and the unfortunate.

Ahead of me, on 14th Street, I can see a large sundial and, to its left, a metronome. Sundials are the world's most ancient clocks, dating back perhaps to 3,500 BC. And the metronome is a modern-day way of measuring time. It has fifteen digital numbers from left to right which count the minutes in a day and also show how much time remains in the day. Watching the people hurrying by on this major thoroughfare, I feel that I'm looking at people in motion trying, in a way, to beat the clock, while the images above chart their progress. An intriguing juxtaposition, I think.

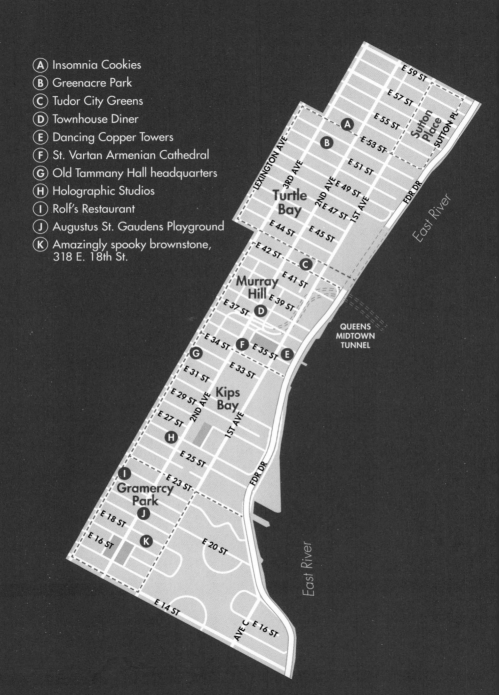

(A) Insomnia Cookies
(B) Greenacre Park
(C) Tudor City Greens
(D) Townhouse Diner
(E) Dancing Copper Towers
(F) St. Vartan Armenian Cathedral
(G) Old Tammany Hall headquarters
(H) Holographic Studios
(I) Rolf's Restaurant
(J) Augustus St. Gaudens Playground
(K) Amazingly spooky brownstone,
    318 E. 18th St.

MIDTOWN EAST

THIS AREA IS BOUNDED BY 59TH STREET ON THE NORTH, the East River on the east, 14th Street on the south, and Third Avenue on the west. As opposed to Central Midtown, it is considerably more residential. The communities here are more distinct, but the boundaries are not so clearly defined and agreed upon. In effect they are "subneighborhoods" that residents clearly identify with. They never say, "I live in Midtown East," but instead say they reside in Sutton Place or Gramercy Park. The communities include Sutton Place, Turtle Bay, Kips Bay, Peter Cooper Village, Stuyvesant Town, Murray Hill, and Gramercy Park. The last two overlap into Central Midtown and have already been discussed in that section.

From the latter part of the nineteenth and into the twentieth century, this part of the city consisted of rundown tenements whose population was impoverished. It was also home to slaughterhouses, coal yards, breweries, power plants, cattle pens, and other business establishments. Beginning in the 1920s living conditions began to improve, and over a period of time the area became much more upscale. Today, there isn't much left of the old days except for older brownstones and row houses that have somehow made it into the twenty-first century, where their owners often wait for a commercial buyer who will make them rich. It's a mixed residential and commercial area that also includes the United Nations at 42nd Street. Commercial streets include First, Second, and Third Avenues, as well as 57th, 42nd, 34th, 23rd, and 14th Streets and many other side streets with small businesses interspersed with residential housing. Ethnically, the residential parts of Midtown East are upper-middle class or wealthy socioeconomically. The population is mostly white and Asian, and the area, which is heavily trafficked day and night, is very safe.

I've seen many streets in Manhattan with flowers in the semipublic areas near the front of the sidewalk, but the large red, pink, and yellow tulips on 55th and 56th Streets between First Avenue and Sutton Place South really stand out. Then there's Sutton Place Park at the eastern end of 56th Street. It's pretty bare, but there's a bench looking out over the East River, with a terrific view of the Queens skyline and the Ed Koch Queensboro Bridge to the left, just another oasis in the midst of Manhattan's cacophony of noise, crowds, and constant activity.

I find myself attracted to 405 E. 54th Street, just east of First Avenue, where the first three floors of this 1920s-style apartment building contain bricks that are of many shapes—oblong, square, rectangular, triangular—and of many shades of red, brown, tan, and black. It looks as though someone threw them haphazardly at the building wall, allowing them to remain wherever and whichever way they happened to have landed. The doorman tells me that this is one of a very few New York City buildings with this type of look. The bricks themselves are actually "clinkers," bricks that were discarded because their color or shape was off. Many have black marks on them, a result of overheating. In the early 1920s, clinkers inexplicably became fashionable, as people decided they were charming. "Famous people lived here," he adds, almost as a disconnected afterthought. "Van Johnson, Noel Coward, Lotte Lenya."

The interior is dimly lit by gas lamps, with Gothic-style vaulted ceilings and arched entranceways. I am greeted by an elderly man who has lived in the building for forty-five years. I ask him what it's like to have lived here for so long and he replies: "You know, thirty-five years ago, there were so many gays living in this building, and now they're all gone." "Where did they all go?" "Go?" he responds. "Most of them died. The AIDS thing killed them. I knew them. It's so incredibly sad. They were full of life and now they're gone forever." The man's remarks are a bitter reminder of the devastation wrought by this disease, especially in the early

The mystery of clinker bricks—triangular, rectangular, square, oblong.

years, when so little was known about it. It peaked in 1993 and then began a long steady decline. Nevertheless, it remains a major health challenge.

On E. 53rd Street, one block east of First Avenue, I come to Sutton Place South and enter another tiny section of Sutton Place Park, one block long, and it turns out to have an interesting history. It was originally owned by the developers of 60 Sutton Place immediately behind it. Not wanting their residents' view of the East River blocked by another tower in front of it, they donated this small parcel to the city with the stipulation that it would be a park. A person walking by might think the park came first, but it didn't.

Certain signs are designed to make you think, and one such instance is a shop at 237 E. 53rd Street, between Second and Third Avenues, proclaiming "Insomnia Cookies." What's that all about? I wonder. Do they keep you up? Will they put you to sleep? Neither, it turns out. Rather, it has to do with the customer's own state of mind, as it continues with: "Warm, fresh cookies delivered until 3:00 a.m." By then, I guess, even an insomniac should probably be sleeping. Inside, a perky young woman studying at the Borough of Manhattan Community College tells me, "Warm cookies will always put you to sleep. We deliver and keep them warm. We have all types of cookies, and the chocolate chip ones are the most popular." They are, in fact, scrumptious. The store's theme, or exhortation, is also posted: "Never leave a craving unfulfilled."

In Turtle Bay, on 51st Street, between Third and Second Avenues, I come across Greenacre Park, a most beautiful little park created by the Rockefeller family in 1971. It's privately owned but open to the public. It's accessible from early morning and closes at 7:45 p.m. Its main feature is a stunning waterfall, where the water cascades over several large boulders. The water fairly roars as it rushes over the top of the rock formation. Off to the side are an ivy-covered wall and some potted plants. A number of trees dot the area, providing both luxuriant foliage and ample shade. People are seated beneath them, usually at small tables, enjoying a cup of coffee with a croissant, talking, texting, reading the paper, or listening to music on their headphones.

Sitting in front of the waterfall, I find that it drowns out every other city sound—trucks passing by, horns honking, construction activity—giving me the feeling that I'm hundreds of miles away, deep in the forests of the Catskills or Adirondacks. The waterfall can become mesmerizing if you stare at it long enough, the streams of flowing water hypnotizing the viewer into staying longer than he or she intended. When the park first opened, the water had to be heated in the winter, but today that's no longer necessary, perhaps because of climate change. Those gathered in the park are a mix of

A waterfall offers up tranquility in Midtown Manhattan.

older and younger people, tourists and natives. One person, a door-man, tells me, "I come here every day on my lunch break and relax in front of the waterfall. It's the gem of the neighborhood." And how many thousands of people walk by the park every day on this very busy street, not knowing the beauty that lies just steps away?

Reflecting on his comment and on the scene in general, I am struck by the importance of what he says. New Yorkers are an en-ergetic lot. They work hard and they lead busy lives. Even getting to and from work is often a challenging and tiring experience. The sights, sounds, and smells of the city assault them at every turn, and living here can sometimes seem like residing in a giant obstacle course. Nowhere is this feeling greater than in Midtown Manhattan.

The fact that in its midst there exists a popular oasis of peace and quiet highlights the fact that people need opportunities to relax. Without them, life becomes virtually intolerable. When people speak about their night off, their weekend at the beach, their vacation, they think of such time as a reward for all their labors, one that makes it all worthwhile.[30]

Tudor City, the first residential high-rise complex in the United States, perhaps in the world, runs from 40th to 43rd Street and from First to Second Avenue. It can best be accessed by walking east from Second Avenue on 41st Street and then turning left or right onto Tudor Place. The style of the buildings is neo-Gothic and very striking. Ironically, given its high-end population, the area was a slum and ruled by gangs in the nineteenth century. The complex was constructed in the 1920s with most of the apartments facing west to avoid the stench from the slaughterhouses to the east. Of course, once the United Nations replaced these foul-smelling businesses, this was no longer an issue.

The crown jewel of this mini-community for visitors is Tudor City Greens, a two-block long private park for residents that is open to the public. The landscaping is lovely, with variegated shrubbery, stone walkways, and flowers of every kind, especially tulips. Unlike Greenacre Park, it's pretty empty, the picture of quiet and serenity in the midst of a crowded and very noisy area. One reason for the lack of people may be that it's not easy to find. There's also a terrific view on Tudor City Place of the entire east-west length of 42nd Street looking west. From where I'm standing on an overpass, it's at a height of three stories and even New Jersey is faintly visible in the distance.

In Murray Hill, on Second Avenue, between 37th and 38th Streets, I come to the Townhouse Diner. The sign outside proclaims it to be "The Best Diner in Town." I've often wondered about signs like these, of which there are thousands in the city. The proprietors put them up—"greatest pizza in New York," or, "voted best Chinese food in New York" (by whom?). Can they be true? In whose opinion(s)? Who believes them? And I think I may have an answer: whoever wants to. If someone is looking for a place to eat and they don't know anything about an eatery, signs like this can help propel them to a decision to step in and have a meal. In the back of their minds they may be skeptical, but hunger and a desire to satisfy it makes them want to believe such claims which, in marketing lingo, give them "permission" to dine there. And so they do serve a real purpose, though not for those locals who already know what they're getting for their money.

I'm attracted to this joint because there are very few real diners in the heart of Manhattan and I want to see what it's like. Much to my surprise it looks like the real deal. There are booths with bright pink plastic backing and green-colored tables. There's a counter with the usual revolving stools. And there are the countless dishes, all made in the same kitchen. And the coup de grace is the Greek immigrant owner, a super-friendly, elderly but very energetic guy named Stavros. I ask the question: "What makes your diner the best in town?"

"Ah, it's the attention we give to everything, the customers, whatever they want, and how delicious we make all the food with great service. I've been doing this for forty years. We started with six brothers, all working in the diner by Lefrak City in Queens along the LIE [Long Island Expressway]."

"So why are the Greeks into diners?"

"I'm not sure, but I know my uncle was one of the early ones, in the 1950s. And one got the idea and then got the others involved when they immigrated here." I have often found that groups who dominate certain industries—like the Yemenis and the delis, the Chinese and takeout places, or Indians and motels—have no idea as to how their people got into these lines of work. The likely answer is probably a combination of factors: a person tries a new business here, it succeeds, he or she brings over some relatives, lends them some startup funds, and the word spreads. Sometimes it's related to the work they did it in the old country, sometimes not. Greece is certainly not full of diners, and Chinese laundries don't dot every inch of the landscape in China.

"That's amazing," I interject. "You started with a place along the LIE service road and today you're still sort of on the LIE, actually just one block from the LIE which begins at the Second Avenue and 36th entrance to the Queens-Midtown Tunnel. And diners are often close to highways, though not ones that begin on Second Avenue in a very crowded part of Manhattan. Do you feel you've made it in America?"

"Sure. I make a good living. Not only that, but more important, my kids have. My daughter graduated St. John's University and is a pharmacist, my son has an MBA from Baruch College and works for AIG, and my youngest son goes to SUNY Binghamton. And that's why it was worth it to come here." The typical immigrant dream, personified—all for the children.

Standing on the northeast corner of First Avenue and 35th Street, I glance west and up, and see, off to the right, the Chrysler building, that critical part of the Manhattan landscape; only it looks very different from here. The classic silver top part of it is there, shimmering against a cobalt blue sky, like it often does. But from this angle it seems to be right on top of a plain square-shaped black building, making it look like one connected structure. It's an optical illusion, and a very eye-catching one at that, because the two structures don't match at all. These interesting juxtapositions appear elsewhere at many locations, depending on where you're standing. It's simply a matter of looking at the skyline where you are when possible. The view can sometimes change even within a single block.

As I'm walking, I notice two forty-nine-story residential towers clad in metal on the eastern side of First Avenue, between 35th and 36th Streets. They have an unusual, eye-catching shape. Each one angles backward beginning at the top third of the building, with the intention of making them appear to be a dancing couple. Does it succeed? Yes, if I use my imagination. Like the Barclays Center

The wedding dance of a skyscraper couple.

and some other buildings in the city, they are connected by a sky-bridge. The material is copper, giving it an orange color. I'm struck by the black sign on a white background, running the length of the building, which reads: "4,250,000 pounds. That's a lot of pennies!" It certainly is.

The largest Armenian church in the city, St. Vartan Armenian Cathedral, the first one built in the United States, is located at 34th Street and Second Avenue. Consecrated in 1968, the exterior features intersecting rooflines and a pyramidal dome with a round base. It resembles St. Hripsime Church found in the holy city of Etchmiadzin, Armenia. On the day I visited, it had a more modern, distinctly American purpose: as a voting center for a New

Can you guess where and what this is?

York State primary election. Walking in, I came upon a gift shop devoted to Armenian items—books, clothing, dolls and other trinkets. As I circled the church complex, I was struck by the fact that the back abuts the block off E. 34th Street that leads directly into the Queens-Midtown Tunnel. This means that every day, tens of thousands of autos and trucks pass by without any idea of what the complex on their left is because there's no sign identifying it. It's odd, in a way, that the building is known to all who pass by on foot on Second Avenue, yet completely anonymous to the many who drive by it every day.

At 204 E. 35th Street, just east of Third Avenue, there's an enterprise called Laser Tattoo Removal, where they do just that. I've always wondered about this: Who goes there? Why? Is it painful? I go through a double door and meet Martin, the receptionist.

"Nice-looking place you have here. I was just wondering, is it painful to have tattoos removed?"

"Yes, but you can manage it. And the people who come in really want to do it."

"Why do most people want them taken off?"

"There are all sorts of reasons. They may have been dating someone. Then they broke up and now they don't want the person's name on it."

"I guess it's sort of like 'Forever' and then 'Not.'"

"Yes, and we get people who are going into the army or marines and they have all sorts of restrictions. You can't have them or they can't be below the arm, whatever. Then you've got people who were in gangs and left them; so they want to get rid of the name. You also have situations, many, where people just got sick of their tattoos and want to have a new start, sort of."

"Is it expensive to do this?"

"Yes. Exactly how much depends on what you have and how it was applied on your skin. But it's not cheap." I think of how many of these people were really committed to something or somebody and then suddenly, or maybe slowly, they decided to end that commitment or relationship. Doing so was very painful, physically. Yet it was worth it to them because they had a chance to literally erase something, though only from their bodies, not their minds or hearts. The place has relocated since I was there to 635 Madison Avenue, but the discussion remains just as relevant and interesting.

The area from 34th to 23rd Street along First and Second Avenues, Kips Bay, is pleasant-looking but not especially interesting in terms of unknown places. It contains a number of medical buildings that are part of New York University and some rather ordinary apartment buildings. There are, however, some things of note on the side streets. For instance, Public School 116 on 33rd Street between Second and Third Avenues looks like a typical school, but, as

I learned, its program is unusual in at least one respect sure to excite many a child, though not necessarily all of their parents: no homework! Instead it initiated a fun program called PDF—Playtime, Downtime, Family Time.

It was a controversial decision among the parents, but Jane Hsu and Gary Shevell, the principal and assistant principal, had done *their* homework. After a year of reviewing the research, they concluded there was insufficient evidence to support the view that homework really mattered. In fact, a 2006 review of sixty-nine studies on the subject headed by Harris Cooper of Duke University, a leading national expert on homework, concluded that there was only a tenuous connection between homework and academic achievement in elementary school.

On Third Avenue I walk south to 32nd Street. Near the corner, on the left, at #207, I see a pretty Beaux-Arts limestone and brick building, uncommon here since it was not historically a fancy part of town. The building in question was the Tammany Hall Twentieth District headquarters and looks pretty much the same as when built in 1902, except it now has even nicer windows and a beautiful polished wooden front door. It was here that politicians, many of them corrupt and led by Richard Croker, met, schemed, and relaxed, eating, smoking, drinking, playing cards, and making use of its gym. Later on it was owned by *New York Magazine,* and then bought by the graphic artist Milton Glaser, who was also a co-founder of the magazine. Above the door is the inscription "Art Is Work." Yes, and it was certainly worth it for Glaser, a Cooper Union graduate who created the famous "I Love New York" logo (with a red heart).

Returning to Third Avenue, I resume my walk downtown and make a left at E. 26th Street. Near Second Avenue, at #240 I see the Holographic Studios, founded in 1979. It is the oldest such gallery in the world. There are hologram displays of various celebrities, including Pierre Cardin, Andy Warhol, Bill Clinton, Edward Koch, the Smothers Brothers. For those unfamiliar with the term, a hologram is a three-dimensional image formed and re-created, in part, by light beams from a laser.

The section between 23rd and 14th Streets and between Third Avenue and the East River is known, generally, as Gramercy Park. It also includes Stuyvesant Town and Peter Cooper Village. On the corner of 22nd Street at 281 Third Avenue, I discover Rolf's German Restaurant. Outside, on the wall there's a well-done impressionistic painting of a bucolic valley in a mountainous setting. Inside, even in April, are some of the most luminous, shining, and colorful Christmas decorations—baubles, bangles, beads, lights, plus many gorgeous dolls, and lots more. It seems as though every square inch of this Bavarian eatery has them. Owned by a family named Hoffman, it's been here almost fifty years. I speak with Bob, the maître d', and ask him, "Why do you leave these decorations up so long after the holiday season?"

"Actually," he replies, "they stay up until Memorial Day, and the reason is that during the holiday season the lines are so long, halfway down the block, that many people don't get to see them. The weekend after Labor Day, they go up again. Even the building itself has a history. Groucho Marx had his first audition here on the rooftop terrace, at the age of fourteen, in 1905. He was hired to be part of a singing vaudeville act, the Leroy Trio. Groucho saw the ad in the paper and he came running down here. And during Prohibition there was a speakeasy upstairs." This is a common story. From 1920 to 1933, speakeasies flourished in many parts of the city in upstairs rooms, basements, and even behind false doors. The name came from the need to speak only in undertones about such places, so as not to alarm or alert the neighbors or the police.

Strolling down Second Avenue, I enter Augustus St. Gaudens Playground, which runs from E. 20th to E. 19th Street, and discover that it has a rather unique theme. It was named for a noted nineteenth-century sculptor who created many well-known landmarks. But the playground honors, in particular, some very important coins that he designed, such as the $10 and $20 gold coins, the

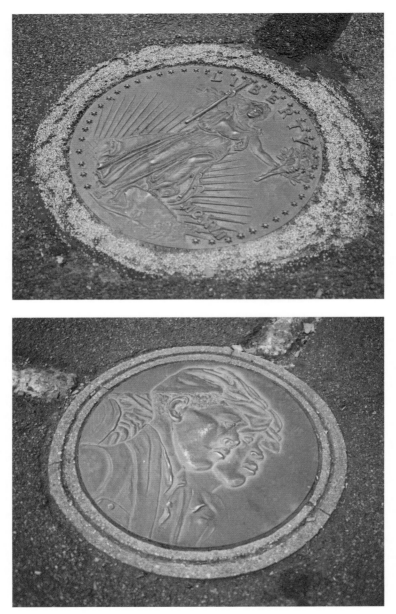

Coins of the realm in a Mid-Manhattan park.

latter better known as the double-eagle piece, which are represented on large porcelain and bronze medallions embedded in the ground.

Just west of First Avenue, on the south side of E. 18th Street, I come to three well-preserved Italianate-style, colorful homes in a New Orleans–type setting, with deep, lush gardens and wrought-iron railings that remind me of homes in Carroll Gardens, Brooklyn. These date back to the early 1850s, located on land that was once part of New York Governor Peter Stuyvesant's farm. These are homes that lasted and they're worth seeing.

I almost miss them, but as I walk by 318 E. 18th Street my attention is drawn to two heads made of stone that have settled in on the stairs of a row house, which is festooned with other statues, fairly clinging to its white exterior. The doorway is wrought iron and ornate in front of what looks like an oak door with a sign, reading "Unwelcomed" and on top of it a skeleton with bat wings. Above it are frightful gargoyles, dragons, and a serpent with a human head, made of different materials. There's also a hooded shroud on the ground floor with scary fingers pointing outward, seemingly beckoning you, not in, but out.

Along the first floor are the names of the owners, Joel Krupnik and Mildred Castellanos. Under the windowsills from left to right, are seven heads, each representing and identifying one of the seven deadly sins—sloth, anger, gluttony, greed, etc. Inside, on the ground floor, two heads stare out from inside two windows. One is of a terrified-looking man, who appears to have seen or experienced some pretty terrible things. The woman looks like the walking dead. In the yard there's a head of a green painted man looking upward with his eyes at four small ducks sitting on his head. By contrast, in the same yard, there's a statue of a wolf guarding a sheep, quite benign considering what else is here. Are these just some unfriendly people discouraging human contact, or is it simply a year-round Halloween exhibit? As I'm leaving, I bump into a young man who enters the gate and ask him, "Do you live here?"

"Yes I do."

"You're just the man I want to see. What's this all about?"

"It's just a collection of items that were built over the years. It was done by me and my parents who have lived here for twenty years. Their names are on the house. On Halloween it's this but with ten times more, with lights, and many more decorations. My mother puts Barbie doll heads inside the plants. It's a fun thing to do. My folks are in business. I work in film and TV and now I'm taking a break from it, running a mixed martial arts place with my brother."

"What made you want to do this?" I persist.

"Well, I guess every neighborhood is missing something, so we decided to change that."

"Has it ever been vandalized?"

"Yes. Somebody stole two of the deadly-sins heads and we were pretty angry about that. So we thought of putting up a high wall but decided against it." Chance sometimes plays a significant role in what I learn, and this is a good case in point. If I hadn't met this person, I would have left without knowing that the owners' reason for doing all this was essentially for fun, as a hobby, in a way, and not the work of an eccentric semi-hermit. Had I left a minute earlier, the meeting would never have occurred.

WEST VILLAGE

GREENWICH VILLAGE

EAST VILLAGE

WEST VILLAGE

THE WEST VILLAGE IS BASICALLY THE western section of Greenwich Village proper, and its general boundaries are 14th Street on the north, Sixth Avenue on the east, Houston Street on the south, and the Hudson River on the west. Houston Street is actually called East Houston east of Broadway and West Houston west of Broadway. Many people are unaware of this and so, to eliminate confusion, it's referred to here and elsewhere in this book as simply Houston Street. It was named after the colonial-era politician William Houston (or Houstoun), and pronounced HOW-ston.

Through the efforts of preservation societies and other community advocates, the West Village has managed, amid all the din and noise of its many nightclubs and restaurants, to maintain parts of its important history. As I traverse some of its cobbled streets, walk under the old sidewalk overhangs on Gansevoort Street, and go tripping down historic byways like Horatio Street that have so many quaint row houses, boasting plaques like "1836" or "1868," I feel almost lost in time. Everywhere you look there are signs and plaques to remind the flaneur that

W 13 ST

12 ST

0 ST

AVE OF THE AMERICAS (6TH AVE)

(A) Liberty Hotel
(B) Jane Hotel
(C) James J. Walker Park
(D) Automatic Slim's
(E) Transplanted nineteenth-century farmhouse
(F) Casa La Femme
(G) Le Gendarme
(H) WXOU Radio Bar
(I) Myers of Keswick

this place doesn't merely *have* history—it *is* history because so much of importance took place here. But that hasn't deterred the developers of glass- and metal-clad behemoths from dragging this quiet enclave into the twenty-first century, thereby making for an uneasy yet fascinating example of geographical and cultural coexistence.

Much of the area has been designated a historic and landmarked district. It has been known as a bohemian area since the early twentieth century, populated by artists, musicians, writers, many of them unconventional types. It was also an industrial part of the city with many warehouses, as well as the center of the meatpacking industry. And in 1969, it became the birthplace of gay rights activism, in the wake of events that took place at the Stonewall Inn, on 53 Christopher Street. When the police raided the tavern, a popular gathering place for gays, lesbians, and transvestites, riots broke out in protest. The Stonewall is now a National Historic Monument and the only one that's focused on LGBT history, a shame given the gay community's enormous contributions to life, culture, and politics in this country and elsewhere in the world.[31]

Attracted, in part, by its rich and scruffy past, plus its central location, gentrifiers began moving in during the 1980s, gradually transforming the area from a rundown, rowdy community where people had to contend with drugs and crime generally into one that is today one of the most expensive neighborhoods in the country. There are numerous points of interest, most famously the High Line Park, which ends here, the previously mentioned Stonewall Inn, and the Whitney Museum. There are many bars, jazz clubs, boutiques, and restaurants here, but much of the community is residential and pretty quiet. The main commercial thoroughfares are Eighth, Seventh, and Sixth Avenues, as well as Hudson, 14th, and Houston Streets. For those interested, it's also been home to a multitude of famous people like Woody Guthrie, Delmore Schwartz, Diane Arbus, Pete Seeger, Nicole Kidman, Will Ferrell, Sarah Jessica Parker, and many others.

A famous publisher's home dating back to 1888.

As I walk along W. 13th Street, I see the sign "P. F. Collier" etched in stone above #416. Immediately recognizing the name of the venerable publishing house, I snap a photo. The large entranceway is supported by four Greek columns. Above it there's a winged globe of the world, flanked by an ink pen made of stone on the right side and a feathered quill on the left, all of which is crowned by a stone torch. Launched in 1888, the company printed 20,000 books a day at one time and had 700 employees. It also published *Collier's Magazine*, a muckraking publication that constantly called for reform throughout its long history. In the mid-1940s, the magazine reached its apex, with a circulation of almost three million, before beginning a long decline and closing in 1956.

The Meatpacking District runs from Bethune to 16th Street south to north and from Greenwich Avenue to the Hudson River east to west. It was home to both slaughterhouses and a large wholesale meat industry and was also the area where farmers sold their crops to New Yorkers. Today, one still sees some wholesale meat outfits like London Meat Company on Little W. 12th Street, which distributes Murray's All-Natural Chicken. There are many visible signs of the storied past of this district scattered throughout, such as the wall drawing on 13th Street near Washington Street which announces the presence of "Dave's Quality Veal 425," with a depiction of a not-too-happy cow in the center.

Just west of Washington Street on 13th is the High Line Park and, towering above the High Line, which it also straddles, is the Standard High Line Hotel. I turn right onto Little W. 12th Street. Why the peculiar name? Because, heading west toward the Hudson, W. 12th Street angles sharply to the left as it crosses Greenwich Avenue. But if it had continued it would have, after a few blocks, again become 12th Street, which is how the block that's there now became known as Little West 12th Street. Most of Manhattan adheres to the orderly grid pattern imposed in 1811, but this area is a throwback to the eighteenth century, when streets were constructed at various angles in no particular order. And so, at the end of the day, Little W. 12th is a block south of 13th Street, while W. 12th is actually three blocks south of Little W. 12th. This haphazard pattern also explains how W. 4th Street goes off in a different direction from the original east-west path of 4th Street. It gives you an appreciation for the grid that prevails in most of Manhattan. Walking this area requires paying close attention to a map to avoid missing key points of interest on its many angled streets.

Midway down Little W. 12th, I come across a small grassy lot on my right. Two elderly men, Novac Noury and Gerry Autry, greet me with a well-harmonized song by Tom Petty called "Wildflowers," looking at me with a heartfelt and intimate expression that makes me feel as if I'm being serenaded—and I am. All the while I'm glancing behind them at a peculiar contraption about six feet tall standing upright. There's a keyboard with a stream of water shooting upward out of small holes bored into the keyboard from its top. As Novac, the creator of this, explains: "In the morning, when the water goes up, the sun hits it at an angle and you can clearly see a rainbow through it. And it looks just beautiful. I used to work for Studio 54 in the music area back in the day, as they say. I was part of the new wave era." Indeed, when I look at the stream of water even now, in the early evening, I can make out the faint color scheme of a rainbow generated by the setting sun.

Novac performs his music at small events and invites me to come and see him do his thing. He's wearing a tee shirt featuring a reproduction of his keyboard. "This musical instrument," he continues, "which I call the Arrowhead Keyboard because of its shape, is my invention. I created it in 1970. It's a wireless keyboard that I made with the help of a New Jersey scientist who worked for the Apollo Mission. I do Gene Kelly, mixed with *Saturday Night Fever*, and then with some Michael Jackson. You have to be stone cold sober, which I am, to do that kind of music. In my opinion the new wave era of the 1980s was the next meaningful period after the '60s. Of course, since I'm 70, I would call myself a hippie." To the left of the keyboard is a Statue of Liberty re-creation. There's also a mannequin on the right with a small colored globe where the head should be.

Novac grew up on Fountain Avenue in the rough East New York section of Brooklyn, a place from which he says he escaped with the intervention of "the good Lord." His mother, he tells me, put him in the church choir. I don't know the details of his journey from Studio 54 to this grassy place, but he's active and healthy-looking and still performs, singing and playing music and getting donations at his location from passersby. He's as much a part of New York's life and culture as Broadway or the Whitney Museum of American Art—not as famous, but always ready to entertain and inform in his own way.

The move by the Whitney Museum to nearby Gansevoort Street, facing the Hudson River, is a noteworthy development. The museum's former building at 75th Street and Madison Avenue on the Upper East Side was a traditional concrete structure that fit in well in that part of Manhattan. The new one, a gleaming metal and glass structure, has adapted architecturally to its new surroundings. The move from the Upper East Side validates the reality that this part of town has become established and that New York's cultural scene now encompasses it. At this point, it's impossible to say whether its geographic separation from the other museums will be successful, which makes the name of its restaurant, "Untitled," seem very appropriate at this stage.

Not far from Novac's mini-meadow on Little W. 12th Street, I come across a bricked-up place with a gleaming metal door. Several young people are waiting for someone else to show up. I engage them in conversation and learn that yet another eatery is about to open here. A twenty-something public relations person, filled with the enthusiasm of youth and hope gushes: "This is replacing another place that closed. But this one will be different. We'll have really great little plates and original drinks. And we'll have terrific live entertainment. We're fixing it up now. It's gonna be *so good*."

I wish them well, but the odds aren't that much in their favor since many new businesses, especially restaurants, fail. If they make it, it will probably be due to their ability to be perceived as "hot" by those who frequent these places. In a way, this is very typical of the area, where the crowds are huge on the weekend and the possibilities seem limitless. An eatery is suddenly "in" because it was written up by a magazine or newspaper, or because certain key opinion shapers decided to dine there. Then, just as suddenly, a few months later, it loses its appeal.

Those who survive generally fall into two sometimes overlapping categories. They have a gimmick, a hook, or they are part of a larger chain of stores and can feed off their brand's success. One example of a gimmick is Bantam Bagel at 283 Bleecker Street, which sells tasty bite-sized bagels with no hole and filled mostly with cream cheese. They ship around the country and sell to Starbucks. Of course, the success of a business also depends on other factors, such as location, quality of product, cost, and the national economy.

Walking along a quiet part of Greenwich Street, I chat with Bart, a bearded chap in his forties, wearing shorts and a tee shirt, who's playing with his kids in a small park. "How do you like living here?" I inquire.

"It's fine. I've lived here since the '80s."

"It must have changed a lot."

"Well, then it was really interesting. We had transvestites, prostitution, and it was a sketchy neighborhood. Today, it's so boring, just like me." He laughs at his self-description, and I join in, as he continues. "Actually, there's still something left from that time period. There was a hotel called the Liberty at 51 Tenth Avenue that was known as a center for hookers and all that stuff. Well, it's still there today. It sits right on a small triangle at the end of 14th Street bordering the West Side Highway. I can't imagine what it's still doing there. It has a big American flag flying over the roof. I swear it's a CIA front."

With that description I hoof it over to check it out. A modest looking three-story brick structure, now called the Liberty Hotel, it turns out to be a rent-by-the-hour hotel, as I learn from a young couple who reluctantly tell me this as they check in with no luggage. Inside, a vending machine dispenses both condoms and cookies while you wait in line for a room. For $90, you can have two hours, while an overnight stay in a "Romantic Interlude" room with a Jacuzzi and lots of well-angled mirrors, goes for $250. These places have been around for ages, but they often look seedy, sort of like walking into a porn shop. The Liberty apparently looked that way in the '80s, but today it's respectable in appearance, low-key, and spotless. Its location on the very edge of the West Village makes it uncontroversial. Thinking it's a CIA front makes it more exciting, but I personally doubt it, large flag notwithstanding. In a way, it reminds me that one can live somewhere a long time and still not know exactly what's happening in every part of the neighborhood.

A nicer establishment of a very different sort is the Jane Hotel, four blocks south on Jane Street and overlooking the Hudson River. An imposing, stolid, Georgian-style, red-brick structure, it was built in 1908 as a sailor's hotel. It also housed survivors of the Titanic while the tragedy was being investigated. Eventually it became a down-at-the-heels lodging house largely inhabited by drug addicts. The latest iteration began in 2008 when it morphed into a boutique hotel. It's the interior that catches the eye. The lobby, smallish and intimate, makes me feel as if I've gone back a century, largely because of the Romanesque stone fountain and the intricately carved wooden designs surrounding the check-in desk, which has those old little boxes for the room keys. A very spacious room used for receptions features memorabilia from various eras, including exquisitely designed chandeliers, comfortable sofas and chairs, a replica of a clipper ship off to the side, and a mosaic made from colored glass tiles near the back. Hanging above the mosaic is a painting of what appears to be a North African officer, with a white beard, and gold medals on his chest. Beneath it, on the left, I notice what looks like a deejay's console. There's also a stunning carving of a ram with perfectly curved horns, its appearance enhanced by a spotlight focused on it. It's standing atop an elaborate fireplace, seemingly looking off into the distance. Next door, a bar runs the length of a smaller space; while off to the side, a beautifully feathered white peacock hangs high from a wall. Finally, as you walk out, there's the Gitane Café, with French/Moroccan cuisine and decor off to the right of the lobby area..

Running along the western border of the West Village is the Hudson River Park, precious land in an area with few parks. It extends along the river from 59th Street to Battery Park, and this portion is particularly scenic. I walk along the park from Jane Street to Leroy Street where I turn left and soon come to a small park on the right, three blocks away. James J. Walker Park is a half-square-block recreational space between Leroy and Clarkson Streets, and running along Hudson Street. It boasts an outdoor swimming pool, up-to-date playgrounds, a bocce court with a sign warning dogs to keep off, plus baseball and soccer fields.

Inside the park is a granite monument with three helmets atop it with an unusually worded story: "This monument was erected by the members of Eagle Fire Engine Company No. 13 in connection with friends of the deceased to commemorate the sad event connected with their death and the loss which they deplore." Nothing is said about the nature of the event, and the word "deplore" sounds like an archaism for "are greatly saddened by" or something similar. If the style sounds somewhat old-fashioned, it's no surprise since the monument was found inside the park, which was used by Trinity Church as a burial ground from 1806 to 1852 and, in 1897, became a public park. Delving into it, I learn that the three young men died when a building on Pearl Street fell on them as they were fighting a blaze. Tragically, it was apparently their first day on the job. It's also worth noting that the cemetery beneath the park contains the remains of thousands of poor immigrants, a good number of them young, buried here in the nineteenth century. Some of the remains were removed by family members and friends, but many were not.

I turn around and head west one block to Washington. Strolling uptown I eventually come to #733, near the intersection with Bank Street. I venture into Automatic Slim's, a small, nondescript place with a black-and-red checkered floor whose appearance belies its substance. The name Automatic Slim's comes from an old blues song called "Wang Dang Doodle All Night Long," written by Willie Dixon. It starts with a man talking about inviting someone named Automatic Slim to his party. This location is a real "happening" place that's been here twenty-nine years and attracts serious bar food connoisseurs in the early evening and wall-to-wall, noisy crowds late at night. But it's the evocative framed black-and-white photos of famous singers and musicians that stand out. I speak with Dave Zinsser, the nattily attired gray-haired owner, who's in his mid-sixties, and get a detailed description of his collection.

"These photos are generally one-of-a-kind photos that either I found, or which friends gave me. You have the Supremes, which I got in Amsterdam. This one's of Bob Marley when he gave his first concert. My friend was there and took the picture. You cannot believe how small the place where he played, in Boston, was. This group is of the Meters playing in New Orleans, one of the greatest funk bands of all time. The bass player was so good he sounded like a guitar player. That one's of Art Neville, and this one is the Rolling Stones in 1964. Over there you have the Five Blind Boys of Alabama. They're a gospel band. Their new lead player is a guy named Jimmy Carter. He's, like, ninety-two years old and he can hold a note longer than a minute, like 1:40. This last band began playing in 1944, is in the Gospel Hall of Fame, and still performs today. They played at the Julliard School a year ago."

Dave certainly knows his stuff and loves to talk about it. He also has photographs of Charlie Parker, Chuck Berry, and Miles Davis. I ask him to describe the scene here on Saturday night. "Well, the best way to put it is that we sell about 600 drinks between the hours of 10 p.m. and 3 a.m. That's insane since we can only have 75 people inside at a time. Just think about those numbers." I also discover that Dave has a PhD in English literature from New York University and worked in publishing for many years. "I love the name of your place," I say to him as I leave. "Taking it from a song is so fitting." "Well, you know," he says, breaking into a wide smile, "people come in here sometimes thinking it's one of those dieting places."

A half-block farther east at 113–115 Bank Street is a pretty, though somewhat spartan-looking renovated white brick building with stars and nautical symbols on it and a round plaque identifying it as a hospital. The backstory is that it once catered to sailors in need of medical treatment. Almost all of these streets in the West Village south of the Gansevoort area are very quiet—Bank, Bethune, Charles, West 12th—in contrast to the northern end of the neighborhood. I make a right at Greenwich Street and one block later, where it intersects with W. 11th Street, I spy an interesting-looking building. It's one of the few in this area that's covered in ivy, and it's beautifully manicured. Even as I walk by, it's being carefully tended by an Ecuadorian gardener who speaks no English and is wearing a hat with lettering that says, "In God We Trust" along with a tee shirt reading "Dutch Masters."

At 360 W. 11th Street between Washington Street and the Hudson River, a condo building rises into the sky. The lower part was once a horse stable. Its upper half is done in a Moorish style, with graceful balconies and arches throughout, and looks like an Italian palazzo. Designed and used as an art studio by the well-known artist Julian Schnabel it has received a mixed reception. Some see it as a gorgeous expression of the West Village's reputation for over-the-top extravagance and nonconformism. Others, namely preservationists, see it as being out of context with both history and contemporary architecture.

Turning around, I head east on W. 11th Street, and turn right onto Hudson Street, walk to Charles Street, and turn right. At #121 I stop short in front of a detached house that looks as if it's

A nineteenth-century farmhouse relocated to the West Village.

been there forever. But things are not always what they seem. It was actually rescued in 1967 before a knockdown of a property on York Avenue and 71st Street. A nineteenth-century farmhouse, it was relocated to this lot and renovated. Farther up, at #140, there's an upscale restaurant, Casa La Femme, probably the most opulent Egyptian dining option in the city, including tented tables for atmosphere, that serves up genuine native food, with a belly dancer thrown in as well. Scattered throughout the dining room are elaborate woodcarvings, and thick drapes along the wall give the place a dark feeling of intimacy.

Across the street from Casa La Femme is a limestone and granite building at 135 Charles Street, built over a century ago. It is named Le Gendarme and appropriately so, since it was a police station until 1969. It then became a condo, but there's ample evidence of its previous life, such as the carved letters announcing "Police Patrol" above a ground-floor window, which was also the site of a watering trough for the horses. If you look through the glass in the front door, you'll see a nice plaque in honor of those who ran the show in those days, including Police Commissioner Teddy Roosevelt. I wonder if living in a preserved building where criminals passed through on a daily basis matters at all to the residents. One of them, who happened to walk out while I stood there, said somewhat airily, almost as if the thought of such an unsavory connection meant a loss in status, "I could care less. All I know is, I have a beautiful apartment." Of course, you could ask the same question in reverse. Does the fact that one of the city's greatest mayors, Fiorello La Guardia, resided at 39 Charles Street for seven years, from 1914–1921, make any difference to current residents? Probably not, except as a conversation piece.

Returning to Hudson Street, I turn right, go left at Christopher, and make a quick right onto Bedford Street. As noted, the West Village has many historical identifiers. Some are larger, even more elaborate than the usual modest-size plaques. Take, for instance, the exquisite raised lettering and elegant coat of arms on a small residential building at 95 Bedford Street. It reads, "J. Goebel & Co. est. 1865." Julius Goebel immigrated to New York from Germany, where he opened a business that produced crucibles, containers in which metal or other substances can be heated in very high temperatures. His son continued in his father's footsteps. A resident told me that some of the crucibles are still in the basement. He also mentioned that tour guides sometimes incorrectly tell their clients that Goebel was a wine distributor. Perhaps they think it makes for an interesting story.

Continuing down to the corner in the same direction, I turn left onto Barrow Street, take it to Bleecker Street, go right and in a block, I'm at the Congregational Neighborhood Church, at #269. As in other parts of the city, there are many churches of historic importance in the West Village. But there are also new ones, like this church, that have sprung up in recent decades. It's on the ground floor of a narrow two-story red-brick row house, nicely kept. The inside is very spare, with a simple gold cross in front of the sitting area. In short, it's an upscale storefront church, the equivalent to the many such houses of worship that are very common in the city's poorer communities. Does this work here? I ask one of the original congregants, who has been a member since the early 1970s, who replies: "We get about thirty people a week. This is an area of wealth. And I think the problem is that people don't want to get in touch with their sins and don't realize that Jesus is the answer. Yuppies don't come here. They're mostly interested in getting good jobs. We do have jazz concerts on Friday night and they're free. In the old days more people came, but the area had more drugs and all." This reveals how complex religious communities are. The church is here even if the market is small because this is where it began, and there may not be an incentive to move. They've also adapted to the current neighborhood, hosting concerts and art shows.

I complete my walk through this richly tapestried part of town on Hudson Street, turning around and heading north to Perry Street, where I go left to Hudson and make a right. The White Horse Tavern, with its glorious long history and great decor, featuring various statues and busts of white horses, is a well-known landmark, But for an unknown place, I go halfway up Hudson to the WXOU Radio Bar across the street at #558. Its old-timey tiled floor and long bar is reminiscent of decades past. The name itself has little to do with anything. As the barista explained: "The previous owner collected antique clocks, and this neon-lit one had a radio station sign under it. Take a look on the wall behind you and you'll see it. So when the current owner bought it, he just kept the name." For the record, WXOU is a real station operated by students at Oakland University in Detroit, Michigan. This dive bar also serves up a top-notch Bloody Mary!

There's a small British expat population in Gotham, and the largest specialty food shop is Myers of Keswick at 634 Hudson between Horatio and Jane Streets. It's like a small Balducci's, only its products are British and Irish. There are freshly made meat pies of all sorts and American brands like Heinz beans whose ingredients have been altered to suit British tastes—that is, less spicy. The place is authentic and a real cure for homesickness, as attested to by the largely British clientele. The people I met there were truly excited to be here. They'd been away from England for several years, were living in Ohio, and had made a beeline for this place immediately upon arriving in the Big Apple as tourists. For those from an ocean away, this is a real opportunity to indulge and connect.

W 14 ST

E 14 ST

W 13 ST

E 13 ST

AVE OF THE AMERICAS (6TH AVE)

W 12 ST

W 11 ST

W 10 ST

E 11 ST

FIFTH AVE

E 12 ST

UNIVERSITY PL

W 9 ST

E 10 ST

W 8 ST

E 9 ST

WAVERLY PL

E 8 ST

WASHINGTON PL

WASHINGTON SQ N

WASHINGTON MEWS

Washington
Square Park

GREENE ST

WASHINGTON SQ S

WASHINGTON PL

MINETTA LN

ASTOR

BROADWAY

W 3 ST

SULLIVAN ST

LAGUARDIA PL

Noho

LAFAYETTE

MacDOUGAL ST

E 4 ST

THOMPSON ST

BLEECKER ST

MERCER ST

GREAT JONES ST

BOND ST

HOUSTON ST

JONES ALLEY

CROSBY ST

MOTT ST

BOWERY

GREENWICH VILLAGE

SOMETIMES REFERRED TO AS SIMPLY "THE VILLAGE," Greenwich Village's boundaries are, roughly, 14th Street on the north, Third Avenue and the Bowery on the east, Houston Street on the south, and Sixth Avenue to the west. Within this is the Noho (or NoHo, for *No*rth of *Ho*uston Street) district, bounded by 9th Street on the north, Third Avenue and the Bowery on the east, Houston Street on the south, and Broadway on the west. Like the West Village, the Village has many landmarked buildings. Its reputation as a center of bohemian culture was established in the nineteenth century, when it was home to many artists and writers.

Nightclubs that showcased, among others, African American performers, flourished in the Village during the 1940s and beyond. In the 1950s, it was the birthplace of the beat generation, including William Burroughs, Allen Ginsberg, and Jack Kerouac, whose iconic work, *On the Road,* inspired me and many others to hitchhike across America in the late 1960s. This was followed in the '60s by the "hippie" or "flower child" generation, which danced and "grooved" to the songs of Joan Baez, Bob Dylan, Judy Collins, the Beatles, and Joni Mitchell, all of whom performed in this part of the Village. These singers often expressed the mood of young people who had joined up with the civil rights, antiwar, women's, and gay rights movements that marked and energized this remarkable era.

For me, growing up in those heady times was an extraordinary experience, and I spent a lot of time in the Village, whose musical epicenter was Third and MacDougal Streets, which throbbed to the rhythms of its residents and visitors, augmented by LSD/acid and other drugs as well as alcohol, until the wee hours of the morning. I even sang in cafes and bars there on numerous occasions. Today, as I walk these lanes—Bleecker Street, Minetta Lane, MacDougal, and 3rd, as well as Sullivan and Thompson Streets—I find a much tamer version of those years, but still a crowded and active scene, especially on the weekends.

The neighborhood is dominated by NYU in the same way that Columbia dominates its environs in Morningside Heights. Although resented by many as an institution that gobbles up available real estate, its schools and centers have enriched the cultural scene in general, as have the New School and Cooper Union, albeit to a lesser degree.

The upper part of Greenwich Village, from 13th to 8th Street, is home to century-old row houses, townhouses, and luxury apartment buildings, especially along Fifth Avenue. The main commercial thoroughfares are Sixth and Fourth Avenues, University Place, Broadway, and Houston, 8th, and 14th Streets. Washington Square Park is the area's glorious gathering place, day and night. The architecture is beautiful throughout this area and worth walking nearly every block to admire. There are many standouts, like 7 and 9 E. 10th Street, two teakwood-accented beauties; but everyone can find their own favorites here on almost any block.

At 67 E. 11th Street, corner of Broadway, I pass the Cast Iron Building, constructed in 1868 as a home for the James McCreery

Dry Goods Store. In 1971, it was the first cast-iron structure converted to a residential building. It's large and imposing, with tall Corinthian columns and arched windows. Perhaps its major contribution was that it persuaded many builders that cast-iron buildings could have a second life as residential complexes.

Heading west, at 18 W. 11th Street, I'm jolted again into New York's past, only it's a very different encounter. This is where, decades ago, five Weathermen terrorists built a bomb factory in the basement. Two of their intended targets were Columbia University's Butler Library and an officer's dance at Fort Dix, New Jersey. Fortunately, it never happened because on March 6, 1970, there was an accidental explosion of dynamite in which three Weathermen were killed and two who survived, Kathy Boudin and Cathy Wilkerson, evaded the law for at least ten years. Ironically, Boudin became an adjunct professor at Columbia's School of Social Work in 2008. As for the townhouse, it was rebuilt and blends in nicely with its century-old (or older) counterparts, distinguished only by the fact that the building has an irregular, angled front.

Known as "the House of Death," the townhouse at 14 W. 10th Street is another notorious location. In November 1987, attorney Joel Steinberg severely beat his adopted six-year-old daughter, Lisa, on the second floor, after getting high on cocaine. She died three days later. But that's not the only reason for its dark reputation. Mark Twain lived there in 1900, and various residents have sworn they had seen him walking around in a white suit. One woman, Jan Bryant Bartell, who lived there in the late 1950s, died under suspicious circumstances shortly after completing an account of the ghosts she had seen there. Others reported strange odors, lights, and noises there and in other houses on the block, especially #16 and #18. And why not? Ghosts can obviously and easily move from one location to another. And if that's not enough, #17 was the last known residence of Edgar Allan Poe, a master storyteller of the supernatural world.

At 36 E. 12th Street, east of Fifth Avenue, I pass by Seidenberg, an antique emporium that's high-ceilinged, carpeted, spacious, and

Site of the Weathermen's former home and their bomb factory.

filled with beautifully displayed merchandise. It's a colorful and stunning collection, more befitting a museum, one of the nicest I have ever seen. It's not one of those antique stores filled with used and sometimes bedraggled cast-offs. Rather, it's replete with fine china, urns, vases, and tureens made of porcelain. There's Limoges, Rosenthal, Wedgwood jasperware, lots of dainty and heavy silver items, vanity brushes, mirrors and combs, crystal and silver candlesticks, and decorative sets of dishes with beautiful drawings on them. Needless to say, my dog, who came along for the exercise, did not enter the store, for while not a bull in a china shop, she's certainly capable of destroying, with one swipe of her tail, a priceless urn.

A magnificent ode to the glory days of antique emporiums.

I speak with Jack Seidenberg, the proprietor. He's wearing a pale blue suit and an elegant yellow-orange tie, very dapper. A handsome man in his sixties, with wavy brownish-gray hair, he greets me effusively. "Welcome," he says in a friendly tone. "What can I do for you?"

"How's business?"

"Well, I make a living. We moved here from Broadway because our lease was up and we renovated this place, which used to be a pool hall."

"Is there anything special about the items you have, or anything else that makes your store unique?"

Jack, who grew up in Washington Heights, answers in a self-effacing manner. He's not interested in impressing anyone at the expense of the facts: "Not really. All antique places carry essentially similar merchandise. If there's anything different, I'd like to think that I might bring an unerring eye or a certain taste. In addition to your taste or anyone else's taste, I try to bring something else to the game that can be helpful and informative. My father started this business in 1940, and I've been at it since the 1970s. It's in my blood. When I was a kid, our apartment looked like a mini-antique shop."

"So you were always in this line of work?"

"No. I graduated law school and practiced for about a year but didn't like it, and then my father, who had wanted me to be a professional, finally relented and let me do this."

"I'm here today at 12:30, we've been talking for a while and no one has come in. Is this usual? Do you get walk-ins?"

"Occasionally I get a walk-in, but that's about it. It's not the most well-traveled street in New York. We'll get collectors or decorators or, when the economy and the currency were better we got Europeans or Asians. But with the Internet it's a new game, and my son will enlarge it. However, with everybody shopping virtually, what do you need a brick-and-mortar store [for], especially with the way rents are going in New York? Every day more and more stores are vacant."

"So you followed your father into the business. Given the current situation of very little business, do you have any regrets?"

Again, a humble and measured response: "None at all and I'll tell you why: after practicing law for a year, I realized I'm not aggressive enough, I don't have that temperament, maybe I'm not bright enough, whatever."

"What do you like most about doing this?"

"I like the exercise of figuring out what everything is, where it's from, what it means to a buyer, the aesthetics of it all, and I like selling. I was always attracted to this kind of stuff. After a while, you know where it's from and what it really is, and it's not just a pair of vases."

"What do you do all day?"

"I read, talk with people on the phone. There's always things to do. Look, this business is clearly not the flavor of the month. You need so much capital, but if you had it why would you do this? It's not a turnover business like Bloomingdale's. It was always meant for the 1 percent or 2 percent. So it's a struggle, but I'm existing."

"And yet, you're happy."

"You know, I have people who come in here and wake me up from my lethargy. They say to me: 'You must have such a wonderful life being surrounded by all these beautiful works of art.' And I'm thinking about the next sale, but they set me right and stop me in my tracks, stop me from thinking despairing thoughts and set me on the right path where I was and where I should be."

Jack mirrors the dilemmas facing thousands of New York small-business owners. Times and tastes are changing, and technology is transforming everything. He's caught in a business that's still solvent but not very profitable. He looks at his investment and worries whether or not it will end badly. Perhaps he should have been an attorney, but then he reflects and decides it wasn't for him. Sales is what he loves, and he feels it's worth the struggle, one that becomes more gratifying as others teach him through their words to see genuine value in what he has and what he does. His words offer a portrait of what it's really like to be in business at this level, to wait and hope that someone comes in on their own and makes your day.

Next I visit the Strand Bookstore, which, besides selling new books, has one of the world's best and largest collections of used books, and at good prices. Located on the corner of Broadway and E. 12th Street, it also features many talks and events of interest to literary folks, I remember speaking there on a cold January night, when the temperature was 7 degrees Fahrenheit. There were about eighty people present, testimony not so much to me as to the store's many fans. Its catchy slogan is "Eighteen miles of books," at least some of which I too have walked over the years.

Turning around, I head west on 12th to Sixth Avenue, and turn left to 9th Street. Ironically, this location achieved its greatest fame, perhaps, as a fictional address in Alfred Hitchcock's classic film *Rear Window*—125 W. 9th Street. And, what today is a peaceful garden at this intersection, was, until 1973, the Women's House of Detention, whose famous involuntary inhabitants included the atomic spy Ethel Rosenberg, the Catholic activist Dorothy Day, and the '60s radical Angela Davis.

The first block on 9th Street east of Sixth Avenue is lined with ginkgo trees, surrounded by black wrought-iron fencing, and planted with coleus and silver lace. It's a quiet street, in sharp contrast to its famous and far more honky-tonk neighbor, 8th Street, or St. Mark's Place. Today, St. Mark's Place has become a popular venue for Asian students. On 9th Street, refurbished tenements and brownstones predominate, some with limestone pillars and friezes under windows. Hanging over them are solemn-looking terracotta faces that appear to be staring at you no matter where you stand. Some of the houses are covered with thick ivy, stretching almost to the roofs of the buildings.

There are quite a few unusual-looking structures on this block. One of them, the Portsmouth, at #38, was home for many years to theater impresario Joseph Papp. Behind a rich brown, mahogany door is a fan light with squares of colored glass in front of it that emit a warm welcoming glow. A stone-carved woman's face with a long-suffering look, lips parted in a faint, enigmatic smile, gazes out from the facade. Another building, #23, with a long balcony, would certainly look at home in New Orleans's French Quarter. Near the corner, a house built in 1859 has wrought-iron wagon wheels in front of the second-floor windows.

One wonders how many passersby appreciate all this. The Korean woman who runs the Farmer's Market near Sixth Avenue, opposite the PATH station, doesn't seem to. I ask her what's interesting about the block. "Nothing," she says, "except a lot of crazy people walking around who come from the train station. I live here thirty years, but you can trust *nobody*. I was robbed five years ago. America is getting really bad." She is unimpressed by my observation that the Big Apple's crime rate is way down.

East of Broadway, on the northern end of Noho, 9th Street temporarily becomes known as Wanamaker Place, named for the famous department store opened at this location in 1896 by John Wanamaker. The cast-iron building, which featured a huge glass skylight at the top, remained there until 1956, when it was destroyed by a fire. It took almost 600 firemen to extinguish the blaze, and the flames almost destroyed the historic Astor Place subway station. Its two separate buildings were linked on an upper floor by what was somewhat grandiosely called "the Bridge of Progress." Whose progress, one wonders? What sort of progress? The renaming of streets has become quite common in this city, and it may please those with the connections to make it happen, but it often goes unnoticed and unappreciated by the masses. None of the dozen or so people I asked on the block had the slightest idea who or what Wanamaker was. Today the block is known for its Ann Taylor Loft store and as a headquarters for both AOL and Facebook. Southward, Noho stretches down to Houston. Most of its expensive apartments are lofts, ideal locations for artists.

As I spoke with the residents, several themes kept coming up. One of them was the gay community, with most people professing tolerance for them but not always in a convincing way. "I'm very discreet about my neighbors," an elderly woman asserts. "But often the gays, the way they dress, are really out there. But I don't care. Whatever they do, that's their problem . . . I mean, their business. I have one I know for twenty-five years, coming for dinner tonight."

Another favorite topic is apartments and their cost. A truly happy Manhattanite is one with a rent-controlled apartment in the city who lets you know that they feel they're making out like bandits. It's the way the average New Yorker beats the system. They lean forward and whisper confidentially, "I'm paying $1,100 a month and if the landlord could get me out, he could sell it for a million."

I walk into the Central Bar, farther east on 9th Street and just west of Third Avenue, and discover that it is full of Irish fans avidly watching a large screen, as Manchester United plays soccer (they call it "football") against a Ukrainian opponent. Bedlam erupts as Manchester scores. It's actually one of several such pubs in the area. As I sit at the bar, musing about how so many nationalities create their own little communities in the city, wild cheering suddenly breaks out as the home team scores the winning goal. Those around me burst into a ditty about the Manchester scorer: "He comes from Serbia; he'll f***in' murder ya."

Why are the pubs here? Because quite a few people from the British Isles—England, Scotland, Wales, and Ireland—and a smattering of Australians and New Zealanders live in the neighborhood and on the Lower East Side generally. I asked a blonde-haired, blue-eyed patron why they chose this as an enclave of sorts. His reply: "There's a lot of variety here in people, stores that sell our foods, marmite and vegemite toast, pubs where you can get great English beer. Plus, we like locales where, as in England, the buildings aren't too tall." Whatever the reason, this part of town and the West Village, too, are the closest it gets to a British community in New York—one that numbers some 35,000 souls.

Neighborhoods are sometimes closely linked to certain sports activities. For example, some of the best basketball in the city is played at the eastern intersection of Sixth Avenue and 3rd Street. It's known as "the Cage" because of the wire fencing surrounding it and its smaller than regulation size. Like Rucker Park in Harlem, it has had iconic status for decades, in large part because NBA stars have occasionally played there. I have watched many a game there, enjoying the scrappy New York style of pickup games marked by sharp elbows, rough jostling, and take-no-prisoners drives down the court. Less well known but equally enjoyable to see are games on the handball courts next to the basketball courts, which sometimes feature A-level players.

I walk down 3rd Street to MacDougal, turn left and arrive at Washington Square Park. A walk through the Village wouldn't be complete without a visit to the park. It has beautiful landscaping, a great fountain, a magnificent arch, and so much history. Near that fountain I meet Paul, known as "the Birdman," who has been feeding the pigeons for the last fourteen years or so. He's in his fifties, dresses very casually in jeans and a tee shirt, and has grown up in the neighborhood. His main occupation over the years was repairing Persian rugs, a trade taught to him by one of his father's friends. When Paul was sixteen his father died, and he left school to support his mother. But, in recent years, with a downturn in that market, he's unemployed and was recently evicted, he says, by his landlord, who drastically increased the rents. As I'm talking with him, Michal, a street photographer from Queens, is filming Paul.

"How do you live with no apartment?" I ask him.

"I stay with friends who help me," he answers, sounding a bit vague. Tall, bespectacled, with soft features, he gives the impression of being a nice man. His greatest love is "his" pigeons, whom he knows on a first-name basis, and whom he's been feeding for many years. They're on his arms, legs, even his head. "I knew and fed their parents." He says, almost matter-of-factly.

"But why do you love pigeons so much?"

"They're better than therapy. They make people laugh and not think about bad things. They're much better than humans, who can be very nasty, offensive, and they want to ruin your life."

"But some of them are nice."

"Only earthlings are. That's what I call them. I'm an earthling. We enjoy the little things in life. But others, teenagers, they beat me up for no reason. They're humans. The cops came and it was like, 'Scratch it off. You live in New York.' People are jealous, and they say pigeons are just rats in the sky. And the pigeons are very smart. They see a hawk and they just take off. They'll make a left or right, and in sequence. How do they know how to do that? Pigeons are doves. You see this one. He likes me and shows it by gently pecking me. They have feelings, they want my affection, but nothing like for each other. You see this one on the ground here? He's puffed up because he's doing the love dance for this female, showing her how beautiful and important he is." A pigeon lands on his shoulder and starts pecking playfully at his face.

"No kissing, no kissing, Cheetah." he says softly. "I know Cheetah a long time. You know, they're just as smart as chimpanzees, in their own way. They have a GPS. They know where to go, how to get there. During the war, if they got oil on their wings and couldn't fly, they'd walk incredibly long distances to get where they had to go." Paul takes pride in what he does and who he is, as the following vignette indicates.

"Two years ago the captain of the precinct came to the park when he was doing his last day on the job and said, 'I wanna hold those birds. I really envy you.' And I said, 'I would be afraid of getting shot my last day. I would be hiding under my desk.'"

"And what did the captain say?"

"He said, 'Everybody talks about you and I just wanna hold the bird.' Yesterday, the cops were here, and they were taking pictures too."

"Would you rather be with a pigeon than a person?"

He pauses before responding, looking at me a bit apprehensively. "Yeah, I'd rather be with the pigeons. They make me happy. I don't entertain them. They entertain me. They're so trusting. They don't have diseases. Humans have the worst diseases. Anyway, take care of yourself." And that's how the conversation ended.

As I listened to him I began to get the feeling that Paul has, in a way, crossed the bridge from the human world to the pigeon world. He interacts with humans because they're there and even necessary to his survival. But mostly his waking hours are spent with the pigeons, and they're what really counts for him. He's gentle, kind, and not at all like the stereotype of the tough, scrappy New Yorker. I suspect that he may have been picked on in school, that he was seen by others as naive, even weird. Perhaps he would be viewed as a misfit by most people. But from his perspective, it's surely the other way around. The truth is that a city this large can and does accommodate all types of humans, or "earthlings." In the end, as I learn from the photographer Michal, and from some Asian teenagers standing here and kidding around with him, Paul has his admirers and fans too, and so he should.[32]

One of the prettiest streets in the Village is Thompson Street, which begins off the south side of the park. There are nice eateries and boutiques, but it's really about the old trees whose branches create a glorious canopy of green. One standout storefront, however, is the Chess Forum, at #219, where I once bought a stunning green and blue chess set. Here for twenty-five years, it is, beyond any doubt, the only shop that I know of that is exclusively devoted to unusual chess sets. I point to one and ask the manager what it costs. "About $6,000. It's handmade in Italy, solid bronze, with gold and silver leaf. Here's a set with golfers and golfing items. There's one that has handblown glass, filled with different colors of neon. Then you can turn the board on, which has a capacitor that excites the glass and makes it either pink or blue for each side. It's on consignment from the artist, who wants $5,000 for it. This one is made of Super Mario figures and it's only $50." These are really works of art, as I know from my own modest collection of four such sets. They're impractical to play a game with because it's hard to keep track of what's a bishop, queen, or pawn since the shapes look nothing like a standard piece.

Chess players are an unusual bunch, as I learned as a teenager, when I was one of thirty people to simultaneously play a game against Bobby Fischer at a college-sponsored tournament. I was the third-to-last player to lose, after forty-two moves, but don't be fooled. He somehow grabbed my bishop on the fourth move, and I just waited for him to finish me off. For some reason, he saved that for the end, which, when it came, was mercifully swift. Everyone suffered the same fate that day.

After the match ended, we asked him if he would ever consider marrying someone. "No," he said. "Women are lousy chess players." That was before the Polgar sisters showed up and upended that stereotype. A couple of us set up a chess riddle. He stared at it for about fifteen minutes and gave up. We were about to tell him the answer when someone realized it had been arranged incorrectly. With great trepidation, we owned up to our mistake. To our amazement, he was a real gentleman, saying, "Oh, that's okay," displaying none of the explosive anger for which he was known.

My reverie is interrupted by an elderly man who complains to the manager: "What's the matter with these people? I was playing with some guy"—the store charges people by the hour if they want to play—"and someone he knew walked in and he just quit the game to play with the other guy. That's really rude." But chess is an idiosyncratic world, and those who inhabit it can be unpredictable.

Two Chinese teenagers enter and ask the manager if they can play. The cost is $5 an hour. "We brought pieces. What does it cost if we only use our own?" "Your own pieces? Then it's $10 an hour," he says with a grin. A typical New York response—half serious, half not. They pay $5, park their skateboards, and start playing.

My last stop is at a place called Meatball Obsession, on Sixth Avenue between 14th and 13th Streets, which I reach by going west on 3rd Street to Sixth and turning right. Wow—imagine centering an entire menu around meatballs. They must be really good, I think to myself. I speak with a young, earnest-looking man behind the counter. Perhaps "counter" is not the right term, since this is literally a hole-in-the-wall joint, where the customer cannot enter, but just orders while standing in the street. I guess it's a permanent cart, if you will. He's been working here for about four years.

"How do you feel standing here all day? Do you ever get bored?"

"No," is the response. "When things are slow, I love people-watching, especially the pretty girls from the Parsons School of Design, which is just around the corner."

"That's great, but, seriously, why are you still here after four years? Do you want to do this for the rest of your life?"

Another employee, a graduate of Long Island University living in Brooklyn, chimes in with: "I like the way they treat you, like family. I want to be in the health field, but I need the immediate income." This is a reality I often encounter. There's an idea that people must be happy with what they're doing, but many folks from modest backgrounds don't have that option.

"What's in your meatballs that makes them so special, I mean, without giving away the recipe?"

"It's nothing special. They're just really good. We have beef, chicken, pork sausage, and turkey meatballs, and they taste delicious. You can get them in a cup, and we give you a little pasta around it. It's a takeoff on the owner's recipe, which is Mama Mancini."

I'm shocked to hear this since, coincidentally, I once did a market research project for this company, which sells frozen meatballs in Costco and other chains around the country. Wouldn't it be better for the company to advertise their meatballs as Mama Mancini? Indeed, the website fesses up to this connection, capitalizing on the brand's marketing pitch in which Dan Mancini enthusiastically tells us: "Our meatballs and Sunday Sauce are made exactly the way my grandmother taught me thirty-five years ago, with real ingredients." So the connection isn't a secret if you look them up.

The absence of the name turns out to be a matter of internal politics between different partners, but in a way, it's irrelevant because customers just loved the idea that they're getting what they think is a one-of-a-kind homemade meatball and might well be disappointed to learn the product has a more mass-produced heritage. The employees agree with my assessment. And so, welcome to New York City, where people's cravings for an individualized, one-of-a-kind experience often outpaces and outproduces the reality that it isn't so. At least, according to the customers, they taste good!

(A) Renewal on the Bowery
(B) Liz Christy Community Garden
(C) Former Evangelical Lutheran Church of St. Mark
(D) Ave. B Garden
(E) La Plaza Cultural Park Garden
(F) Ray's Candy Store
(G) Tompkins Square Park

3RD AVE

STUYVESANT ST

2ND AVE

ST MARKS PL

1ST AVE

AVE A

AVE B

AVE C

E 14 ST
E 13 ST
E 12 ST
E 11 ST
E 10 ST
E 9 ST
E 8 ST
E 7 ST
E 6 ST
E 5 ST
E 4 ST
E 3 ST
E 2 ST
E 1 ST

HOUSTON ST

BOWERY

Tompkins Square Park

EAST VILLAGE

OF THE THREE PARTS OF GREENWICH VILLAGE, the eastern portion, namely Avenues A through D, has changed the least. That's in relative terms, however, as the pace of gentrification picks up. It's known as Alphabet City or Loisaida, Spanglish for Lower East Side, in recognition of the large Puerto Rican presence in the area.[33] The boundaries of the East Village are, generally, 14th Street on the north, the East River on the east, Houston Street on the south, and the Bowery and Third Avenue on the west. Historically, parts of this area were viewed as part of the Lower East Side and others were counted as part of Greenwich Village. Earlier groups, such as the Irish, Germans, Italians, and Jews, had departed by the early 1950s, but the Eastern European presence, mostly Ukrainian, remained strong until recently, when it too began to decline. By the 1960s, people were moving here, primarily because artists, musicians, writers, and young people in general were priced out as rents rose in the center of Greenwich Village. It also became the scene for beats, hippies, radicals, and the counterculture in general.

The artists and countercultural populations informally renamed the area the East Village, not wanting to be associated with what was seen as the poverty-stricken Lower East Side. The change was also supported by real estate agents, who thought it made the area sound more appealing. Of course, that reasoning no longer applies as the Lower East Side gentrifies even faster than the East Village. Moreover, the East Village still has a rough, edgy feel to it. The history of the area can be summed up in the following two wry jokes: In the 1980s, the lettered avenues stood for Adventurous, Brave, Crazy, and Dead. Today, they stand for Affluent, Bourgeois, Comfortable, and Decent.[34]

The western part of the East Village is where most of the gentrification is taking place. It extends southward from 14th to Houston Street and eastward from Third Avenue to Avenue A. The latter street has many bars and restaurants that cater to young urban professionals. Of course, the area also has many old-line residents who continue to reside in the same cheaper apartments in the five- to six-story buildings that they've always been in. East of Avenue A, the area, also known as "Alphabet City," becomes much more Hispanic, with a smaller black population as well. The main commercial streets are 14th, 8th, and Houston Streets, as well as Third, Second, and First Avenues, along with Avenue A. The main recreational area is Tompkins Square Park. Cooper Union College and NYU are also a presence here.

I come across a hotel called the Standard on Third Avenue and E. 5th Street (Third Avenue becomes the Bowery below E. 4th Street). The words are upside down, and I soon learn that this is an essential part of the logo. As the desk clerk explains: "It's because we are the *opposite* of what our name is. We are not standard. We are better than standard." It's part of a chain of five hotels, in New York, Los Angeles, and Miami. It's pricey, very well appointed, and has a nicely designed bar and lounge. As a gimmick it works, having caught my attention.

Not far away, at the corner of E. 4th Street, I pass Phebe's Bar, which has a different but even catchier gimmick on a chalkboard outside: "A banana is 105 calories. A tequila shot is 64 calories. Choose wisely." I walk into this pretty, spacious bar and ask a young woman working there with blondish hair and black rimmed glasses about the sign. "Well, actually I thought of it after seeing a statement to that effect on the Internet; I don't remember where. It gets a lot of comments; and don't forget, a tequila is an upper and a banana is sort of a downer." These types of quips are quite effective because once you walk in, you're more likely to imbibe there.

On the Bowery, at E. 3rd Street, I come to another boutique establishment, the luxurious Bowery Hotel, with its beautiful rooms and exquisite wood-paneled sitting areas in the lobby. But what resonates with me is a shelter for the homeless as well as a detox facility called Renewal on the Bowery, almost next door on 3rd Street. This place was around in the 1960s when I first became interested in sociology, and in those days it was popularly referred to as "the Muni." In those days, the Bowery was full of homeless people or, as they were then called, "derelicts." As it happened, in 1966, some friends and I decided to found a magazine for college students in general, and I found myself looking for a good story to write. Moved by a TV program with talk show host David Susskind, that had the politically incorrect title of "The Six Bowery Bums," I decided to do an in-depth story for the magazine about those who appeared on it and on the community in general. Most of them lived in $1.10-a-night hotels called "flophouses," many of which had wildly inappropriate names like the Majestic, the Palace, the Prince, and the White House. One of them, the Pioneer, was reserved for women. Later on, I worked as an interviewer of the homeless, for the Columbia University Homelessness Project. That's how my career as a sociologist began.[35]

On the northeast corner of the Bowery and Houston Street, I enter the large Liz Christy Community Garden, which runs a full block east to Second Avenue. It features nice wooden benches, birch trees, vegetable gardens, a fish and turtle pond, and gently winding walking paths that give one the feeling, briefly, of walking through a natural forest. Founded in 1973, it was also the very first community garden in the city and actually sits on what had been the southern portion of a farm owned by the Dutch governor Peter Stuyvesant hundreds of years ago. In New York terms, that qualifies as hallowed ground![36]

One notable and very sad chapter in the history of the German community that once lived here was the *General Slocum* disaster, as it has come to be known. On Wednesday, June 15, 1904, the *General Slocum* steamship set out for an excursion to the Locust Grove Picnic Ground in Long Island's Eaton's Neck. The passengers were members of the German Evangelical Lutheran Church of St. Mark, on 6th Street between First and Second Avenues. Those on board, mostly women and children, had no inkling of the terrible fate that was about to overtake them.

As the ship approached the Hell's Gate Bridge near Astoria, Queens, a fire broke out, most probably ignited by a lit match or cigarette. As music played in the background, the passengers on board screamed for help, but their cries went unanswered, as people on shore thought they were just having a good time. Those who donned life jackets found them to be filled with rotten cork, which actually weighed them down in the water, thereby hastening their deaths. Lifeboats that had been painted over stuck to the ship, and the incompetent crew was of little help. When the day was over, 1,021 out of 1,358 souls had perished, making it the single greatest human disaster in New York City's history, until 9/11.[37]

The community never recovered, and what had been known as Klein Deutschland faded into obscurity as most of the German community relocated north to Yorkville. The parish merged with a Yorkville church in 1946 and the church was sold to an Orthodox Jewish synagogue, the Max D. Raiskin Center in 1940. Walking by the location of the church on 6th Street gave me the chills as I thought about the services, parties, and many community events that had once been held here. All that remains today is a small fountain in Tompkins Square Park, a plaque on the shore of the East River in Astoria telling the story of this tragedy, and a stone memorial in the shape of a steamship at Lutheran All Faiths Cemetery in Middle Village, Queens. I took my graduate students there to see the memorial and was shocked to find my own name on a gravestone elsewhere in the cemetery. When I inquired if there were other people with my name buried here, the woman in the office said: "Yes, a William Helmreich, a baby, died on August 25, 1898." August 25 happens to be my birthday. A strange coincidence, to say the least.

I continue on east on 6th Street, and on the corner of Avenue B, I see the Avenue B Garden—well tended, with vegetable plots, a gazebo, and musical performers and lectures on the benefits of using hemp. Community parks are everywhere in this sprawling neighborhood, but often they're locked, with keys available only for the locals, though sometimes they have special hours for the public. On the next block, Avenue C, I go left, and near 9th Street I discover the marvelous La Plaza Cultural Park Garden. It has many sculptural works and a huge weeping willow tree. There are hundreds of cans, canteens, and bottles painted in many colors, along with tubing and piping in very unusual designs, all along the top of the fence.

The term "Belgian fries," as opposed to French fries, has come into vogue recently. These are fries that are fresh, irregularly shaped, and have been deep-fried twice. They're crispy on the outside but smooth on the inside. They're a bit pricier than your average fries, but the portion, served in a plastic see-through box held together with a rubber band, is three times the regular size. A number of places serve them, but the ultimate insider location for the fries is a tiny 24/7 joint called Ray's Candy Store at 113 Avenue A, near 7th Street. It's been there for forty-three years and is owned by a Turkish guy named Ray. The woman behind the counter is Polish. Are there any Belgians working here? No, and why should there be? After all, this is New York City, where everyone believes they can do anything. They also have delicious egg creams and deep-fried Oreo cookies.

Cans, bottles, canteens, and more, like you've never seen before.

Ray's is opposite Tompkins Square Park, the site of labor riots in 1874 over an economic depression touched off by the panic of 1873. Locations sometimes have an identity of their own that transcends specific events, and this park has always been viewed as a place for both the downtrodden and the avant-garde. There's a grove of American elm trees in the park, and one of them has a special role in history. It was here, in 1966, that the Indian Swami Prabhupada, founder of the Hare Krishna society, sat and held the first chanting group outside of India.

More recently, in the 1980s, the park had filled up with homeless people, drug dealers, and petty criminals. The volume of complaints against the disorder and filth in the park reached a crescendo, with people demanding that the police make the park safe for ordinary residents of the neighborhood. Some felt this violated the progressive history of the East Village, but most thought something had to be done. In August 1988, the police moved in to enforce a curfew. But a riot ensued in which thirty-eight people were injured, and the curfew was promptly lifted.

I decide to check out this historic venue, entering on 9th Street, which goes right through the center of the park. It is a multi-use place, with skateboarding, basketball, chess and checkers, nice gardens, and performances. Its peaceful, almost tranquil appearance contains no hint of its turbulent, sometimes violent history when people struggled over control of the space. The dog parks are separated into one for small dogs and another for larger ones. I talk to a woman working in one of the gardens. She proudly informs me that her garden was given an award at Yankee Stadium. The elm trees are still flourishing, rising to about twenty feet.

I strike up a conversation with a man who's here with his dog, Pluto. Jim is a heavyset man with thick glasses who was raised in the South Bronx. In his early 60s, he comes here a lot. I ask him if the yuppies are snobby. His reply is revealing: "They don't bother me none. I mind my own business and that's it." I soon learn that he does resent them for having made the area so expensive. He certainly doesn't see them as moving in his orbit. "Do you like steamed vegetables?" he asks out of the blue. "Yes, I do," I reply. "Over on Avenue A and 7th Street, they got a place, open 24 hours a day, where you can get cheap steamed vegetables. And it's dog-friendly too."

Exiting the park on the east side, I pass 151 Avenue B, near 10th Street, a brownstone where Charlie "Bird" Parker, the legendary alto saxophonist who co-founded bebop music in the 1940s with Dizzy Gillespie, lived in the 1950s. Musical continuity of a sort was established in 1979 when Judy Rhodes, who bought the house and who booked jazz concerts, allowed the players to practice in her parlor. At 236 E. 3rd Street, there's a famous hangout, the Nuyorican Poets Café, between Avenues B and C, which has showcased jazz, poetry, and comedy for many years. It welcomes visitors and performers of all backgrounds, prompting the famed poet Allen Ginsberg to dub it "the most integrated place on the planet."

Farther north, at 412–414 E. 13th Street, between Avenues C and D, I come to a place where the great performer Lead Belly lived in the 1940s. Born in 1889 in Louisiana, he played a twelve-string guitar and popularized songs like "House of the Rising Sun" and "Goodnight Irene." Beatles star George Harrison paid him the supreme compliment when he said, "No Lead Belly, no Beatles." It's worth mentioning that you can hear great jazz in so many places in the area. I remember going to a terrific jazz performance a few years ago at the Blue Note Jazz Club at 131 W. 3rd Street, by Jimmy Haslip, a well-known musician who plays the six-string bass guitar. The audience wouldn't let him leave!

I detour east to Avenue D, a place where few tourists venture. Much of the avenue is lined with public housing, and fast-food joints and bars predominate. Thus, I'm surprised to discover the shop of Jutta Neumann, at 355 E. 4th Street, a boutique specializing in leather goods, just off the avenue. Walking in, I ask a young fellow working there, "Can you really make it here, selling high-end leather products so far away from the center of the East Village?" "We've been here twenty years and we do okay," he responds, somewhat defensively. And he's telling the truth. Despite the modest disclaimer on their business card—Visit Our Tiny Store—this place has an outstanding reputation for high-quality sandals, handbags, and wristbands, as well as jewelry combining leather with silver. Jutta's designs have been featured in *Mademoiselle*, *Vogue*, and other leading style publications. The lesson here is that location isn't always the most important determinant of success. If you have a high-quality product and can attract clients through word of mouth, you can make it here and pass on the savings in rent to your customers. People have, in fact, commented on the Internet how you get far more for your money with Jutta than with many name designers.

Next, I enter an arts and crafts shop up the street and meet the owner, Doreen. She teaches in the store and received her BA from Queens College, where she did a double major in art and English. She's been in the East Village for thirty-one years and observes: "In that time, the East Village has gone from a scruffy unappealing area to a scruffy extremely appealing area. Many of the stores have been here for a long time. We put up business lights on the block. If people get sick, we visit them. We're a community. Sure, we have political differences, but they're within the liberal-radical orbit. No one's a Republican as far as I know." And yet, there are exceptions to this air of bonhomie. I see a Russian shoemaker's shop. An Orthodox Jew from Uzbekistan, he wears a kipa. And he knows no one on the block, despite having been there for years. Doreen says, "He's not really social."

I walk back to Third Avenue, where my journey began. There's a small triangular fenced-in park on the east side near 9th Street. The park is called the George Hecht Viewing Gardens, after the man who donated the money for it as a gift, together with the City Council of New York. He was a Cooper Union College alumnus of the class of 1930, and the school is two blocks south of the park. The top of each fencepost has a gold gilt design that looks like leaves, thus making each black iron post appear like the handle of a sword. Immediately beneath the gilt-edged top is a taupe-colored bow, also made of iron, in the shape of several thick elongated, scalloped leaves and what appears to be a band designed to hold them together. Inside the fence are various plants, including ilex, burning bush, ivy, and sea grass. In the center is a round concrete fountain that contains a compass, indicating North, South, East, and West. The middle of the compass is painted pink and the points are a dark green. Rings of cement surround the compass, painted white, peach, gray, and purple. It's a design, not a functional compass. Off to the side stand two bedraggled-looking pigeons, staring at the compass, as if to say, "Where's the water? We wanna take a bath."

Starting at this intersection and heading east is Little Tokyo or, as some call it, "J Town," the Japanese commercial and residential center. It's a tiny area, but it has the largest concentration of Japanese shops and markets in the city, as well as a good number of Japanese residents in the general area. Ownership of the real estate here is in the hands of a few Japanese businessmen, I learn. Some of the business establishments have been here for twenty-five years. Japanese people have lived on the Lower East Side for many years, in part because a commercial center was built here but also because the area was inexpensive in the pre-gentrification period. To learn more, I meet with Bon Yagi, president of a business firm known as TDC that owns a number of Japanese businesses, including nine restaurants, most in the immediate vicinity.

"This all began in the late '60s when a dozen people came in 1968," Yagi explains. "We chose this area because it was cheap. Sony, Nikon, et cetera, came here when Japan started expanding worldwide. So diplomats came first to negotiate with the government and open up the market. They needed a place to live, eat, shop. In the beginning, as single men here just for business, they lived in Manhattan. But then they established families, needed more room, and some moved to Flushing. At that time this area was cheap and accepting of newcomers. So, the midtown employees and students came here. In the East Village there were a few thousand Japanese living here in the '80s and '90s. We even had festivals here then. My concept in building Japanese stores—restaurants, specialty supermarkets—was that here you can come to enjoy Japan without going to Japan." Though some might miss seeing Tokyo and the islands that make up Japan, he has a point. At least they're getting a taste, literally, of Japan and its culture.

Yagi employed a strategy common to new groups entering a neighborhood. He worked with local businesses, supported the block association, the churches, and the local police. He sold vegetables at low prices to the Second Avenue Deli. This is similar to what Betty Park, the owner of Manna's, the famous Harlem soul food chain did. To win over the locals there, many of whom were hostile to the Koreans, she gave free food to the poor through the local churches, who, in turn, supported her stores. It's the same tactic utilized by the Weinstein Hardware store in Bedford Stuyvesant, which allowed local artists to create a memorial tribute to people in the community on the wall outside its store. The result? Community support and no graffiti.

I arrive at Whiskers, a place on 9th Street, near Second Avenue offering holistic pet care: "For all your pets' nutrition and supplies. You can order from 1-800-WHISKERS." "We're not a pet store," says Phil Klein, the owner. "We're a holistic information reference center that sells products." They have food, but not the brands typically found in a supermarket. The emphasis is on foods with no toxicity or allergens, "They're a lot closer to the natural system designed for the animal." He shows me a book filled with letters of thanks from people all over the world—"stories of miracles," he tells me. I peruse the correspondence and indeed, the enthusiasm and gratitude to Phil is real and palpable. And the store carries thousands of items for sale, along with conducting a huge mail-order business.

East of Second Avenue, 9th Street becomes a jumble of small shops, art galleries, tenement buildings, lofts, and murals, with everything painted in all sorts of psychedelic colors. The streets are so filled with people walking, talking, and just hanging out that you feel you can't contain them within their normally defined boundaries.

Here you'll find Mud, a popular local coffee house. The creation of Mud is a perfect example of how a new place nevertheless remains true to the East Village's roots. It used to be an empty storefront, with the back half serving as a one-room apartment for Perry Gewirtz. Gewirtz was an old-style beatnik of the Jack Kerouac era. In fact, Kerouac was a friend of his. Gewirtz was surrounded by his two favorite loves—books and a black and white cat. He had been a bit actor in various films including *Putney Swope*, *The Hospital*, and *Marathon Man*, a career that had been enhanced by an eerie resemblance to Woody Allen, which got him minor parts in various advertisements. He also played the role of an aging hippie alongside Madonna in *Desperately Seeking Susan*. The son of an Orthodox rabbi, Gewirtz had rebelled early, telling his father that the biblical parting of the Red Sea was actually a tidal wave, and then departed Brooklyn bound for the East Village. As with many "street characters," Gewirtz is not forgotten. A photo of him with Donald Sutherland hangs on Mud's wall. And about three doors west there's a mural of people in the neighborhood, featuring Gewirtz and others, like Billy, owner of a store that sells Middle Eastern garments. Billy is a Muslim who plays the saxophone and the piano.

I ask Mike, a worker at Mud, about the area. His response: "9th Street is possibly one of the most interesting streets on the planet." An argument can be made for that. The Beastie Boys recorded their first album, *Polly Wog Stew*, in the basement of #307. Astor Piazzolla (1921–1992), an Argentine tango composer born in Mar del Plata, lived at #313 until 1936. And #321 was once home to Jimi Hendrix. Until a few years ago, a sign told passersby to feel free to write letters to Jimi and place them in the orange mailbox in the front garden where they will go directly to heaven. Mike says: "Nobody on this block is into religion, because it's a faith-based kind of thing and there's just too much reality going on around you. The time I walked out of church was when the pastor said God demands 10 percent. I moved to the East Village, where my grandmother lived, in the third grade. But things have changed. In the last five years, all that's been moving in is upper-class privileged kids whose parents paid for their apartments."

These characters, the famous anti-establishment types and entertainers who have made this community their home through the years, are what gives this part of town its unique flavor. As I walk on 9th and the surrounding streets, the smell of marijuana wafts through the air, day and night. It might as well be legal here. Blue, purple, and green hair are the norm, as are lavishly tattooed folks. All this is augmented by the many stores offering tarot card readings, acupuncture, folk music, ceramics and pottery classes, dive bars, exotic eateries, boutique shops, and the like.

The area also has a certain old-world charm, all the more so because there are remnants of older communities—Ukrainians, Poles, Germans, Irish, among the older people. Sometimes it's a two-generational phenomenon, like a Ukrainian woman born on the block, who's always lived there and has her chiropractic practice there. With their numbers dwindling, it is an open question how long the community, once centered around E. 7th Street, can survive.[38]

I'm now east of First Avenue and still on 9th Street. I walk in to Herb and Roots at #406 and discover that it's is filled with jars of a multitude of herbs, many of them medicinal—couch grass and colt's foot for the urinary tract, and herbs that can help break up a kidney stone. "We're a famous place amongst a certain crowd," the owner tells me. The block is relatively quiet, with lots of trees, and kind of plain-looking four- to five-story old-law tenements. A pet-store owner shows me a four-leaf clover on a green piece of paper, and tells me about a block resident, Hilda, who gives them to firemen for good luck. He is proud that she gave him one too when he first moved in. It shows you that a present doesn't have to cost much to be meaningful. It's more about how and why it's given.

Neighborhood Barbers, at 439 E. 9th Street, exemplifies the block. It's run by Bukharian Jews, who've taken over this trade all over the city from the Italians. The owner, thirty-one-year old Eric Uvaydovs, runs a three-chair operation and charges $12 a haircut. He has an impressive clientele of entertainers and writers who prefer to remain anonymous. He's also known as a Mohawk haircut expert. Inside is a picture of Boxer, a canine who received a shave in the shop. This may be indicative of the area's general friendliness to pets. Coffee shops rarely say anything if someone walks in with a dog. "Hey, sure it's illegal," said one owner, "but this is the East Village. We don't operate like the rest of the city."

On the southwest corner of Avenue A and E. 9th Street is a place known as Doc Holliday's Bar, named after the famous gunslinger. "It's a local hangout," explains one patron named Damian. "By the time you make it from the door to your stool, there's a drink waitin' for you." There is a mural of bad guys, drawn by the well-known mural artist, Chico. On the wall next to an ad for Jim Beam is a suggestion written in chalk: "Embrace your inner redneck." Beneath that, in neat script, potential customers are exhorted to "Ask about our daily specials! Cold beer plus hot girls." A poster advertises Doc's "legendary sexiest costume contest, offering a top prize of $300," held on Halloween. I attended. It was wild and lots of fun, with young women, some of them NYU students looking for a little cash and fun, probably unbeknownst to their parents, dancing along the bar.

I speak with Joanna Leban, the manager, who's been working here since 1994. An NYU graduate with a major in sociology, she really understands the rhythms and culture of a bar. She's seen and heard everything in this milieu. Rather than present my discussion with her, I'm quoting from an unpublished essay she wrote about one of her patrons, with first names changed. To me, having been a bar habitué myself, it's the kind of crazy yet totally believable tale that make bars such fun places.

Lou, one of our regulars that could be called "furniture," with questionable grooming habits, also seems to have a way with the ladies. He can be quite charming, when he applies himself. Having been married three times, once to a playboy bunny (or something), he certainly has had his share of women. Although he is sometimes rude and cranky, he does know how to treat a lady with proper manners, and respect. Lou is rather old school, and knows how to be a gentleman when duty calls.

This Tuesday, like so many others, he was hitting the Pabst and Kentucky Gentleman at his leisurely pace. Late night, he was still in full swing, as he headed outside for a cigarette break. Shortly, the doors to the entrance swung back open, and low and behold, Lou had a lovely-looking old lady in his company.

"Tanqueray martini straight up—very, very cold, no olives, no nothing," she politely ordered. Apparently, Lou had approached her on the sidewalk, and asked her if she would like to come in for a drink, AND she accepted. It wasn't long before I was intently listening to this woman, entranced by her mannerisms and utterings. Her name was Sue, and as Lou quickly pointed out, their names rhymed . . . was it a match made in heaven? Over the next few hours, I tried to absorb as much as I could about Sue. This is her story:

She was born in Manhattan in 1939, and has lived on 11th Street, a few blocks away, for seventy-seven years. Both Lou and I comment, how she looks better than him, a man twenty years younger than her. She was married to a man who smoked and passed away in 1991. She never had children, because as she told it, they were too busy having a good time, and by the time they were ready to consider it, she had passed her childbearing years. Sue has some unusual facial expressions: an odd crinkling of the nose, and a wide smile that appears at strange times. . . .

This excerpt from the story exemplifies how bars serve as places where people of all types gather and, in the haze of what happens in a bar after a few drinks, become very chummy despite never having met before. These encounters are often only possible in such circumstances, and they are a staple of life everywhere; after all, what little town doesn't have a tavern? But in each case, the discussion reveals the culture of the community. Joanna's story presents her bar as a place where characters are accepted in all their eccentricities.[39]

LOWER EAST SIDE

SOHO

HUDSON SQUARE

PRINCE ST
MOTT ST
SPRING ST
KENMARE ST
BROOME ST
STANTON ST
HOUSTON S
RIVINGTON ST
ESSEX ST
NORFOLK ST
SUFFOLK ST
CLINTON ST

Little Italy

CANAL ST
CENTRE ST
BAXTER ST
MULBERRY ST
ELIZABETH ST
BOWERY
CHRYSTIE ST
FORSYTH ST
ELDRIDGE ST
ALLEN ST
ORCHARD ST
LUDLOW ST
DELANCEY ST
BROOME ST
GRAND ST

BROADWAY
LAFAYETTE ST

Chinatown

WORTH ST
BAYARD ST
PELL ST
HESTER ST
CANAL ST

DIVISION ST
E BROADWAY
HENRY ST
RUTGERS ST
MADISON ST

CATHERINE ST
ST JAMES PL
MARKET ST
CLINTON ST
MONTGOMERY ST

CHERRY ST
SOUTH ST

WATER ST

R F WAGNER SR PL
FDR DR
BROOKLYN BRIDGE
MANHATTAN BRIDGE

East River

LOWER EAST SIDE

THE LOWER EAST SIDE'S general boundaries are Houston Street on the north; Brooklyn Bridge, St. James Place, Worth Street, and the East River on the east and south; and Broadway and Lafayette Street on the west. In the late nineteenth and early twentieth centuries, the Lower East Side became the area of first settlement for millions of new arrivals from every corner of Europe, especially its eastern and southern regions. Poor as they were, the new immigrants settled here because the crowded buildings already here were cheap and could be further subdivided. As each new group began to adapt to life in the New Land, they would move out to better areas, only to be replaced by other newcomers. By the 1960s, however, most of these people had departed for literally greener pastures—Queens, Brooklyn, and the suburbs. The neighborhood declined and became crime ridden until the 1980s, when new groups settled in significant numbers from China and various Hispanic lands, becoming a new melting pot, with a different mix and flavor. Today it is reinventing itself as a trendy hip neighborhood for a new generation of urban professionals.

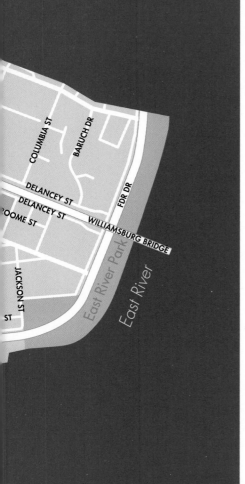

Although these changes are occurring, it is not the overwhelmingly gentrified place that many people envision when they think about it. Moreover, while the area is safe, I recommend caution about walking east of Pitt Street at night, especially between Houston and Delancey Streets. The same holds true for the section south of East Broadway to the FDR Drive and from Rutgers Street east to the FDR Drive. For now, the main, mostly commercial section, where all the eateries, bars, and boutiques are located, is bounded by Houston on the north, Ridge Street on the east, Delancey on the south, and the Bowery on the west.

I start my walk at Cheese Grille at 188 Allen Street. The emphasis here is on fine cheeses—asiago, gruyere, cheddar, goat, and gouda. Even the pencils used in this place have small, yellow, triangle-shaped, rubber cheeses as erasers. But what drew my attention was a strikingly artistic creation immediately above, and outside the store. Spray-painted on white-colored, fine wood, it portrays dozens of young people looking upward, through rainbow-colored raindrops, searching for salvation. The artists are the legendary Iranians Icy and Sot. Misha, the general manager, tells me the work was commissioned by the restaurant. The message, according to Misha, is one of peace. I ask him about his place.

"We use the finest cheeses, of course, and we buy from local places. Our artwork is also local. These large jars of bottle caps are sent to our Queens warehouse, where we store them to be turned into commissioned works of art, which we'll display here. We have different varieties of grilled-cheese sandwiches, and they're really works of culinary art. We're open until 3:00 a.m., and we have great wines and beers too. And we get fresh bread every day from Balthazar's French bakery." Their menu looks really good; it's inexpensive, and it's centrally located just off Houston Street. The sign outside their bathroom reads, "Hi Neighbor," as opposed to what I usually see in such establishments—"Customers Only" or the often untrue "Out of Order." Misha says they allow noncustomers to use it, "unless you look like you're gonna do drugs or something in there."

In casual conversation, I learn that Jewish and Muslim store owners in the area get along quite well, though they steer clear of sensitive issues and situations. Locals note that Muslim grocery stores sometimes use a space in their basements for daily prayers, and others attend as well. But a Jewish restaurant proprietor who mentions this says, "Even though I'm quite friendly with this Yemeni shopkeeper I know, I would never ask if I could see his prayer space. I don't want to get into an uncomfortable situation in case he doesn't want me to see it." I respond, "But you get along well with him." "Oh yes," he says, "we get along great. I go in there and buy stuff, and we talk and kid around." This is, after all, the Lower East Side, as multicultural a place as you can find.

At Stanton Street, I turn right and go to the Bowery, turn left, and in a few steps find myself in front of the Bowery Mission, founded in 1879 under Christian auspices to serve the needy and the homeless, in particular. It has an extensive program of providing outreach and shelter for the homeless. Entering, I see that it has been nicely refurbished, but still attracts many real down-and-out people. In the front rows, several younger women are singing a song with great feeling. It begins with: "The more I see you, the more I love you. The more I find you, the more I love you." The audience, consisting mostly of lone black men, is visibly moved, seeming to find solace in the stirring music. One man leans forward, as if intently focused on every note.

Rounding the next corner onto Rivington Street, I see a great mural across the street. Nina Pandolfo is a Brazilian artist who is married to one of the Os Gemeos twins, famous Brazilian graffiti artists whose works also grace the walls of the East Village and the Lower East Side. Pandolfo's work features children with large, yet delicate, almond-shaped eyes, that reminds me of the well-received film, *Big Eyes*, a biography of the American artist Margaret Keane. This is one of Pandolfo's murals between the Bowery and Chrystie

Eyes you can't avoid—or forget.

Street. It makes me think of the open-eyed wonder with which a child greets the world.

Freemans Sporting Club Barbershop, a very different place, is also on this block. I ask a young man waiting for a haircut and re-clining on a leather sofa, if the haircut is really worth the $48 price tag. "Oh yes," he replies. "I mean, just look at this place. Everyone who works here is gorgeous. They give you a hot towel around your neck. And listen to the great music they're playing. And that beau-tiful woman at the counter—I know she's listening, or I hope so—really makes the place. They'll do your beard, whatever. And look how it looks—the wood paneling, the chair itself, the cabinets, the whole mellow feel of the shop." For some people, atmosphere is a powerful incentive, extending even to the attractiveness of the staff, as is being treated like a king.

About ten yards down, I come to an alleyway, at the end of which I see some decorative lights in a store window. Curious, I walk down what's called Freemans Alley, a private path, to the end. There's really nothing on either side. It turns out to be a restaurant named Freemans. Inside, it's beautiful. "How can you survive?" I ask the manager. "How does anyone know you're here? I wouldn't have walked down if not for the lights." "It's word of mouth," is the answer. "We've been here for eleven years." The place certainly looks beautiful. It has trophy heads of rams, elks, bucks, etc., mounted on the wall, and birds—none of them killed by the owner, I'm assured. There are also expensive-looking old prints scattered through this wood-paneled establishment. In addition to all the usual menu offerings, like Caesar salad and filet mignon, they have a variety of unusual dishes. These include mushroom donuts, lobster bake, and squash salad, not to mention a selection of craft cocktails.

Farther down Rivington, at #113, between Essex and Ludlow Streets, I take note of El Castillo de Jagua, a well-known Dominican establishment that's been serving hearty Dominican food for decades. It's an insider place, with simple decor and white painted walls, whose survival in the midst of massive gentrification is silent testimony that certain things can buck the trend. Why? Sometimes it's an owner with an outsize personality, or the fact that a loyal group of patrons is made to feel welcome, or the food itself, and sometimes it's a combination of these characteristics.

At 148–154 Rivington Street, at the corner of Suffolk Street, there's a piece of Lower East Side history that reminds me of the days when the area had a large Jewish presence. It's the Streit's Matzo Factory, and the original sign is still there on the top floor of the red brick building. When Aron Streit opened his first factory in 1916, almost half a million Jews resided here, making it the largest Jewish community in the world at that time. Over the years, thousands of people have taken tours of this factory. For students in Jewish day schools, a trip of that sort was considered essential for their education. Other signs of that era include scattered tenements once built and owned by Jews, whose exteriors displayed carved Stars of David. Good examples are 47 Orchard Street and 375 Broome Street.

I turn around and head west up Rivington to Orchard Street, where I go right half a block to Shut, at 168 Orchard. Reportedly, it was the first skateboard shop in the city. The selection of skateboards is colorful and beautifully designed, and the employees have a reputation for being super helpful and knowledgeable In the past, they designed boards for high-profile clients, including Pepsi and HBO. They've also designed a skateboard for Russ & Daughters, the famous 103-year-old appetizing store on Houston Street. It has a shiny smoked whitefish—one of the store's specialty items—on the skateboard. In the last eight years, though, they've been focusing on retail.

Retracing my steps, I head south on Orchard Street and, in a few blocks, cross Delancey. The Lower East Side Tenement Museum, located on Orchard just beyond Delancey Street, is home to one of the city's most unusual attractions. It owns a tenement in which tours of apartments where people once resided are given, with the goal of showing visitors exactly how these people lived. The families include Jewish, Italian, Irish, and German immigrants. The museum researched which families lived in their building at 97 Orchard Street and, if possible, they got in touch with the descendants of these families to learn about how the living quarters were furnished, what foods were eaten, and the like. The result is amazing as one is transported back in time by looking at the furnishings, items of clothing, fixtures, etc.

In one case, at least twenty attempts were made to get in touch with the children of a family of Holocaust survivors who happened to have lived in an apartment there. They resisted cooperating with the museum. Repeated calls requesting an interview went unanswered. Finally, an outside expert on the Holocaust was engaged to solve the problem. Through contacts with intermediaries, the researcher determined that the woman who had lived there didn't want to speak with museum representatives because she thought all they wanted was a donation. Once the purpose was explained she readily cooperated and gave them a detailed description of what her place looked like.

The Essex/Delancey Street subway station, two blocks east on Delancey, where the J, M, and Z lines run, is home to a project called the "Low Line," a verbal takeoff on the High Line. The idea is to showcase life in an underground park, where plants and other living organisms can flourish in what seems like an inhospitable environment by using the latest techniques and bringing sunlight into the park. In February 2017, the Low Line, which had been approved by the city in 2016, closed. The developers asserted that the closure was only temporary as the project entered another phase.

Heading west up Delancey, at #47A, I discover the Tribes of Morocco, probably New York's largest such store and one of very few selling exclusively Moroccan products of all kinds. The place is chock-full of vases, urns, custom-made bras, hand-painted silk scarves, rugs of every imaginable color, tiled end-tables, cushions, sconces lit from the inside, serving dishes, and a tagine cooking pot.

Two blocks later, Delancey Street intersects with Sara D. Roosevelt Park, which runs for seven blocks, from Houston to Canal Street, between Forsyth and Chrystie Streets, making it the largest open space in the neighborhood. It was originally supposed to be used for public housing by the city, which purchased the land in 1929, but because of lack of support for the housing, it became a park instead. This is very important because there's no Central Park or Prospect Park in this crowded part of the city. The park has ball fields, including a synthetic turf soccer field, walking paths, and playgrounds, but the crown jewel is, in my view, the M'Finda Kalunga Garden, between Rivington and Delancey Streets, named after an African-American burial site near the intersection of Stanton and Forsyth. The words mean "Garden at the Edge of the Other Side of the World," in the African Kikongo or Kongo language. It is spoken in the Democratic Republic of the Congo, a region from which many Africans were forcibly brought to the Western Hemisphere. The garden is a lush place, with many varieties of bushes and flowers, and nice trellises. It has about forty separate plots cared for by gardeners.[40]

On the corner, at 126 Forsyth Street, at the corner of Delancey, I come upon the Spanish Delancey Seventh Day Adventist Church. In the front is a white cross and immediately behind it is a Jewish Star of David. This poignantly illustrates the idea of one ethnic generation departing and then being replaced by a new one. The newer group could have removed the Star of David, but it clearly chose not to. This can be inferred from the very visible four Stars of David I see above the large windows running along the Delancey side of the church. This is actually fairly common, as many people with whom I've spoken don't see it as affecting their own beliefs. Some have told me they want to respect other religions too. Although there's no name on the building, this was once the home of Congregation Poel Zedek Anshei Illiya. Illiya was a small village near Minsk in Belarus, and the congregation was one of the wealthiest in this area, owing in part to its foresight in building a number of retail shops on synagogue property. The building was sold to the Adventist church in the 1960s due to declining membership.

Generally, one thinks of this as a one-generation phenomenon. The Jews leave the Lower East Side and more Hispanics move in; end of story. But this isn't always the case, certainly not here. The synagogue had actually bought the building from the Forsyth Street Church, which had been designed in 1890 by the noted architect Josiah Cleaveland Cady, who had a hand in the design of many important structures, including the Metropolitan Opera House and the American Museum of Natural History. So, at this point the building has now been a church, then a synagogue, then a church again. In 2016, the current church announced its intention to sell part of the building, keeping the first three floors as a church. But what if they can't find such a buyer? It wouldn't surprise me if they sold it to a hotel, community center, or even a synagogue with a membership made up largely of gentrifiers. Why does this happen so often? Because when a building is a house of worship, it's more adaptable to other religious buildings, regardless of what religion they belong to. That said, the Lower East Side has an impressive number of historic synagogues.

The hub of the small Jewish community that's left lies along Grand Street, with most residents living in Cooperative Village, a development built by labor unions. Their main house of worship is the Bialystoker Synagogue at 7–11 Willett Street (now known as Bialystoker Place). Their building, originally a Methodist church, dates back to 1826, making it the oldest structure in the city that is used as a synagogue. The congregation consists mostly of strictly Orthodox Jews.

I continue along Forsyth to Grand Street, where I turn left and discover, at #281, a shoe repair shop. I almost missed it because of its minuscule size. In a space about five feet high and five feet wide, a short Chinese man sits, putting a new sole on a shoe. Literally a hole in the wall, this has to be the smallest shoe repair shop in the city. Does he feel claustrophobic sitting there all day? Do his legs cramp up? He speaks no English, so I can't talk to him, and I settle instead for observation outside his shop on the sidewalk. After sizing me up as a noncustomer, he ignores me. Over a half-hour period several customers, all of them Chinese, approach and either drop off or pick up items. He seems to know them and gets up several times to find things. He never leaves the place or stretches his legs, giving no indication that he finds being there in any way unpleasant. As I'm leaving, he takes out a sandwich, sits down, and eats it with great relish, sipping tea as well from a small porcelain cup. He seems to be completely content, and I feel like I'm watching a TV program, with him as the star.

As I stroll down nearby Hester Street, one block south and east of Allen Street, a sign at #72 catches my attention: "Mendel Goldberg Fabrics, since 1890." It is one of very few survivors from the days when there were so many fabric and clothing stores, most of them Jewish-owned, that Orchard Street was closed to traffic on Sundays to accommodate the throngs of shoppers who came to look, bargain, and buy. How and why has this place survived, I wonder. I

NYC's smallest shoe repair shop.

enter and meet Louis Ortega, the manager for twenty-eight years, who lives in the community. The most recent incarnation of this family dynasty, Sam Goldberg, died recently at age eighty-eight, but when I visited the shop, he still came in once a week for a few hours. There are family photos in the back, and the fabrics are indeed beautiful.

"How have you lasted for more than 125 years?" I ask Louis.

"We have an excellent reputation that we built up over many years for selling quality goods. We get people from all over the country and the world. You know who was in here the other day? Nancy Kissinger. I didn't even realize who it was until I looked at her credit card. One time, a couple of years ago, two Secret Service guys came in and bought hundreds of dollars' worth of expensive fabric. They had come from Kennedy Airport and said they only had an hour to buy stuff. And who was it for? A Saudi Arabian princess! And she was buying from a Jewish store. Just yesterday someone from the cast of *Hamilton* came in and bought some items for the stage set." I have encountered this pattern of well-known people buying in a shop before, but here it's somewhat different. The store isn't a fancy place, and this part of the area is by no means upscale. Coming in here is a very deliberate act and one needs to know it's here.

A block later, on Hester Street, I pass Public School 42, built in 1898. It's a perfect representation of what schools looked like a century ago, but its red-brick exterior, many French windows, and richly designed friezes are also in mint condition. Diagonally across the street I enter the Classic Coffee Shop, and it's definitely a classic. The store looks as if it's in a time warp. The counter is wooden, the rotating stools are from the distant past, as are the small wooden tables, with black-cushioned chairs, and the sign offers an egg cream made with Fox U-Bet chocolate syrup. I meet Carmine Morales, the owner, a man in his sixties with a neatly trimmed gray beard, attired in a black apron with matching tee shirt. Carmine went to PS 42 and so did his mother. A '60s music tape put together by Carmine is playing "That Loving Feeling," "I Got You Babe," "Wooly Bully," "Runaway," and "The Lion Sleeps Tonight," among many others. He also has tapes from the '50s and '70s. The menu has the usual luncheonette staples: ham and eggs, salami and eggs, tuna melt, and individual tins of sardines. On the silver wall behind the counter are various signs, one of which advertises Wrigley's Doublemint and Spearmint Gum, with the following accompanying poem:

Little Miss Muffet sits on a tuffet,
eating her curds and whey.
After she's through, she will Double-mint chew.
It keeps indigestion away.

To the left are photos of Yankees stars Joe DiMaggio and Mickey Mantle. Carmine, however, is a Mets fan, so he knows what suffering is about. There's a poster of the film *Casablanca* and, on the right, a poster of James Brown performing at the Apollo Theater in Harlem.

On a shelf in the back are old cameras including a Brownie, an ancient toaster that is manually operated, an original Pepsi bottle. Carmine loves old stuff, which he gets at flea markets as well as from friends. His eyes light up as he talks about how he got the bottle: "This bottle also has an original cap. This guy I know was working in construction in Brooklyn, and he went down to the basement and they had these cases of Pepsi bottles because the basement used to be a grocery. And the next day he brought me a can. In the old days when you bought a soda, there was a can opener outside by the door of the store. You opened the bottle and the cap fell into a can that held the caps. And he found the caps." This is what animates collectors. There's always a story, frequently involving an-out-of-the-way location, where the object is rescued from oblivion and brought back to life in someone's house or store. Looking at it, the person feels he can now live both in the past and in the present. To emphasize the point, Carmine points proudly to a photo of his graduating class from PS 42. In a way, the fact that these items are sold, decorate his place, and are the subject of comments and compliments by people who walk in, are proof of their worth and, by extension, his own.

I see a poster advertising the historic Max Schmeling–Joe Louis bout, another featuring Wonder Woman, and an ad for a staple of the '50s, Bond Bread. Carmine's favorite comedians are up there, smiling out of framed photographs—a likely trio of Abbott and Costello, the Three Stooges, and Jackie Gleason. One intriguing sign grabs me. It's an old ad for Lucky Strike cigarettes that proclaims: "20,679 physicians say: 'Luckies are less irritating.'" The ad features a woman in a revealing negligee enjoying a cigarette and opining, "I, too, prefer Luckies because the toasting removes dangerous irritants that cause throat irritation and coughing." The idea of having physicians endorse cigarettes—and unfiltered ones at that—seems startling when measured against today, with every cigarette box warning that smoking causes cancer. On the other hand, it took countless deaths and at least seventy years to get to this point.

Carmine is from a working-class family, half Italian and half Puerto Rican, and his wife is Jewish. He's liberal in his views. His grandfather made gin, stirring it in his apartment bathtub, and sold it to people in Little Italy. Given that he grew up in an immigrant community, his openness on this issue isn't surprising: "Prejudice is foolish. You gotta get to know somebody. My son has continued our ways. He's dating a woman who's Italian and Palestinian, and my daughter's going with someone who's a Muslim from Nigeria. So we got all the bases covered. Growing up I had friends who were all different—Irish, Polish, Jewish, Chinese. When you grow up in that environment, you come to realize everybody's in the same boat as you are—poor, but lookin' to succeed. The only difference I found was food." Carmine is living evidence of the contact theory, namely, that contact with others often increases tolerance. And despite his humble origins, his attitudes on this topic are remarkably similar to those of the gentrifiers who are moving in. In a sense, Carmine's story makes clear just how far America, and New York for that matter, have come. The old days of ethnic turfing are mostly gone, replaced by an attitude of not only live and let live, but live and explore, and maybe even love.

"What do you love about what you do?" I ask.

"It's like we're doing now, chatting. People come in, sit at the counter, strangers, and before you know it, everybody's talking to each other. And we all have different opinions and that's nice. The truth is it's crazy. I don't even make much money here. I'm struggling to make it. *I don't care because I'm havin' a good time.*" As they say, life isn't just about making money.

Around the corner and down the block, at 7 Ludlow Street, just before Canal Street, is the Metrograph Theater. It's a perfect fit, reflecting the changing community. It features old and new films, with an emphasis on that which isn't shown in the chains. Old films include Brian De Palma's 1981 classic, *Blow Out*, and current documentaries like *Los Sures*, which is about the slow disappearance of the Hispanic part of Williamsburg across the river. There's gourmet popcorn available in small containers with tempting flavors and popped in olive oil. Upstairs there's a bookstore dedicated to film, run by Arthur Fornier. It's where, as the ad says, "the screen meets the page." There are rare first-edition biographies and other books on films. On the other side of the walkway, there's an attractive eating space called the Metrograph Commissary.

Turning right at Canal Street, I head up to the corner of Orchard, where there's a tall building that's under construction when I walk by. The bottom portion, however, reveals its past with the sign, Jarmulowsky Bank Building. As is still true today, immigrants in the nineteenth century founded banks that tried to attract their own brethren. Many Jews invested in Sender Jarmulowsky's bank. In 1907, twelve years after its founding, there was a financial panic and the bank collapsed, causing financial ruin to thousands. Today, it's just another relic of the area's past, with no evidence of what happened behind its walls, or of the thousands of people who lined up in a desperate attempt to withdraw their money.

From here I go left onto Orchard Street, make a right onto Division and take it west to Catherine Street, where I turn left. Then, at Henry Street, I swing left again, turn, and find, to my surprise, another Henry—that is, O'Henry—displayed. Amazingly, it's in the form of an enterprise at #37, called O'Henry's Laundromat! O. Henry himself would probably, as they say, turn over in his grave if he knew. Then again, maybe he'd see the humor in it and think of it as one of his "shirt stories." I drop in and ask the middle-aged Chinese proprietor how he thought of the name. He's reading an English newspaper, so I assume he knows who this was. "It wasn't my idea," he says, looking a bit uncomfortable. "It was my sister-in-law. She thought it would be good for business since people know who he was. But I'm not Irish."[41] It's perhaps the most unusual effort

I've encountered among countless stores trying to attract business by name-dropping!

Farther down at 165–167 Henry Street, I pass by a sign identifying the Rabbi Jacob Joseph Yeshiva, one of New York City's oldest Jewish schools, or yeshivas, dating back to 1899. The school was named after New York City's first Chief Rabbi. Beginning as an elementary school, it developed into a prominent high school and seminary, educating hundreds of rabbis. Many of its high school students came from the rough-and-tumble neighborhood in which it existed, as well as from other parts of the city. Its most famous graduate is Robert Aumann, winner in 2005 of the Nobel Prize in Economic Sciences.

Not so well known is Captain Jacob Joseph, after whom the city playground nearby on Rutgers Street is named—a grandson of the illustrious rabbi. Reflecting the patriotism that prevailed in World War Two, as well as the Americanization process, Joseph enlisted in the Marines, leaving Columbia University in his junior year. He was killed in action in 1942 at Guadalcanal. The park serves mostly Hispanics living in the immediate area, but is also visited by gentrifiers and Chinese residents.

It's worth mentioning that the area, below, or south of East Broadway all the way south to the FDR and east of Essex and Rutgers Streets is overwhelmingly made up of co-ops and public housing. Standing on Rutgers, I go a few yards to my left from Henry Street and hit East Broadway, where I make an immediate right and come to a place of great historical importance for the Jewish community, the old *Forward* building at 175 East Broadway, built in 1912. Founded in 1897, the Yiddish-language socialist-oriented newspaper was read by hundreds of thousands of Jewish immigrants. There's still a bas-relief facade over the entrance, featuring carvings of Karl Marx, Friedrich Engels, and Ferdinand Lassalle. Today, indicative of the changing times, it's an English-language liberal weekly, with offices at 125 Maiden Lane. This location became a condo building in the 1990s, and I ask the concierge about that: "Is there anything in the building that suggests its rich history?" "Not really," he replies, "though there are some apartments I've seen with stairs leading to what was once an auditorium. But it's a desirable address, and our condos, depending on size, go from $800,000 to $2 million. Basically, it has a Jewish exterior with an Italian-decorated interior. A great combo, don't you think?" he says, laughing.

Turning around, I head up East Broadway and step into Weilgus & Sons Hardware Store at 158 East Broadway. It has been here since 1932. Its customers come from all over the metropolitan area, and it specializes in hard-to-find items. I speak with the owner, Lenny Weilgus. "Why do you think you're one of the last surviving Jewishly owned stores in the area?" I ask him. "Narrowness," he says chuckling softly. "No, seriously, in Hebrew, the sages say you're a rich man if you're happy with what you have. We made a good living, we were closed on all of the holidays since we were in a Jewish area. We weren't hungry. My father told me: 'You can only drive one car at a time, eat three meals a day, and wear one suit at a time.' What's the whole desire to become rich? Rich. Rich. Rich. We never had that fire. My father had the place and passed it on to me. I'm happy, but I'm 68; so I don't always jump out of bed. The business has changed. The local customers are a mix of Jews, Hispanics, and Chinese." Does he have any regrets about how his life turned out? "Not really," he says.

East Broadway has become a commercial center, of late, for the Fuzhounese, New York's newest arrivals from China, who are concentrated in this area, in Brooklyn's Sunset Park, and in a few other Chinese neighborhoods. To the south for several blocks lies a tenement neighborhood, teeming with more recent, low-income arrivals from China. I walk east on East Broadway about fifty yards and turn left onto Essex Street heading north to Broome Street where I turn left. Up the street on my right are 252 and 254 Broome, old tenement buildings. I notice small, rounded-off fire escapes with intricate, wrought-iron curlicue designs. In fact, the buildings themselves have complex friezes, with floral designs, human faces, and terracotta rectangles, positioned beside some of the windows, thus making the entire block a visually appealing detour.

On the next block, at 280 Broome Street, there's an unusual synagogue, Kehila Kedosha Janina, whose members are Romaniote Jews and whose original language was Yevanit, a Greek dialect. Some sources date their presence in Greece to before Christian times. Others date their origins to a group of Jews sent to Rome on a slave ship after the Jewish Temple in Jerusalem was destroyed in AD 70. On the way, according to one version of the story, a storm forced the vessel to land in Greece, where they remained until modern times, settling in the town of Janina. They have unique customs and traditions and are neither Ashkenazi nor Sephardic, the two main groups of Jews historically and in today's times. Their house of worship, a replica of the one in Janina, looks beautiful and has been at this location for over ninety years, and restored in 2006 by an architect. In what is now an overwhelmingly Chinese and gentrifying community, this place is an example of what people can do to survive through sheer determination.[42] And from whence does such determination come? Most often it stems from charismatic individuals who also had the financial means to support such endeavors.

Of course, the Chinese village associations, one of them a few doors down, as well as the old Italian social clubs here in Little Italy, make it clear that other groups have the same goals too. Looking at a Chinese-Hispanic grocery store, I also see that there are no ethnic barriers when it comes to attracting customers. At the same time, things aren't always what they seem. I pass a restaurant at 303 Broome with an Italian menu, called Louie & Chan. The owner informs me that Chan isn't the name of his co-owner, but simply "a nod to the Chinese population so they'll come in and eat here."

Entering a Cantonese Buddhist temple at 294 Broome, I see, in front of several statues, donations of fruits, Poland Spring bottles of water, and an opening in a large, red-painted wooden box for coins and bills. In the back of the temple sits a large statue of a fierce-looking bearded man named Guan Gong, dressed up in a resplendent blue robe covered with spangles. Red lanterns and plants surround the statue. Briefly, Guan Gong was a third-century Chinese general who represented the ideals of courage and loyalty. He is revered and popular in many Chinese expat communities. Interestingly, when I walked in, the man working there claimed not to know English. But after I made a small contribution, he became quite fluent and readily gave me information about the temple. In general, people talk more when you're nice and respect them.

Nearby, Nolita (or NoLIta, for *No*rth of *Li*ttle *It*aly) extends from Houston Street, south to Broome Street, and from the Bowery west to Lafayette Street. The name was created by real estate people looking for a catchy name. It is a gentrifying area with many bars, cafés, boutiques, and shops catering to the tourist trade. It also has some spillover from Little Italy in the form of Italian eateries. Most of those living here now are Chinese, along with a smattering of young people priced out of more expensive areas like the Lower East Side and Soho; very few Italians remain. That said, the Feast of San Gennaro is still held here annually in September. For the local eateries, bakeries, and novelty shops, the festival is a lucrative source of income, attracting many tourists, and as long as that's the case, it will remain. If nothing else, areas like this are a lesson about New York's history, however superficial. It should be noted that even in its heyday at the beginning of the twentieth century, the Italian population was about 10,000, compared with more than 100,000 Italian residents in East Harlem.

At Broome and Mulberry Streets, I turn right, and at 39 Spring Street, near Mulberry, I see a small blue mural of John Lennon covering both sides of a doorway to a nondescript building. There's a brightly colored butterfly on his forehead. Two silver teaspoons hang down from the spectacles over his eyes, giving the impression somehow that he's crying. Below it is a peacenow.com inscription. Above his head are a number of spray cans with red hearts, and on them, the identifier "Peace Spray." The bottom of the can says "WARNING: Contents May Be Dangerous." Since this is the avant-garde and liberal Lower East Side, the mural is perfectly fitting, reflecting the sentiments of many locals.

At 217 Mulberry Street, I step into the Tea Shoppe. It sells mostly tea kettles, along with matching cups, primarily from China. Its "hook" is that it sells both traditional and modern varieties. Customers include both locals and tourists. The manager, Melvin Fong, is a young man of Cantonese origin, who grew up here. His background lends the place an air of authenticity. The shop also has an interesting bit of history. "In the old days," Melvin tells me, "back in the eighties, Mafia criminals used the bathroom to stash stuff or hide out when the heat was on them." He invites me to look at it and while nothing remains to indicate its past role, my imagination gives me the feeling that I've connected with the past.

Due largely to the expansion of Chinatown from its original northern border of Canal Street, Little Italy has today been basically reduced to a three-block tourist attraction on Mulberry Street, running from Broome to Canal Street, with restaurants like the once infamous, but now tame, Umberto's Clam House at #132. The place was run by the mob, and the government took over the restaurant at various times. It achieved almost instant notoriety shortly after opening in 1972 when the gangster Joseph Gallo was murdered while having a meal.

I have my own story about "Crazy Joe." While working as a bar waiter at the Concord Hotel in Kiamesha, New York, to help pay my way through college, I had the nerve-racking honor of serving him, one of his brothers, and about ten other guests, on a summer night in the mid-'60s. They drank Johnny Walker Black and gave me a $24 tip, a very generous amount in those days. I remember hoping and praying that I wouldn't spill anything on them and being very relieved when they departed after the show.

Just south of Little Italy, Chinatown was originally settled in the 1800s by Cantonese people who often came here from Hong Kong. In the 1980s, Chinese entrepreneurs, fearing a communist takeover of Hong Kong, sent money overseas to the United States, snapping up tenements, so that their countrymen immigrating here would have places to live in. Chinatown has been increasing in size over the years beyond its traditional boundaries, north of Canal Street to beyond Broome and east of the Bowery, all the way to Essex Street. But there's still a large presence in the original area, west of the Bowery to Centre Street and from Canal Street on the north to Worth Street on the south.[43]

I continue farther down Mulberry and cross Canal, where I walk along Mott, Mulberry, Baxter, Bayard, and Pell Streets, the heart of Chinatown. It's bursting at the seams with stores selling meat, fish, and vegetables; restaurants; bakeries; Buddhist temples; and souvenir shops. Throngs of visitors wander along the narrow, sometimes winding streets, snapping photos and pointing excitedly at shop windows and other sites. Besides touring the contiguous areas of Little Italy and Chinatown, they are likely to walk along Canal to purchase knockoff Gucci or Louis Vuitton pocketbooks and other name brands from street vendors, many of them Senegalese.

In the midst of this shopping paradise, where there's a feeling that all the stores are selling very similar versions of the same thing, there are, nevertheless, some unusual places, beginning with the only kosher *and* vegan restaurant in Chinatown, Buddha Bodai, at 77 Mulberry. Chinese owned and operated, it serves dim sum, the usual vegetable and rice dishes and mock offerings of pork, beef, chicken, and shrimp. While not the real thing, it's a decent imitation for those who want to avoid meat and fish, which includes lots of Chinese vegetarians. There's also an upscale Mexican restaurant, Pulqueria, at 11 Doyers Street, which is two blocks east of Mulberry, the only one around here. At 50 Mott, I discover an exquisitely designed shop called Yunhong. It is the only establishment in the city dedicated almost exclusively to the sale of chopsticks. They are colorful, made of sandalwood, bamboo, and other materials, with many different motifs, and are all elegantly presented.

This entire area is rich with history, and Doyers Street, off Pell Street, is a perfect example. It's featured in the excellent thriller film

A Chinatown shop devoted to the sale of chopsticks.

about Manhattan's bicycle messengers, *Premium Rush*. Until it was closed off, there was a tunnel near the Nom Wah Tea Parlor that ran from Doyers to nearby Chatham Square. Gangs, also referred to as tongs by the Chinese, fought and often sneaked up on each other at the point where this one-block street curves sharply, dubbed "the Bloody Angle." The gangs, who also preyed on the innocent passing by on the Bowery or Pell Street, used the tunnel to escape pursuing policemen. Today, the tunnel entrance is gone, but the route it followed can be partially accessed by walking on Chatham Square, and turning mid-block onto a very bland passageway, consisting of some retail shops. Also on Doyers, at the corner of Pell, is Ting Yu Hong Gift Shop, where an opium den flourished in the 1950s, shut down only when Ting's was raided in 1958.

I head east down Pell Street and turn left, walking north on the Bowery, past Confucius Plaza, where I spot the Mahayana Buddhist Temple at 133 Canal Street. It's home to New York's largest statue of Buddha, a gold edifice, surrounded by a circular, electric, blue-colored halo. Until 1996 it was an adult movie theater. Locals swore

Home to New York's largest statue of Buddha—gold with a blue halo.

that the theater was haunted at the time and that's why, in part, the temple was erected here—to chase away the ghosts. Mahayana Buddhism's belief system includes spirits, so there is a connection here. It is not uncommon, for example, for monasteries to have spirit houses, whose origins may lie in folk traditions incorporated in Buddhism. In any case, from what I hear, the effort was a rousing success.

Walking west on Canal Street and turning left onto Mulberry, my tour of this incredibly diverse and fascinating neighborhood ends in Columbus Park, at the intersection of Bayard and Mulberry Streets. As I enter, I'm greeted by the haunting and mellifluous sound of traditional Chinese music on banjos and other instruments. The musicians are elderly and in no way intrusive, not even looking at those who watch them play. Their diffidence gives the impression that it's nice to give a tip, but not terribly important. I sit under a tree and contemplate the scene, looking at a statue of Dr. Sun Yat-sen, the founder of the Chinese Republic in 1912. This is, after all, Chinatown's center of outdoor recreation. Chinese men stand around concrete tables where Chinese chess and games of mahjong are played. Off in a corner I see Chinese women engaged in a game of poker. It's a gorgeous day and the world seems at peace, at least in this urban oasis, surrounded by graceful trees and chirping birds.

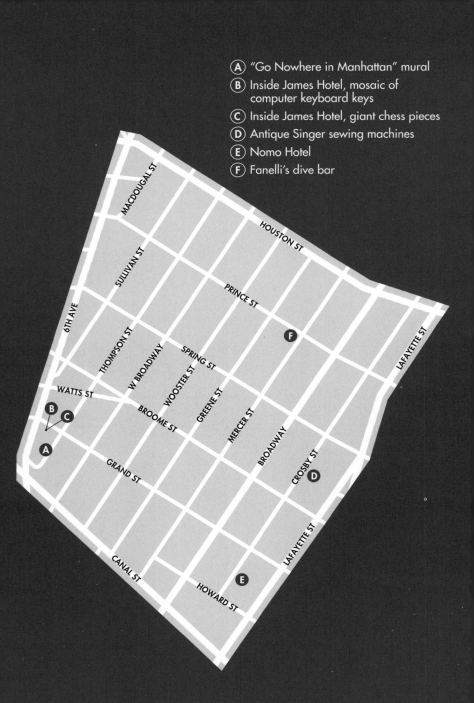

(A) "Go Nowhere in Manhattan" mural
(B) Inside James Hotel, mosaic of computer keyboard keys
(C) Inside James Hotel, giant chess pieces
(D) Antique Singer sewing machines
(E) Nomo Hotel
(F) Fanelli's dive bar

MACDOUGAL ST
HOUSTON ST
SULLIVAN ST
PRINCE ST
6TH AVE
THOMPSON ST
W BROADWAY
SPRING ST
WOOSTER ST
WATTS ST
GREENE ST
BROOME ST
MERCER ST
LAFAYETTE ST
BROADWAY
CROSBY ST
GRAND ST
LAFAYETTE ST
CANAL ST
HOWARD ST

SOHO

SOHO (OR SoHo, FOR *So*UTH OF *Ho*USTON STREET) IS A SMALL, highly gentrified neighborhood whose boundaries, generally, are Houston Street on the north, Lafayette Street on the east, Canal Street on the south, and Sixth Avenue on the west. The Soho Cast-Iron District makes up about 95 percent of the area. Cast iron is used as an ornamental facade for buildings. Its features also include large windows, often flanked by Roman columns. Between 1840 and 1880, hundreds of cast-iron buildings were constructed in Soho, of which about 250 remain. Cast iron was eventually replaced by steel, which is a stronger material. These buildings are easily recognizable, with some better preserved than others, and are the most distinguishable feature of the neighborhood, along with hundreds of boutiques, upscale chain stores like Bloomingdale's, and art galleries.

In the nineteenth century, Soho was arguably New York's primary entertainment venue for shopping, theater, and general nightlife. This was followed by a period in which it was a center for dry goods. As the city's center gravitated farther uptown and the textile industry migrated to the South, it entered a long period of decline, changing over to repair shops, sweatshops, and abandoned buildings and empty lots. In the 1960s artists, attracted by lofts with high ceilings, big windows, and low rents, came here in large numbers.[44] This was the main center for art galleries until the late 1980s, when retail shops selling high-fashion clothing and accessories moved in. And this is what it is today, though some artists still remain in the places they acquired decades ago. The epicenter lies on Broadway, with throngs of shoppers and tourists crowding the avenue, especially from Houston Street south to Broome Street.

From Broome to Canal, Soho is a quieter place. There are boutiques along Crosby, Mercer, and Greene Streets, but the foot traffic there is much lighter.

Emerging from the subway at Canal Street, I start walking up Thompson Street and find myself drawn to a small billboard to my left on a brick wall belonging to the James Hotel at 27 Grand Street. It's a color photo of a rural wooded area and beneath it is a sign declaring: "Go Nowhere in Manhattan." I walk into the lobby and meet the doorman, Jay Jimenez, an enthusiastic young man of Dominican and African American descent who lives in Washington Heights. He elaborates on the message.

"It basically means that you don't have to go anywhere else to find a quiet place because we have it right here. It's like an oasis. We have a beautiful garden upstairs that we call the Birds Nest, because there are all these birds that have chosen to make their home in the trees. We also have a pool on the rooftop and a great restaurant and bar." This is, in a sense, the hotel's rationale for having the mural placed there. A visit to the Internet reveals that "Go Nowhere in Manhattan" is the brainchild of the photographer, Matthew Jensen. The site includes more than 200 such images of places in Manhattan "where the city disappears." It's interesting to note that I might well have not entered the hotel had the sign not drawn my attention. Jay continues telling me about the James.

"We're into servicing the community too, and some of our facilities are open to the public at selected times. We use local artists and food suppliers, and we're also environmentally friendly." As I'm listening to him, I notice what appears to be a mosaic along a back wall of the hotel check-in area. A closer look reveals a very unusual mosaic, consisting of thousands of plastic computer keyboard keys—letters, numbers, shift, and page-down keys. The effect is mesmerizing since they are arrayed in random

Thousands of plastic computer keyboard keys—letters, numbers, shift, enter.

order and there are so many of them. The artist, Sarah Frost, calls them "QWERTY Installations," and she gets these and other items for her creations from garbage bins and garage sales. Her goal is to reuse objects, thereby giving them a second life. As she puts it: "Each key has a unique history and bears the imprint of the thousands of taps by countless users." The effect is to give one the full appreciation of the many ways in which things can be recycled.

Next, I walk into an outdoor sitting area and discover a giant chess set with two-foot-high brown and black pieces on a board. "This looks great," I say. "Nicely polished too. But do people actually play here?" "Yes," says Jay. "The area gets very crowded with people looking at this great view we have of the city, river to river. But people like playing with these pieces." I point out to Jay that in my travels I discovered that chess is very big among black residents of the city, telling him how I observed people playing with fanatical devotion to the game, day and night, in parks located in some of the city's poorest neighborhoods. I tell him that the game's popularity may stem in part from blacks wanting to combat negative stereotypes about them and demonstrate, as Maryland's black State Senator Ulysses Currie asserted, that "we are intellectual, cerebral people and that we are interested in something other than basketball."[45] Jay gives me another possible explanation for their interest: "Well, I guess that's true, but there's another reason too. A lot of young black people have been in prison and, you know, while they're in there they have a lot of time on their hands. And chess is one of the time-consuming games they like to play. That and another game called spades." I tell Jay about one black drug dealer whom I observed as he watched a game with intense interest even as he discussed a drug deal on his cell phone, seemingly oblivious to my presence.

The hotel, where nightly rates range from $200 to $500 depending on the season, attracts guests from all over the United States and from abroad, including celebrities looking for a quiet understated place, yet one that's near everything in Manhattan. Jay ticks off some names like the actress Kathy Bates and the director Ridley Scott, adding that some wealthy people and a couple of Middle Eastern princes have also been guests in the past. This gives the hotel cachet, something every business wants. Sometimes it's a catchy name, of which there are plenty, the type that can even cause the passerby to step into the establishment.

I turn right from Thompson onto Broome Street and go east until I come to Mercer where I make a left. A short distance away, I discover the chain retailer Sweaty Betty at 77 Mercer Street, which sells sports and exercise clothing as well as accessories, and Georgetown Cupcake, at 111 Mercer. The latter motivates me to stroll inside, where I learn of the many flavors that these cupcakes come in. Returning to Broome, I go left two blocks to Crosby Street and turn left again. As I walk up Crosby Street, my attention is drawn to some antique Singer sewing machines in a window at #56. When I walk into the store—a jewelry store called Broken English—I find it shares space with All Saints–Spitalfields, which owns the sewing machines. As I walk through the aisles, I discover at least 100 more sewing machines along the walls. They're not for sale; only the expensive handbags and clothing are. The Singer machines are there, a salesperson tells me, because in the old days they were considered the finest machines to use for sewing leather jackets and other items.

Meandering back down Crosby in the opposite direction, I come to 9 Crosby where there's an outdoor café, part of the Nomo Hotel, that has a wrought-iron arch with hanging lanterns and a long, ivy-covered trellis. The tables are interspersed throughout the lush garden, and one of the tables is actually in the form of a wooden porch-glider for two. I find myself wondering if the glider is for those wanting to take a rest or to have a romantic experience, or both?

At the corner, I go right on Howard and then right again at Broadway, going all the way to the corner of Houston Street, and enter Hollister, a clothing emporium. Three years ago, when I stepped in there, I entered another world, one where finely muscled and chiseled young men beckoned as they stood bare-chested alongside beautiful young women wearing nothing more than bikinis, and everyone dancing with abandon. I was the oldest visitor by forty years. As a tourist couple from Berlin walked by, their mouths dropped open in amazement. The cavorting models willingly signed autographs.

Today all that is gone. Apparently, people whose bodies were more in the ordinary category felt uncomfortable. They said that most people just weren't built that way. But who *is* built like the models we constantly see in magazines and TV ads? Perhaps seeing them in person was more annoying, store employees said. So today the store still looks great, but no more models, although the salespeople are still very good-looking, in my opinion. I speak with a young woman named Naresa Bharrat who tells me her favorite part of the job is working in the fitting room where you get to interact with the people.

One of New York's classic dive bars is Fanelli's, at 94 Prince Street, just west of Mercer Street. It operated as a saloon as early as 1863. It became known as Fanelli's in 1920 and was a speakeasy until Prohibition ended in 1934. A dive bar, for those unfamiliar with the term, is a neighborhood hangout, devoid of any pretension, where the food is basic, cheap, yet still good, at least in some cases. All this is true of Fanelli's. Inside it's cozy, with both quiet and noisy areas. The ceiling is made of pressed tin, the floor has ancient tiles, as manifested by the long, cracked lines running through them. There are colored fleur-de-lis designs. The bathroom is classic—old with wooden swinging doors and tall urinals. The walls are lined with faded photos of boxers, like Rocky

Graziano and Rocky Marciano. It's a great way to end this trip, for it represents something from out of New York's past that in a strange way harmonizes perfectly with what so many people who have gentrified the city seem to hanker after—a touch of authenticity.[46]

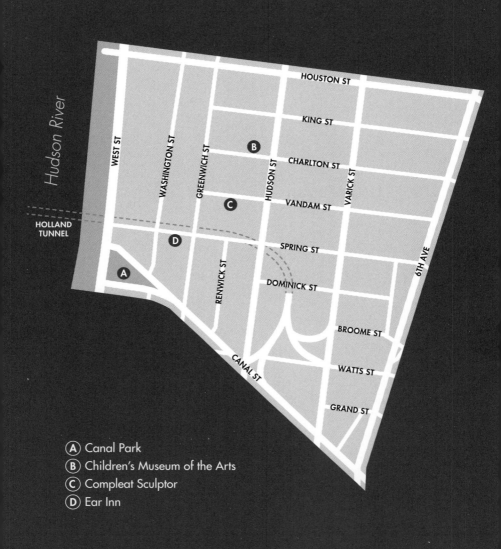

Hudson River

HOUSTON ST

KING ST

WEST ST

WASHINGTON ST

GREENWICH ST

B

HUDSON ST

CHARLTON ST

VARICK ST

C

VANDAM ST

HOLLAND
TUNNEL

D

SPRING ST

RENWICK ST

DOMINICK ST

6TH AVE

A

BROOME ST

CANAL ST

WATTS ST

GRAND ST

A Canal Park
B Children's Museum of the Arts
C Compleat Sculptor
D Ear Inn

HUDSON SQUARE

THIS IS PROBABLY THE LEAST-KNOWN NEIGHBORHOOD IN MANHATTAN even though it borders on some pretty famous communities, like the West Village, Soho, and Tribeca. Geographically small, its borders are Houston Street on the north, Sixth Avenue on the east, Canal Street on the south, and the Hudson River on the west. Adding to the confusion is the tendency of some people to call it West Soho, a term seemingly coined by real estate agents. Its superficial claim to fame would probably be that it encompasses the entrance to the Holland Tunnel on Varick Street, near Canal Street. It also boasts a large collection of Federal– and Greek Revival–style row houses dating back to the early nineteenth century, located largely along Charlton, King, and, to a lesser degree, Vandam Streets. And, of course, there's Hudson River Park, which runs from 59th Street through this neighborhood to Battery Park City.

This area was once a hub for printing companies. Today, there are still some communications outfits, graphic designers, and advertising agencies, like Saatchi & Saatchi, but nothing like the old days. UPS has a huge facility here, along Washington Street; there's a large sanitation facility, as well as a mix of small and large apartment buildings, restaurants, bars, and the usual stores present in any inhabited neighborhood, and even a few boutiques. The main commercial streets are Varick Street and Sixth Avenue. As I was walking here, several hotels were under construction, too, and the future looks bright for those desiring a trendier place.

One of the quietest streets here and in Manhattan generally, is the one-block-long Renwick Street, which runs from Spring to Watts Street. This wouldn't be worth mentioning except for the fact that it's a block west of the entrance to the Holland Tunnel, one of the city's noisiest places, as thousands of vehicles converge to gain entry to it. I spent an hour on Renwick during the rush hour from 4:30 to 5:30 p.m. and there were hardly any cars driving along it. It's a lesson in how space is destiny. The one-way street leads to Canal Street, but because you can't turn left toward the tunnel, only right to the river, it's pretty useless in that regard. There are few establishments on Renwick, save for a catering outfit, an architecture firm, a dentist, a modern furniture store, and a quiet little eatery. It's primarily residential, with small buildings. When I commented on how peaceful the street was, a resident said: "Shhh. Don't tell anyone."

There is a small reward, however, for those who do make the right turn from Renwick onto Canal Street. There are small parks everywhere in the city that lack the range of activities and size of a Central Park but are a vital part of a community. A block west lies Canal Park, right where the street dead-ends at West Street. Canal Park was among the city's first public spaces, having been created in 1686. The name comes from an actual canal that was situated on Canal Street. Calvert Vaux, of Central Park fame, was one of the architects who redesigned it in 1888. In the 1920s, this 234-year-old park became a construction site and also a parking lot. Later the community wanted to restore the historic park. In 2000, they won a case against the New York State Department of Transportation to make it a park again, and now that's a reality. The new design retraces the park's path in 1888. It has a decorative planter and engraved images of the original park. Had the area not become gentrified, I wonder if the effort to retake the space would have succeeded.

Heading east from the river on Canal Street, I turn left at Greenwich, walk up to Charlton Street, and go right. At #103, I take a look at the Children's Museum of the Arts. It claims to be the only interactive museum of its kind. For example, children sit on bar stools at the Clay Bar, where they are instructed in how to make items out of clay. There are interesting exhibits as well. The building in which it is housed (the main address is 345 Hudson Street) is

The only interactive museum of its kind.

one of the finer examples of Art Deco construction in the city. I turn right onto Hudson and go one block to Vandam Street and again turn right.

At 90 Vandam Street, I come to the Compleat Sculptor, the only place in the city offering a complete array of molds, casts, actual rocks in its basement made of alabaster used by sculptors, and anything else relating to sculpting. Its customers range from schools to filmmakers to sculptors. The statue of Raphael, the painter, situated right in front of the place, was so realistic that I thought it was alive.

Continuing west on Vandam I turn left onto Greenwich and turn right a block later on Spring Street, where my last stop is at the Ear Inn at #326, near the river. It's one of the oldest taverns in the city, dating back to 1817. The building itself is landmarked, having served as the residence of James Brown, reportedly an African-American aide to George Washington. The bar has a unique history, having been, at various times, a brothel, a physician's office, a boardinghouse, a speakeasy during Prohibition, and a smugglers den! It's called the Ear because the bar had no formal name for ages and the owners didn't want to go through the Landmark Commission's lengthy process of approving name changes. So they blacked out the round parts of the B on the "BAR" sign, so that it read as "EAR." Today, it's best known, according to the waitress, for "our burgers and jazz entertainment on Sunday nights." To me, it's a nice way to end a long day, as the atmosphere is very convivial.

TRIBECA

BATTERY PARK CITY

CIVIC CENTER

SOUTH STREET SEAPORT

FINANCIAL DISTRICT

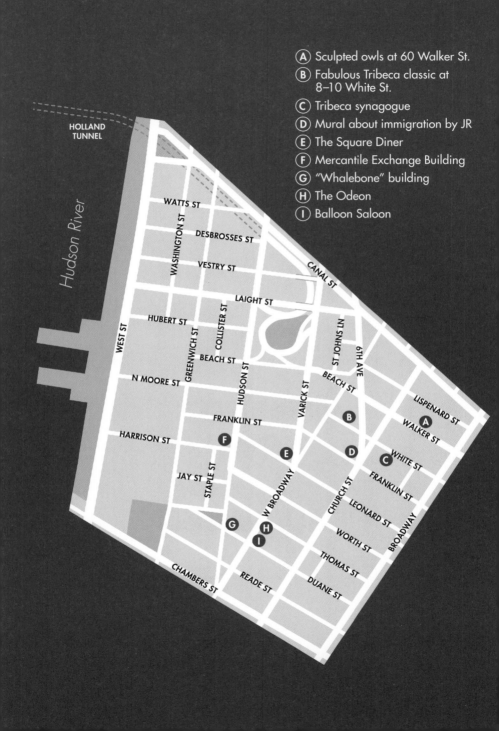

Ⓐ Sculpted owls at 60 Walker St.
Ⓑ Fabulous Tribeca classic at 8–10 White St.
Ⓒ Tribeca synagogue
Ⓓ Mural about immigration by JR
Ⓔ The Square Diner
Ⓕ Mercantile Exchange Building
Ⓖ "Whalebone" building
Ⓗ The Odeon
Ⓘ Balloon Saloon

HOLLAND TUNNEL

Hudson River

WATTS ST
WASHINGTON ST
DESBROSSES ST
VESTRY ST
CANAL ST
LAIGHT ST
HUBERT ST
COLLISTER ST
ST JOHNS LN
6TH AVE
WEST ST
GREENWICH ST
BEACH ST
BEACH ST
N MOORE ST
HUDSON ST
VARICK ST
LISPENARD ST
FRANKLIN ST
Ⓑ
WALKER ST
Ⓐ
HARRISON ST
Ⓕ
Ⓔ
Ⓓ
Ⓒ
WHITE ST
JAY ST
STAPLE ST
W BROADWAY
CHURCH ST
FRANKLIN ST
LEONARD ST
BROADWAY
Ⓖ
Ⓗ
WORTH ST
Ⓘ
CHAMBERS ST
READE ST
THOMAS ST
DUANE ST

TRIBECA

TRIBECA (OR TriBeCa) IS ONE OF NEW YORK CITY'S BEST-KNOWN neighborhoods. The area, shaped like a trapezoid, takes its name from the words *Tri*angle *Be*low *Ca*nal. It is bounded by Canal Street on the north, Broadway on the east, Chambers Street on the south, and the Hudson River on the west. In the mid-1800s it became a business district and the center of the dry goods trade. In those days it was known as the Washington Market area, encompassing several mercantile exchanges devoted to the butter, eggs, and cheese business. After these and other industries relocated to other parts of the city, many of the old buildings were razed and replaced by high-rise commercial and residential buildings. Most of the remaining factory structures became lofts, occupied mostly by artists.

As the two communities closest to the World Trade Center, Tribeca and Battery Park City were severely affected by the events of 9/11. Not only were buildings, air quality, and financial aspects impacted, but the psychological trauma was great. People were forced to evacuate the areas and allowed to return only after services had been restored and dwellings repaired or rebuilt.[47] But many never came back. This was brought home to me by an acquaintance who was a podiatrist with offices in the area. He was hit by flying debris, which may have included body parts. But his most searing memory was that of his patients who had died in or around the towers on 9/11. He found himself wondering over and over whether any of them might have died because he didn't do enough for them. Could foot problems have affected their efforts to escape from the Towers? He knew it was irrational, but it bothered him nonetheless. He never worked again. His story is surely one of many unpublicized responses to the tragedy. Good friends of mine left Tribeca after 9/11 and retreated to a farm in upstate New York. They loved the city, but at that point they'd had enough. Eventually, they returned to live in another part of Manhattan.

In Tribeca, life did gradually return to normal, helped along by government grants, free counseling services, and rebuilding projects. Symbolic of its recovery is the Tribeca Film Festival, founded in 2002 by Jane Rosenthal, Craig Hatkoff and Robert De Niro. By 2008, Tribeca had become New York City's most expensive neighborhood. Walking by the boutiques, chic restaurants, and art galleries, it's easy to forget what happened, unless you happen to look up at the new gleaming One World Trade Center building, which can be seen from almost anywhere in the vicinity. People are resilient and New Yorkers perhaps even more so.[48]

To explore the streets of Tribeca—Lispenard, White, Franklin, and Leonard Streets—is to see a collection of buildings from another time in New York, to step back into the past in this highly landmarked district. It's eminently worthwhile to stroll through the neighborhood and look at the structure and the ornamentation of the cast iron and Art Deco creations that line these blocks. To take just two examples, the sculpted owls on the third floor of 60 Walker Street, on the corner of Broadway, stare unblinkingly into the eyes of anyone gazing upon them. Built in 1930, the edifice also features beautiful stonework and sandstone. Heading west on Walker, I make the first left onto Church Street, go one block and then make a right onto White Street. Up the block, at #8–10 is a grand-looking Doric-columned, light-beige building with filigreed keystones. Because of its foreshortened design, it looks taller than its five-story height. Built in 1870, it is today a residential building.

I turn around and go east on White Street to #49. I stop short and gape at the Tribeca Synagogue because the exterior design is so unusual. It's a multistory structure that curves outward and upward from the bottom, appearing to be suspended between its more conventional neighbors. I meet one of the congregants, Ken Paskar, just as he is leaving for home after morning services. He explains, "This

These owls stare right back at you.

is a Modern Orthodox synagogue, but we attract all types of people. Many of them have a traditional background even if they're not Orthodox. These people are residents who come here on the Sabbath and holidays. Then you have Orthodox judges, lawyers, and others from the nearby Civic Center who want to pray with a minyan [a quorum of ten men]. It was designed in 1967 by William Breger."

Ken, an airline pilot living in nearby Little Italy, invites me to see the sanctuary, which shows the curvilinear design from the inside in front of the auditorium. It succeeds, as it was meant to, in giving the impression of a flame rising into the light-filled skylights. The ark is also unusual—two tall graceful columns made of wood and metal, inside of which are the temple's Torahs. Ken adds that many show-biz celebrities and well-known politicians have prayed here.

Having seen these three amazing structures, I retrace my steps west on White Street to Church. Turning south, I go one block to Franklin. Here, across the street, there's a large mural by the French artist JR that catches my eye. The image looks like a photograph and captures twelve children, clearly immigrants, wearing what appears

A wave-shaped synagogue suspended between its more typical neighbors.

to be garb from their respective homelands. The faces are serious, hopeful, at the same time as they are grim, especially the youth with the black Russian hat, reminding me of the photos on Ellis Island of the newcomers to this land. It was put up in the summer of 2016. It replaces a previous mural, also by JR, of a soaring ballerina that was based on a short film, *Ellis*, directed by JR and starring Robert De Niro. Hopefully, the children will probably still be there by the time this book comes out—or at least replaced by another, equally worthy creation.

Leaving the mural, I go west one block on Franklin to West Broadway, turn left and soon come to Leonard Street, which is also where Varick Street and West Broadway meet. Here across the street on Varick, is the Square Diner. This is one of the few old and old-fashioned diners left in the city. The caboose, with plywood wainscoting, Art Moderne glass blocks, and silver all around, is classic. Inside, it's a warm, and welcoming place, with plastic-covered stools, Formica tables with gray plastic booths to sink into, a polished wood ceiling made up of floorboards, or, I guess, "ceilingboards." There are signs from yesteryear, one reading "Phone Call, 5¢." Diagonally across the street by contrast, is the gleaming, spanking new New York Law School, next to a similarly designed tall residential building.

The waitress points out the owner, Ted Karounos. "How long have you been here?" I ask Ted. He's a tall, well-built man with a neatly trimmed dark beard and a big smile, displaying gleaming white teeth. "I've been here fifteen years as the owner, and my family's been here forty-five years. Plus, the diner's been here for over 100 years. Here's a photo from 1905, when they put the subway underground. My father-in-law took it over from an Irish guy in 1971. Our family story is like a template of the American dream. We're Greek, and he came over here and started as a dishwasher and then he bought the place."

Ted then launches into the familiar neighborhood history: "Back then it was a much seedier place, pretty dangerous, and that's why it was cheap to buy the place. My father walks around the area today, now that he's in his seventies, and says, 'I coulda bought this place for 200 Gs, or that place for 150.' It's great. I mean, we were lucky to get it then because nobody knew what would happen to Tribeca back in those years." This is always a source of pride to individuals. They know they were lucky, but then again, they chose to be here and that must imply some degree of foresight. I glance at several framed photographs on the wall, one of the actor Jerry Orbach.

"What are these photos for? Customers?"

"Not necessarily. Mostly they're from film shoots that were done here. Location scouts looking for the real 'diner look' find us, and these are from the films or TV series that were shot here. They're wonderful income for small businesses. We're in both seasons of Netflix's *Daredevil*."

"Do you ever think of selling for a nice profit?"

"Not yet, because what would I do? I have young kids still, and the place will only increase in value. We're doing great, knock-on-wood, but the real estate pressure to sell is very strong. You could put up a five- or six-story building here. I've had architects come here and tell me, 'I want to build my dream one-family house here.' But I'd like to be here another twenty years at least."

Ted's a happy man. He has a job that's fulfilling and satisfying, not only economically, but also in terms of the very idea of it. "I love it when people come in here and tell me how unbelievable it is to have a place like this from the old days, preserved." It's clear from his enthusiasm that life isn't just about money, at least not as long as the diner's cash register keeps ringing!

I head west on Leonard Street, just past Varick Street. Here I see, at #18, emblazoned above some second-floor windows in large capital letters, the words "The Juilliard Building." Could this be connected to the famed Juilliard School of Music on 66th Street, off Broadway? I ask the concierge (it's been converted into a condo residence) and he responds, "No, no connection at all. That's a music school." But he's wrong, as a little bit of research proves, and once again, I learn that you can't take a person's word, often well-meaning, at face value. The building was once owned and operated as a dry goods establishment by Augustus Juilliard, who donated quite a bit of money to the famed musical academy.

At the end of the block, on Hudson Street, slightly south of Leonard, is the Mercantile Exchange Building at 97 Hudson Street or, if you will, 2–6 Harrison Street. With its dark red-brick exterior, it looks a little like the city's old, late-nineteenth-century public schools. But this Queen Anne beauty is far more ornate, with gables, keystones, granite pillars, and terracotta, as befits an institution with its special place in commercial history. These exchanges were created to regulate various industries and to maintain standards. By 1885, it had over 1,000 members from various trades. By the late twentieth century, its business had greatly expanded to include coins, a variety of food products, and the commodity trading of futures. Today, the building has been converted to condos, and all that's left is the name above the third floor on Hudson.

As I stroll south on Hudson, I think to myself, this is the fun of walking through Tribeca. When you see old names of buildings, there's often a history lesson to be learned. At 161–163 Duane Street, just off Hudson, there's a building with the word "Whalebone" above what had been the kitchen of, several years ago, the famed Bouley Restaurant, and it too is historical. According to Dan, a chef at Bouley, who lived at this address: "You can clearly see what was there because they prepared the whalebone here, and the floor had a glossy sheen to it from the whale meat. When I moved in I cleaned the place up and it was fun."

Backtracking one block from Duane, I walk a block north along Hudson to Thomas Street and turn right, taking it to West Broadway. At the intersection, I see the sign "Hollow Sidewalk," admonishing truck drivers not to park at that spot on the sidewalk. As these signs are common in areas like Tribeca and Soho, it's worth explaining. If a truck were to park there, the sidewalk could collapse. These signs are serious, and the sidewalk is hollow because the ground beneath it may have contained a basement or storage area that was never filled in. The city is responsible for maintaining the sidewalks but not what's under them. When people jumped from the building on Washington Place in Greenwich Village where the 1911 Triangle Shirtwaist Company fire occurred, with 146 workers perishing, quite a few of them fell through the pavement into basements. They jumped from the upper floors because the stairwell doors had been locked to reduce theft and to prevent people from taking breaks during working hours. The tragedy resulted in major changes regulating building safety and was responsible in part for the creation of the famed International Ladies' Garment Workers' Union (ILGWU).

On the southeast side of West Broadway and Thomas Street, there's a restaurant called the Odeon. Part of the sign also reads, "Cafeteria." For those wishing to imagine a slice of the early 1980s scene in Tribeca, it's worth walking inside and sitting at the bar, which retains many of the original features. During that period, the Odeon was a hangout for a who's who of New Yorkers, including Andy Warhol, Tom Wolfe, Calvin Klein, Giorgio Armani, John Belushi, and Robert De Niro. In those unsafe times, Tribeca hadn't become gentrified and the Odeon was one of a very few upscale places.

At 133 West Broadway, at the corner of Duane Street, I come across a marvelous, really fun place, called Balloon Saloon. Outside the store, balloons of every type float in the air, including some that are translucent globes of the world. I walk inside, which is very crowded with mothers and their young charges. Three young people are manning the counter, all of them eager to help.

"Are you the only place in the city devoted primarily to balloons?" I ask.

"I don't know," answers a young goateed man in a black tee shirt. "But I'd like to think we're one of the best." Surveying the scene, I see board games of the past for sale—Yahtzee, Concentration, Easy Money, and others—along with card games and hundreds of novelty items.

"What's your best-selling item?'

"Fake dog poop."

"You're kidding!"

"No. Go take a look," he says smiling and pointing to the location. I walk over and see some very realistic-looking poop, which I resist buying for my dog or anyone else, opting instead for a fake chocolate donut with sprinkles. This place has been around for forty years, so it's safe to assume they know what they're doing. This clearly isn't part of historic Tribeca, but it's a pleasant diversion for the young and for the young at heart.

(A) Metasequoia trees
    memorial to 9/11
(B) Tom Otterness artworks
(C) Teardrop Park
(D) Irish Hunger memorial
(E) Skyscraper Museum
(F) "Cool Globes"
(G) Castle Clinton
(H) SeaGlass Carousel
(I) American Merchant
    Mariners' memorial

Hudson River

CHAMBERS ST
RIVER TERRACE
WARREN ST
MURRAY ST
NORTH END AVE
VESEY ST
LIBERTY
WEST ST
SOUTH END AVE
ALBANY
RECTOR PL
W THAMES ST
3 PL
BATTERY PL
2 PL
LITTLE WEST ST
1 PL
STATE ST
Battery Park

BATTERY PARK CITY

BATTERY PARK CITY IS A PLANNED, state-funded, largely residential and middle-class neighborhood adjacent to Tribeca. It's bounded on the north by Chambers Street, on the east by West Street, and by the Hudson River on the south and west. Sitting as it does, west of the Financial District, it seems to be an island of its own. Many of the streets are quiet. The only really commercial center is Brookfield Place, with its office towers and shops, as well as the area immediately around it. The area sits on millions of cubic feet of landfill, created in the 1970s. The apartment buildings, with their various hues and shapes, are graceful and inviting, and together with its ample and well-designed parks, it has become a very popular community for people with young children.

The area was severely affected by the collapse of the World Trade Center, which was literally across the street from it. Almost all of the people were evacuated from their homes and not allowed to return for months, and with no provisions made for temporary residence. The events had a traumatic effect on the inhabitants, and a good number never returned. Walking through the area you'd never know that anything in particular happened here, unless, as happened to me, a longtime resident spoke about the way the homes were damaged or vandalized, and the extent of the environmental pollution in the aftermath of the tragedy.

A good place to begin a visit to Battery Park City would be Chambers and West Streets. Walking toward the river along Chambers, I pass Stuyvesant High School, one of the premier schools in the city. Battery Park City has a network of parks, all of them well designed and beautifully landscaped. They are jointly operated and managed by the city and the state. Speaking with Sandra and Sarah, two park employees who are working on the flora and fauna, tidying up, putting down earth, and pruning, I find out more about the park.

"This is the beginning of the park," Sandra tells me. "Here you have some small boats in the marina and ahead of you there's Jersey City. As you can see, there are lots of mothers, nannies, and little kids playing in the grass. And there are these five large trees at the Hudson River's edge. They're metasequoias, which are a type of redwood tree. We got the cuttings, I believe, from China. As you can see, they're five of them, and I personally like to think of them as memorials to the World Trade Center buildings that were destroyed on 9/11." This is yet another indication of how deeply rooted 9/11 is in the minds of people. It doesn't have to be a site or a memorial to those who died. It need only be some trees nearby.

Behind me, in what is actually Nelson Rockefeller State Park, is a children's playground with something special added. It contains many works of art by the well-known sculptor Tom Otterness. I start my walk along a winding bronze-inlaid path featuring little bronze footprints that runs through the playground. It is lined with many different items sculpted in bronze. These include a four-foot profile of a man's head. Two children are shouting into its ear. Next to a concrete table with a chessboard are bronze carvings of large chess pieces, one of which has been fashioned so that it appears to be falling down. Another has a bird ready to snap up a worm, while a bronze cat prepares to spring on it. There's a functioning water fountain whose base is a huge human foot.

A few yards farther down is what might be called the centerpiece of these displays. It's an intricate large sculpture, featuring a tall building with Humpty Dumpty sitting atop it, playing on a violin as pennies are falling out of his pockets. Otterness's creations often have a political angle and this is no exception. Scattered everywhere are piles of oversize pennies featuring only the side with the Lincoln Memorial. The other side, with the motto "In God We Trust," was reportedly not to his liking. The building, according to a park podcast, represents the financial center of the city, only a few blocks

Bigfoot on the loose in Battery Park City.

away, and the violin fiddling may be designed to remind people of
the song "If I Were a Rich Man" in *Fiddler On the Roof,* or of the
saying "Nero fiddled while Rome burned." A number of the many
small bronze figures look like bankers and radicals, the latter of
whom are presumably opposed to capitalism. Basically, Otterness is
satirizing a world where money rules. Children can, and do, tour this
place by walking barefoot around the building, which is encircled
by two inches of water.

I continue my walk along River Terrace, the street that is the
eastern boundary of the park. Making a left onto Warren Street I
enter Teardrop Park. I sit on a curved bench and look out upon a
grassy, downward-sloping area surrounded by tall graceful, brick
apartment buildings. It feels as though I'm sitting inside a deep
canyon. Only instead of high cliffs, there's brick and mortar, as
though nature was interacting with the city. It's an oasis of peace
and quiet. At the bottom of the slope is a wall made from blue-
stone from which water flows downward. A built-in passageway
cuts through the park and provides access to its southern section.
Here I meet another park employee, who shows me a large space

containing maintenance equipment, workshops, and storage space, adding, "What's really neat about this is that our place is located within the rock, as opposed to being a stand-alone building, like in most parks." Her thoughts turn to 9/11, for no apparent immediate reason. "You know, after 9/11, on September 13th, we came back to this area to protect it. Otherwise who knows what would have happened."[49] She has a point, as some residents who returned later to their apartments found them vandalized. Above the space is a small playground with a long slide, where kids glide down an incline flanked by cobblestones and small boulders.

Returning to River Terrace, I continue south, and the street soon merges into North End Avenue. Where North End crosses Vesey Street is the entrance to a special exhibit. The Irish have been coming to New York City since the 1840s, when the potato famine forced them to leave their impoverished homeland by the millions. The memorial to that great migration is on display in the form of a re-created field that resembles the Irish countryside and even includes Irish limestone. It features the names of all the counties in Ireland—Mayo, Cork, Sligo, etc.—as well as a wall on which the trials and tribulations that afflicted the Irish are recounted. To most, the Irish immigration is seen as something from the past, along with that of the Jews and Italians. In truth, however, the Irish have never stopped coming, their numbers ebbing and flowing according to the economy of Ireland. Their knowledge of English and the fact that America has a large Irish population has made it a primary destination.

I enter the commercial center that bisects the northern and southern section of Battery Park City. Called Brookfield Place, it has office buildings and restaurants, and is anchored by a large indoor shopping mall with upscale shops like Gucci, Hermès, and Burberry, all in a huge atrium. The floor is made of multicolored marble. Gazing upward, I see fake but pleasant-looking birds suspended from wires and, conceptually parallel to that, on the ground, tall artificial palm trees. It's all very modern, chic, and charming, with throngs of people parading through.

A few blocks south, I speak with a man who is described by his friend as "the mayor of Battery Park City." "What's it like to live here?" I ask. "I came here from Brooklyn and I love it," he declares. "First of all, it's always 10 degrees cooler here than elsewhere in the city. There's this great breeze coming in from the river. And I've got a great view of the Hudson and the Jersey skyline. Another thing is that when Hurricane Sandy hit, all of Lower Manhattan lost power, but we didn't because of the weird way the grid and power stations work. Finally, there's a certain culture here of respecting quiet. The cabs here know not to honk their horns even though there are commercial areas all around. They know it's a residential area."

This self-description of a person's community is revealing in several ways. Cool breezes may be only temporary, but when it's hot they can mean a great deal, as I can attest to, since, when I met him on a hot and humid July afternoon, the temperature was 93 degrees. As to views, this simply reinforces the importance of space in a crowded city where a view is a space. For many people in this teeming city, the view from where they live is important. The comment about Hurricane Sandy suggests that, at least in this respect, the neighborhood has something over all the others in the area. And the idea of cabbies not honking their horns means that their physical space is respected by others. Individually, none of these issues are as important as matters like safety, affordable rents, etc., but as a whole they reflect the intangible aspects that can often tip the scales when it comes to choosing a community in which to live.

South End Avenue is the street where residents do most of their local shopping. There are cafés, preschool programs, delis, dry cleaners, and the like. This gives the area a kind of intimacy and sense of community. It's a place where people who know each other meet and talk. One such place, highly regarded by the natives for its excellent pizza, is Benvenuti. One local said: "This place is better than Lombardi's, or Di Fara, especially if you're looking for that old-style pizza." There are also a couple of well-tended mini-parks where people can sit and chat. The community seems to have experienced an explosion of young families with small children, perhaps, in part, because it has lots of state-of-the art playgrounds and programs for kids.

The Skyscraper Museum is located at 39 Battery Place, the southern boundary of this neighborhood. From 1996 to 2004, it occupied several spaces, all of them in lower Manhattan. Its focus is on the architectural history of the city, how skyscrapers are designed, built, and used. The museum also has temporary exhibitions like one on the history of the World Trade Center, Shanghai as a metropolis, and one called "Supertall," about the world's tallest buildings. In the years after 9/11, people questioned the wisdom of having such tall structures. Recent years, however, have seen an increase in such construction in New York and elsewhere, highlighted by the completion of One World Trade Center. All this makes an understanding of skyscrapers and their contributions to urban life all the more relevant.

A bit farther down on Battery Place, near West Street, I come across an exhibit called "Cool Globes," supported by Governor Andrew Cuomo, that consists of twelve colorful globes emphasizing different aspects of climate change. One describes the power of ocean waves; another urges people to support the protection of rain forests; a third one discusses urban issues. A globe that encourages wearing sweaters and adjusting the thermostat is covered in material that looks like a sweater. Battery Park City in general is quite conscious regarding issues of sustainability. Its library, at 175 North End Avenue, was the first "green" branch in the New York Public Library system, and was certified by LEED (Leadership in Energy and Environmental Design) for its contributions to the environment. The community also has an award-winning building at 20 River Terrace—the Solaire was the first one in the country to be recognized for its environmentally friendly design and construction.

Of course, no one should come to this neighborhood without seeing the World Trade Center Memorial. Its history is forever etched into the city's history. While obviously well known, it's so central to this community and to its collective experiences and memory that I feel an obligation to make mention of it.

Ellis Island is what generally comes to mind when people think of a place through which immigrants were processed when they arrived in the United States. But less is known about Castle Garden, the point of entry for about eight million people who came here between 1855 and 1890. Before that, in 1815, it was used as a fort to ward off a potential invasion by the British. As we now know, that invasion never happened. From 1896 to 1941 Castle Garden was the home of the New York City Aquarium. Today, it's called Castle Clinton and serves as a reminder of the city's history. It's in Battery Park, which is just south of Battery Park City, and I can see the walls of the fort and the openings from which American soldiers might have fired on the British had they attacked.

Whether by design or not, ticket offices for ferry rides to the Statue of Liberty and Ellis Island are sold here, thus insuring a captive audience for this national monument. Battery Park itself has become a venue for many people to ride bicycles, have picnics, and just relax. There's also a ride called the SeaGlass Carousel, where visitors ride on specific fish through an area resembling an under-water garden. This attraction is entirely fitting, since the New York Aquarium, located today in Coney Island, Brooklyn, was housed here from 1896 until 1941.

Another site, lost among the many attractions of Battery Park, is the American Merchant Mariners' Memorial. I asked a federal employee of the Castle Clinton facility, and he had no knowledge of it despite the fact that it was less than a city block away from where he was standing. It features four life-size bronze figures clinging to a lifeboat. When I was there, one of them was almost completely submerged in the water, clutching the outstretched hand of another man on the boat. Whether or not his head is visible depends on the tide at the time. It's based on a true World War Two story about a Nazi attack on a Merchant Marine boat. The Nazis photographed the sailors struggling to stay alive as the boat slowly sank, leaving the men to perish in the water. This memorial honors their memory.

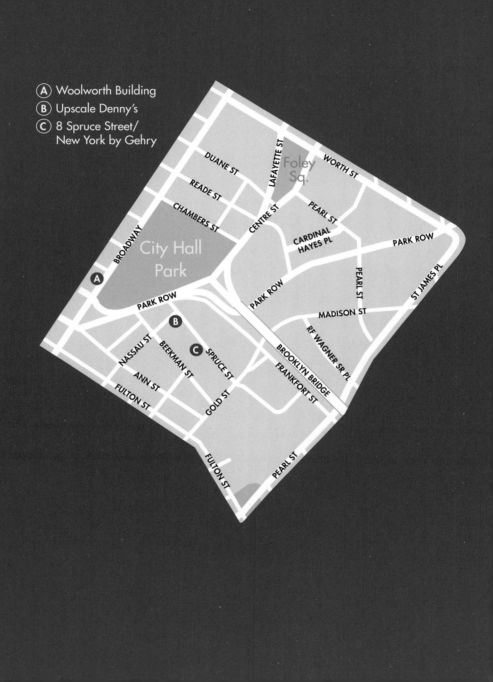

(A) Woolworth Building
(B) Upscale Denny's
(C) 8 Spruce Street/
New York by Gehry

DUANE ST
READE ST
CHAMBERS ST
LAFAYETTE ST
WORTH ST
Foley Sq.
CENTRE ST
PEARL ST
CARDINAL HAYES PL
PARK ROW
BROADWAY
City Hall Park
PARK ROW
PARK ROW
PEARL ST
ST JAMES PL
MADISON ST
RF WAGNER SR PL
NASSAU ST
BEEKMAN ST
SPRUCE ST
BROOKLYN BRIDGE
FRANKFORT ST
ANN ST
GOLD ST
FULTON ST
FULTON ST
PEARL ST

CIVIC CENTER

THE CIVIC CENTER CONTAINS WITHIN IT THE POLITICAL NERVE CENTER of the city. The centerpiece is City Hall near City Hall Park, which houses the mayor's office and the City Council's chambers. It is the oldest building in the United States that still retains its original functions. Adjacent to it is the Municipal Building, home to the municipal agencies overseen by the mayor. The boundaries of this area are Worth Street on the north, St. James Place and Pearl Street on the east, Fulton Street on the south, and Broadway on the west. Its history as a seat of government goes way back to 1700, when the first city hall was built here. Unfortunately, that history also includes the fact that slaves lived here too. An unpleasant but important reminder of this legacy came in 1991 with the discovery of a burial ground for thousands of Africans on the site of what is now 290 Broadway.

Today, the Civic Center has many city agencies and related offices, as well as commercial enterprises of every sort and educational institutions such as Pace University, whose campus flourishes in the shadow of City Hall, east of City Hall Park. There's spillover from the financial district, but it retains its identity as a place where city government predominates. This also includes Police Plaza on Park Row where the police commissioner's offices, those of the Major Case Squad, police intelligence units, and other divisions are headquartered. On Foley Square, there's the Federal Office Building, which is where the offices of Homeland Security, the FBI, the Social Security Administration, and other agencies are located. Finally, the area is also home to various courthouses at the federal, state, and municipal levels.

My walk begins at the intersection of Park Row and Broadway, where the truly iconic sixty-story Woolworth Building may be found. This is a splendid structure that has earned the informal name of "the Cathedral of Commerce." It was dedicated in 1913, with President Woodrow Wilson pressing a button in Washington DC, whereupon those gathered witnessed 80,000 electric bulbs lighting up. The style is classic Gothic with arches, buttresses, and gargoyles. As opposed to so many buildings in New York, the designs prevail on every single floor of the structure, not just the lower and uppermost floors. It is a building that can be appreciated from a distance but also offers beautiful detail on an up-close walk. The interior, with its sparkling, multicolored vaulted mosaic ceiling, and gold-leaf cornices, is truly impressive. Everybody knows what Woolworth's sold and to drive the point home, there's a sculpture of F. W. Woolworth holding on to a giant nickel. Let's not forget, however, that this man, who began his career working in a general store, paid $13.5 million in cash for his monument to American capitalism.

I cross the street and enter the nicely landscaped City Hall Park. It's a hot August day, near 90 degrees, and I'm lucky to find a bench in the shade near a pretty fountain, designed by Jacob Wrey Mould, co-creator of Central Park's Bethesda Fountain. The site has a history. It was at various times a prison, a location for public executions, an art museum, and a concert venue. In the 1600s, the western edge was a trail for the Lenni Lenape Indians, which eventually became Broadway.

At 38 Park Row, I enter a small stationery shop, with the classic large-lettered "Optimo" cigar sign common twenty-five and more years ago. The sign turns out to be an original, but there are no Optimo cigars in the place. Nonetheless, for anyone interested there are cigars available for sale under lock and key, with the best one being a Cohiba, a Dominican cigar selling for $25.99. This little store also has picture postcards and smartly sells American *and* European stamps.

Next door is a building occupied by Pace College, and just to the left I spy a small carved bronze figure of a dog, which reads, beneath it, the "The Pace Setter," a rather clever play on words. The statue and plaque were donated by the class of 1953. The brothers Homer St. Clair and Charles Ashford Pace established the institution in 1906. Today, the campus has quite a presence in what must be one of the busiest locations for an educational complex—the entrance to the Brooklyn Bridge, located right next to City Hall. Given its

A joyful fountain replaces a former site for executions.

focus from the beginning on business and finance, the choice would seem to be entirely appropriate.

Around the corner on Spruce and Nassau Streets is a Denny's restaurant, which opened two years ago. I've seen Denny's all over the country but never in Manhattan. In fact, it's the only one in the borough and one of only two in the city, with the second location in East New York, Brooklyn. Unlike most other Denny's, this one also has a bar, with a nice selection of alcoholic beverages, including Maker's Mark, Jameson, Hennessy, Cherry Heering, and Grand Marnier, not to mention a couple of TV screens.

Just behind the Denny's is 8 Spruce Street, an award-winning residential tower. The seventy-six-story structure was designed by the architect Frank Gehry. In front of it, running from Spruce to Beekman Street is an outdoor plaza with plastic chairs and some nice trees. What catches my eye are the fountains. They're actually five sets of twenty small spouts on the concrete ground in various parts of the space, each no more than a foot high, with water coming out of them. The height of the water seems initially unimpressive, but that is what makes them so noticeable. I find looking at the twenty jets almost mesmerizing.

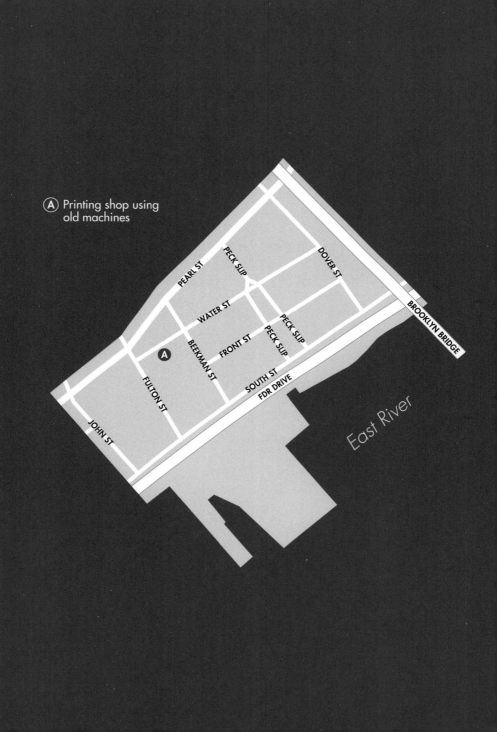

(A) Printing shop using
old machines

SOUTH STREET SEAPORT

THE SOUTH STREET HISTORIC DISTRICT is far too well known to be a feature in this book, but it bears mention here because it's located where Fulton Street meets the East River, right next to the Civic Center and to New York's Financial District and walkers in this area should at least know where and what it is. The Seaport borders are roughly the Brooklyn Bridge on the north, East River on the east, John Street on the south, and Pearl and Water Streets on the west.

The adjacent area, located on the northeast, is known as the "Two Bridges" section because it lies between the Brooklyn and Manhattan Bridges. From the 1600s until the 1950s, it was a center for shipping and commerce. Today, with its quaint cobbled streets and both preserved and renovated buildings, it's a major tourist destination in the city. It's also the former site of the Fulton Fish Market. Visitors can explore its history in condensed form by visiting the South Street Seaport Museum.

To better understand this community's history, I walked into a printing shop on Water Street, where I met Inbal, a young graduate of the Parsons School of Design. The printing presses are very old, dating back a century or more, yet they are still humming along, perhaps not as well as today's creations, but certainly in keeping with the seaport's long history. As Inbal explains: "We do all of our printing on these old machines because we're part of the museum and it wouldn't really make much sense not to use them if they're working. It's part of our history here. We do a lot of custom work. The business cards and stationery we do often have a unique old-time feel to them. It's kind of a rough weathered feel. It also has the impression into the paper. The newest machine is from 1958 and the oldest one is from 1830."

"How does such a machine continue to function?"

A printing shop that still uses century-old presses.

"You just gotta keep using and oiling it. It's like maintaining an old car. You can't just let it sit."

"Why did you go into this type of work?"

"Printing is just what I'm interested in. It's what I studied at Parsons."

"Well, I write books. So I'm definitely interested in this topic."

"Oh wow! You see, these drawers all contain different types of letters, which you won't see in a Kinko's. That's why we stand out."

Inbal hails from a small town in Wisconsin. She loves the history of printing and this job allowed her to pursue her love. When I ask her what she would like to do in the future, she says: "I'm already doing what I want to do." It reminds me that New York has opportunities for all sorts of nonstandard professions, like urban parks management, aquarium design, tour guides, and so many other occupations unavailable in smaller towns.

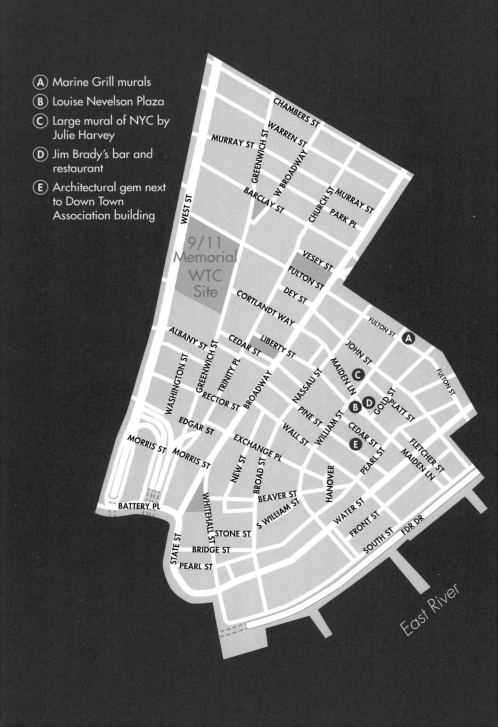

Ⓐ Marine Grill murals
Ⓑ Louise Nevelson Plaza
Ⓒ Large mural of NYC by Julie Harvey
Ⓓ Jim Brady's bar and restaurant
Ⓔ Architectural gem next to Down Town Association building

CHAMBERS ST
WARREN ST
MURRAY ST
GREENWICH ST
W BROADWAY
BARCLAY ST
CHURCH ST
MURRAY ST
PARK PL
WEST ST

9/11 Memorial WTC Site

VESEY ST
FULTON ST
DEY ST
CORTLANDT WAY
LIBERTY ST
CEDAR ST
ALBANY ST
JOHN ST
FULTON ST
Ⓐ
Ⓒ
WASHINGTON ST
GREENWICH ST
TRINITY PL
RECTOR ST
BROADWAY
NASSAU ST
MAIDEN LN
FULTON ST
GOLD ST
PLATT ST
Ⓑ Ⓓ
EDGAR ST
PINE ST
WILLIAM ST
CEDAR ST
Ⓔ
FLETCHER ST
MORRIS ST
MORRIS ST
EXCHANGE PL
WALL ST
PEARL ST
MAIDEN LN
NEW ST
BROAD ST
HANOVER
BATTERY PL
BEAVER ST
S WILLIAM ST
WATER ST
WHITEHALL ST
STONE ST
FRONT ST
SOUTH ST
FDR DR
STATE ST
BRIDGE ST
PEARL ST

East River

FINANCIAL DISTRICT

THE FINANCIAL DISTRICT'S BOUNDARIES ARE, roughly, Chambers and Fulton Streets on the north, the East River on the east, State Street and Battery Place on the south, and West Street on the west. It is the home of the one of the world's leading financial centers, anchored by the Stock Exchange (the world's largest) and top corporate law firms like Sullivan and Cromwell, Fried Frank, and the like. There's also the New York Board of Trade and Nasdaq. One of the favorite activities of tourists is to have their photo taken in front of the statue of a charging bull, at Broadway and Morris Street, symbolizing Wall Street's ethos of optimism and prosperity. It's always crowded in the daytime, especially because the location is right near the National Museum of the American Indian and the Museum of Jewish Heritage, as well as the ferries to Staten Island and the Statue of Liberty.

Whereas other parts of Manhattan were more residential in the nineteenth and early twentieth centuries and became heavily commercial in more recent times, here, the opposite is true. In the twentieth century, the area was almost completely commercial, but it has become much more residential in the last twenty years, with close to 50,000 permanent residents. It's especially attractive to young families where the parents work in the community. It has many restaurants and taverns that cater during the daytime and early evening hours to the thousands of employees that are concentrated in the narrow, yet busy streets.

I begin my journey at street level by the exit for the 2, 3, and A trains on Fulton and William Streets, where there's a glazed terracotta work of art at street level. It's easy to miss because it's just above and behind the station stairs. There are other works, too, farther inside the station. Called "Marine Grill Murals," they were originally commissioned in 1913 by the famous McAlpin Hotel at Broadway and 34th Street. At the time, the McAlpin was the world's biggest hotel, with accommodations for 2,500 guests and 1,500 employees. In 1989, it became an apartment building. The MTA's (Metropolitan Transit Authority) Arts for Transit Program had the tiles reassembled by a group of college students. The themes are nautical history and this one, visible from the sidewalk, features Robert Fulton's steamship and Henry Hudson's vessel, both in New York's harbor. It reminds us of the relationship between the city's harbor and commerce.

From here I walk east one block to Gold Street and make a right. Halfway up the block I see the red-brick Excelsior Power Company Building at #33, on my right. Built in 1888, it housed one of New York City's first electrical power companies. Now it's a perfect example of how buildings are preserved and transformed into residential units. On the left I turn up Ryders Alley. It's a very short lane that has nothing in particular on it (except the backs of some buildings) and is deserted even by day. It soon becomes Eden's Alley as it swerves left and quickly leads out to very busy Fulton Street, all this in the space of a city block. And that's why I'm touching on it. No section of the city is busier than the financial district. And yet, this curving alley is one of the quietest places in the entire city, including Queens and Staten Island!

I head west on Fulton to Church Street, make a left and continue until it becomes Trinity Place. The immigrant experience in this area is relatively unknown when compared to that of the Lower East Side. This neighborhood, especially the area along Trinity Place and from Cedar Street on the north to Morris Street on the south, was once home to immigrants from Ireland, Slovakia, Syria, Greece, and Lebanon, who came here from the mid-nineteenth to early twentieth centuries.[50] Today, the area, with its skyscrapers, bears no resemblance to the residential community that was once here and that teemed with immigrants from Europe. Very few tenements are left in this area, but there are two located on Trinity Place, almost

Across from Edgar Street, Manhattan's shortest thoroughfare.

perpendicular to Edgar Street, the shortest street in Manhattan and directly across from Elizabeth Berger Plaza. Many of the immigrants worked on Wall Street and did their shopping in the nearby Washington Market.

From Edgar Street, I walk one block up Trinity to Exchange Place, make a right and walk to William Street. Here I turn left and go five blocks up to John Street. At the intersection, there's a plaza on my left with a building wall alongside it. It's devoted to a large mural, about seventy-five feet high, by the artist Julie Harvey. First, it depicts some gentlemen and ladies, riding in horse-drawn carriages and strolling through nineteenth-century New York. In an interesting juxtaposition, the mural also contains elements of lower Manhattan through the centuries, including the upper half of the Statue of Liberty reflected in a skyscraper and ships in the New York harbor.

I turn around and head south on William Street one block to Maiden Lane. Formerly owned by Pace University, the AKA long-term residence hotel sits at the intersection. What catches my attention are the many beautiful lions adorning this gorgeous structure,

A 75-foot-tall mural of horse-drawn carriages from the nineteenth century.

built in 1907. As lions are a symbol of power around the world, it's entirely fitting that they're located in this seat of great financial influence. Above the entrance, at the fourth floor level, there's an elaborately carved stone Roman numeral clock, which, though it looks strictly ornamental, actually gives the correct time. A lion and a unicorn flank the clock.

Turning left onto Maiden Lane, I soon come to Louise Nevelson Plaza where it intersects with Gold Street. Nevelson's black-painted steel sculptures dominate the plaza, and together they're known as "Shadows and Flags." The material came from a foundry in Connecticut, and the abstract designs are intended to remind people of flags waving in the breeze.

Across from the plaza I see Jim Brady's bar and restaurant on my left, at 75 Maiden Lane. Inside, I meet the proprietor, Paul Quinn, as he's having a quick early dinner. He has steely gray hair and very alert, almost dancing eyes that manage to be both intense and warm at the same time.

"What can I do for you?" he asks in a friendly Irish brogue.

"I'd like to know why so many young families are living in the Financial District."

"I know exactly why, as I was here when it happened. You see, after 9/11, this place became a ghost town. No one wanted to work here. You couldn't. There was no subway service. The companies all went to New Jersey, Connecticut, wherever they could find space. And many never returned. The stock market has hundreds of people on the floor today, whereas in the old days they had thousands. So the city had to step in. They offered the owners of office buildings all sorts of incentives if they would convert their buildings to apartments. People were attracted to it, especially since the rents were somewhat lower than elsewhere. Plus, the universities, NYU and Pace, for example, bought space here. Today, you have lots of families. From what I hear, it's one of the fastest-growing residential communities in the country. The population has just about doubled in the last ten years to maybe 50,000 people. There are schools, good shopping, day care centers, and playgrounds. And you just have to adapt. In the old days before 9/11, business was great here, with all the workers, and we had great entertainment, Irish bands like the Clancy Brothers."

"Do the people who live here work in the immediate vicinity?"

"Not necessarily. For some it's a reverse commute. They work in Jersey and they come home here."

Paul's absolutely right, as confirmed by articles in the *New York Times* and the *Wall Street Journal.* Doormen tell of a continuing baby boom. Businesses have returned too, though the new jobs are more likely to be in the retail and hotel sectors than in finance. And the Stock Exchange is still a shadow of what it once was in terms of numbers of people there. The population has at least doubled and new schools have been built. Tax incentives were given to both buyers and real estate developers. It's the same in the neighboring communities of Tribeca and Battery Park City, but it's more noticeable here because this area was once far more commercial. This resurgence is augmented by a burgeoning nightlife that finds its expression in places like historic Stone Street, once home to breweries and now crowded with restaurants that attract the young from all over the city. There's even an effort to rename it Soma—South Manhattan. Has it caught on? Not yet, but perhaps it will.[51]

"Does your bar have anything special that would make it different from others?" I ask Paul.

"Well, of course we have very good food. And the decor, wood paneling, stained glass, and all the seats are meant to recall the days of Diamond Jim Brady, who lived in the late nineteenth century. But one thing that's really special is that we have the original bar— the mirrors and paneling and all—from the old and famous Stork Club, which closed over fifty years ago. It was put in storage and later auctioned off. We bought it for about $5,000."

"Just wondering. How do you put something like that together again?"

"Simple. You just get excellent Irish carpenters. But it was hard, like putting together a jigsaw puzzle." True enough, and it demonstrates how aware merchants are that they need to differentiate themselves from other establishments, and the connection to the Stork Club, once one of the world's most distinguished nightclubs, is a great hook.

There are also places that have not changed much since they were first established. Take the Down Town Association, established in 1859, one of the city's first private clubs and the oldest in Lower Manhattan. Past members have included Thomas Dewey, John Foster Dulles, Franklin Delano Roosevelt, and Grover Cleveland. None of this fazed me in the least as I walked south on William about three blocks and made a left toward its sacrosanct precincts at 60 Pine Street. In writing these books, I've always been guided by two principles: if you act like you belong, then you do; and people of my age are generally invisible to others. Whether it's a snooty club or a fancy hotel.

Unfortunately, in this case, that only worked for about two minutes. I sauntered into the bar and lounge area, sat down in a plush easy chair, and began perusing the list of drinks available for purchase. Almost immediately, I noticed two men seated on a divan about twenty feet away, one elderly, with silvery hair and rimless glasses, the other middle-aged and dressed in neat trousers and a button-down shirt, staring intently at me. They began whispering to each other, all the while eyeing me with some degree of suspicion. Curious and seeking to allay their anxieties, I walked over and asked them if anything was wrong.

"I'm the manager of this club," said the older gentleman politely and in a very friendly tone. "Are you a member here?"

"No. I just walked in because I'm writing a book about Manhattan and I was very impressed by the interior, the mosaic tiled floor, oak panels, and oil paintings. Are you perhaps publicity shy?"

"No. It's just that," he said, pausing for a moment as if searching for the most diplomatic way to say something, "just that, there's a policy here, strict policy, that people are not allowed to wear shorts inside; nor are they permitted to use their cell phones. And you seem to have violated, or at least disregarded, both of these rules."

"Well, I'm very sorry. I didn't know. I won't do it again. Could you tell me something about the club and its history?"

"I'd be happy to if you called me, but not when you're standing here dressed like this." I happily obliged, apologized, and began leaving. As I was doing so, he said, "Just one question—How did you gain entry into our club?"

"Well, in truth, I didn't realize it was a club at first because some workers up the block told me this was a beautiful hotel and I should check it out. The door was unlocked, and the man at the desk gave me only a passing glance. I walked farther in and sat down in the lounge area near the bar. Anyway, how does one get to be a member here?'

"Well," said the younger man in an annoyed tone. "It's open to the right sort of people." And that was it. Frankly, I was surprised that I'd even gotten this far. He wasn't sure who I might be, perhaps one of "the right sort of people," who just didn't know the rules. The "right people" comment perfectly captures the dilemma of such places. They want to nourish an aura of exclusivity because that makes gaining entry a real accomplishment for those who make the effort. But they also really need members who have the money that will help the club thrive.

This experience is also an example of one of the most common aspects of big cities. With everything in close proximity, such faux pas are fairly common. You walk into a bodega, buy something, look for a bathroom in the basement and stumble upon an area where Muslims are praying. You lie down on the grass in a public park, not realizing that a group uses the area all the time and considers it as their property even if it isn't, thereby defining you as an interloper. You wander into a midtown hotel and enter a ballroom where your US senator is greeting invited guests at a party. In this particular case, I took note of the fact that this club, which emphasized its exclusivity, was directly across the narrow street, separated perhaps by a mere twenty-five feet from one of New York's largest subway stations, Wall Street, where anyone can access the heavily used 2 and 3 trains by entering an atrium and riding the escalator. Are people's intrusions in these instances all that wrong? Who can say, but they are, in any case, inevitable in a metropolis.

And yet inevitable as they are, the human element cannot be ignored. Within organizations and bureaucracies like the Down Town Association or a Dunkin' Donuts, people still have options. They can, within limits, ignore rules and customs. In contrast to the Down Town Association, my experience with another institution was entirely different. I walked into a McDonald's on Cliff Street in need of a restroom. The sign above it was clear: Restrooms are for customers only. I stepped forward in the line and said to the man behind the counter:

"I need to use the restroom so I'm buying a bottle of water. Can you unlock it, please?"

"Sure. But you don't need to buy anything. I'll let you use it anyway." I was surprised because I have not always found such expressions of kindness in other McDonald's or Burger Kings.

"Thank you. I guess you took pity on me because I'm an older guy."

"Not really," he said. "I let people use it all the time. Some buy, some don't. No matter." Luis happened to be the manager. His parents are from Venezuela, though they are actually Dominican. He's an immigrant and explained to me. "I believe in being nice to everyone whenever possible." This attitude filters down to everyone. As I sat at a booth drinking my water, I noticed how respectful he is to his workers, politely telling them to fill an order in a certain way, yet never raising his voice or showing impatience. In turn, the employees are friendly and considerate of the customers. This man has chosen to flout a rule rather than enforce it. Is he going to get in trouble for that? I don't know, but he doesn't mind that I take note of it for this book.

In a way, this reflects changing values in society as a whole. People today are more apt to protest against rules that make no sense and which they perceive as unfair. They live in a world where there's greater protection for individual rights, especially for members of groups that suffer from discrimination. There's also more room for individual expression. One byproduct of this change is that dress codes have been relaxed. Restaurants that once required jackets for men no longer do, and many companies have no dress code. I visited the Condé Nast offices in the Financial District, and the employees were wearing shorts and tee shirts and playing Ping-Pong for relaxation. At Google headquarters in Chelsea, there's an ice cream truck where employees can sit inside and, under the influence of a favorite childhood memory, get their creative juices flowing. It's a new world, and I suspect that even the Down Town Association will get on board one day.

Next to the Down Town Association, there's a beautifully preserved reddish-brown office building, circa 1893. Its entrance is surrounded by a filigreed design with several carved heads, looking sort of sternly down at those who enter its portals. There are beautiful terracotta accents, rounded arches, and many other elegant features. More important, I noticed that most of those entering and leaving are women with young children, reflecting the demographics of the area. While visitors perceive this part of town simply as the home of finance at the highest levels, for thousands of people it's just home.

ACKNOWLEDGMENTS

I want to first thank all of the people at Princeton University Press who have helped and guided me through the process of writing this book. They are an incredibly talented, committed, and professional group of folks who have been very supportive in so many ways. First and foremost, I want to express my deep appreciation to my editor, Meagan Levinson, who greatly improved the manuscript, both conceptually and in the hundreds of details that are involved in this process. In addition, I want to express my indebtedness to Mark Bellis and Molan Goldstein, both of whom did outstanding work. Special thanks as well to Julia Haav, Samantha Nader, Bob Bettendorf, Laurie Schlesinger, Chris Holewski, Amy Reeve, Debra Liese, and Shane Kelley. I also owe a debt to the Princeton reviewers, Harvey Molotch, Jonathan Wynn, and Graham Hodges, who carefully read the manuscript and made many helpful comments and suggestions.

I also want to express my gratitude to the following people who read portions of this book and/or who made helpful comments and suggestions, Jeff and Joseph Helmreich, Esther Friedman, Josh and Deborah Halpern, Paul and Irene Marcus, Sheldon and Tobie Czapnik, Nathan and Pearl Halegua, Karin and Gerald Feldhamer, Jeff Wiesenfeld, Susan Philips, Morris and Sondra Silver, Phil and Joyce Levine, Joan and Steve Goldberg, Allan and Annie Rudolf, Jack Nass, and Rob Katz.

I especially appreciate the sage counsel and support in various ways from my academic colleagues/friends: Mitchell Duneier, Ruben Rumbaut, Richard Alba, Eli Anderson, Phil Kasinitz, Vince Boudreau, Eric Weitz, Pyong Gap Min, Bill Kornblum, Nancy Foner, Roger Waldinger, Terry Williams, James Katz, Sharon Zukin, John Mollenkopf, Mary Clare Lennon, Cynthia Fuchs Epstein, Juan Battle, Roslyn Bologh, Jack Katz, Gabe Haslip-Viera, Ramona

Hernandez, Parmatma and Rupam Saran, Iris Lopez, Maritsa Poros, Mehdi Bozorgmehr, Keith Thompson, Jeff Gurock, Sylvia Barack Fishman, Moshe Shokeid, Judy Baumel, Peter Moskos, Francis Terrell, Morton Weinfeld, L'Heureux Lewis-McCoy, Gwen Dordick, Leslie Paik, Katherine Chen, Jim Biles, Norma Fuentes, and Yana Kuchova.

Many people helped me in different ways with contacts, ideas, suggestions, leads, and more. They know what they did and how much it means to me, and I'm happy to mention and thank them here: Ivan Kaufman, Tom DiNapoli, George Tzunis, David and Diane Rein, Helen and Harvey Ishofsky, Zach and Ros Dicker, Maris and Stu Blechner, Phil and Margie Jacobs, Daniel Vitow, Avi Hadar, Avery Modlin, Jon Ohebshalom, Eli Goldschmidt, Sydelle and Robert Knepper, David and Martin Werber, Sam Roberts, Joseph Berger, Connie Rosenbloom, Dan Frankel, Alan Helmreich, Murray Gewirtz, Barry Singer, Kenneth Cohen, Itzhak Haimovic, Russell Warren, David Dare, Baruch and Pam Toledano, David Hoenig, Lance Grieff, Eric Schwartz, Gary Knobel, Stanley and Anne Lupkin, Peter Dougherty, Mary Curtis, Nina Johnson-Mende, Joseph Svehlak, Hershey and Linda Friedman, Allan and Judy Halpern, Richard Bienenfeld, Laura Bowman, Sandee Brawarsky, Johanna Holman, Evan Blum, Jeff Marcus, Alison Brown, Charles Matkowsky, Charlene Darbassie, Kevin Matthews, Emily Walz, Maike Zimmermann, John Reddick, Alison Brown, Behfar Ehdaie, and Karen Ward-Gamble,

Saving the best for last, I want to thank the love of my life, my wife and very best friend, Helaine. A talented novelist, biographer, and historian in her own right, she not only read every word I wrote, but she frequently accompanied me on my walks (along with our dog, Heidi). As a result, she found many things that escaped my attention and made innumerable valuable suggestions. Thus, she was also my intellectual partner, a role she has played ever since we married forty-seven years ago. Who can ask for more?

APPENDIX

Most of Manhattan is very safe to walk in, day or evening. Late at night, however, caution should be exercised on the narrow side streets of Washington Heights east of Broadway, East Harlem, and Harlem north of 135th Street. Public housing projects should also not be entered during these hours. Keep in mind that the city is very safe and that the murder rate in the city as a whole is about 300 a year. Also, 80 percent of murders are committed by people who knew their victims.

Some walkers will be motivated by curiosity about what life looks like in these communities. Also, these areas are actually quite interesting in terms of buildings, stores, and life there in general. The vast majority of residents are honest, hardworking folks who will be friendly if approached the way you would anyone else. And then there are risk-takers who look for adventure, which is fine, provided you understand the risks involved. That said, if you're the type of person who worries a lot about crime, then my suggestion is to avoid these areas.

So, if you decide to "go for it," I offer the following tips:

1. Be alert at all times.
2. Dress innocuously and not very well—no loud colors, especially gang ones—bright blue or red.
3. Never stare at anyone, but if you should make eye contact, and the person isn't looking at you in a hostile manner, smile and say "Hi." It's a counterintuitive, disarming approach that has served me well, though gauging this can sometimes be tricky.
4. Avoid groups of people congregating on the street, especially teenagers, but do not cross the street if you feel they've already seen you approaching. You don't want to

look nervous or fearful. This is obviously not easy to determine with certainty.

5. Walking at night, on weekends, and in the summer, is riskier than at other times.

6. Do not walk with more than one person, since you don't want to attract attention.

7. Avoid areas where it's difficult to exit, such as neighborhoods without nearby transportation.

8. Avoid deserted areas.

9. Don't carry a lot of cash, but have some. Having nothing on you may increase the likelihood of physical attack from a disappointed assailant. Never fight back unless all else is lost.

10. Be careful about giving money to panhandlers. Generosity can lead to trouble, especially if others take notice.

11. Always be respectful. If someone is walking toward you be ready to give way as you are not on your home turf.

12. Never try to project an image of toughness. It won't work and, in fact, people may judge you as insecure if you try it.

These are not hard-and-fast rules. Circumstances may dictate a different response or approach. Each situation is, by definition, unique, and one needs to be flexible and adapt. Having and using common sense is an essential quality.

Women, as a rule, should exercise more caution and should not walk in these areas alone. Walking with a man is less likely to attract attention. Walking with a man and a dog is even better. It suggests that you are local, or at least visiting someone local. Older people, provided they are physically fit and can walk at a reasonable pace and without using a cane are actually at less risk than those who are younger. A younger person who looks like an outsider—that is, of a different race or ethnicity—may be seen as a challenge to a resident of similar age. People who look like they could be a cop or a worker in the area—a teacher, social worker, delivery person, or store employee—are at less risk.

On a personal note, I walked 7,595 miles of city streets at all times and was never attacked. Why? I grew up in a rough area of the city and was familiar with life there. I hung out on the streets and developed the usual sixth sense about danger. Plus, I'm a trained and longtime ethnographer. Even more important, perhaps, I was just plain lucky. One incident brought this home to me. I once walked into a public housing project at midday. As I passed a teenager who glanced at me, I said "How ya doin?" His face was expressionless as he said something in Spanish into a walkie-talkie. I looked around and saw seven heads go up about fifteen yards away. Without any hesitation, I said, "Have a nice day," and walked out, not quickly or slowly, toward the street, never looking back. I had, I suspected, interrupted a drug deal or other illegal activity. My goal was to indicate that I wasn't a threat to what they were doing. In this case, being perceived as a cop might have made things worse.

Nothing happened to me. I was fortunate.

NOTES

1. Wynn's book sheds much light in its excellent analysis of the work that the city's tour guides do and how they shape peoples' views of New York. Wynn 2011.
2. Hodges 2007.
3. Roberts 2017a.
4. Grynbaum 2012.
5. See Snyder 1996.
6. Indeed. Sabas is a Greek name that traces its origin to the Hebrew word Saba, meaning old man or grandfather. It may also be of Egyptian or Spanish origin. Saints with this name include a 4th Century Gothic martyr, a 5th Century Cappadocian hermit, and a 12th Century archbishop of Serbia who happens to be the country's patron saint.
7. For an excellent novel about Dominican Washington Heights, read *Let It Rain Coffee* by Angie Cruz (2005). See also Snyder 2015.
8. See Lowenstein 1989.
9. See Marable 2011.
10. Marable 2011.
11. Roberts 2010.
12. Beveridge 2008.
13. Sherman 1973.
14. Stoller 2002.
15. Vergara 2009.
16. Min 2008.
17. This is similar to a description of the Hispanic food vendors in Red Hook, who "cook with the soul and with the heart, just as if they were cooking at home. This is how you get what you get over here: *fresh* authenticity" (Zukin 2010).
18. Gentry 2009.
19. Berger 2001.
20. For those who can't find the time to go there, one alternative is to get a copy of Sandee Brawarsky's beautifully illustrated work, *212 Views of Central Park* (2002). The color photographs are truly outstanding.
21. Martin 1997.
22. Roberts 2017b.
23. Clinton 2004: 73.

24. Stern, Fishman, and Tilove 2006.
25. Stoller 2002.
26. Churchill (1906) 2013.
27. Singer 2012.
28. Reed and Morrone 2011.
29. Wertz 2017: 24–25. Wertz has a fascinating discussion about pinball, which was illegal for several decades in New York City.
30. Whyte 1988.
31. Armstrong and Crage 2006.
32. Jerolmack 2013.
33. Hassell 1996.
34. Murphy 2016; Williams 2016.
35. Bahr 1973.
36. Smith and Kurtz 2003.
37. Schulz 2016.
38. Remnick 2016.
39. Ocejo 2014: 98–100.
40. Smith and Kurtz 2003.
41. O. Henry was actually the pen name for William Sydney Porter. He was an American poet, and his parents were both American-born.
42. Israelowitz 2014: 65.
43. Kwong and Miscevic 2005.
44. See Zukin 1982.
45. Helmreich 2013: 153–55.
46. Ocejo 2014: 46–50.
47. Mollenkopf 2005.
48. Kasinitz, Smithsimon, and Pok 2005.
49. Alexander 2004.
50. Rizek, Rizek, and Medvecky 2004.
51. De Avila, 2011; Toy 2009; Shapiro 2011.

BIBLIOGRAPHY

Alba, Richard D. 2009. *Blurring the Color Line: The New Chance for a More Integrated America.* Cambridge, MA: Harvard University Press.

Alba, Richard, and Nancy Foner. 2015. *Strangers No More: Immigration and the Challenges of Integration in North America and Western Europe.* Princeton, NJ: Princeton University Press.

Alexander, Jeffrey C. 2004. "From the Depths of Despair: Performance, Counterperformance, and 'September 11.'" *Sociological Theory* 22: 88–105.

Anderson, Elijah. 1999. *Code of the Street.* New York: W. W. Norton.

———. 2011. *The Cosmopolitan Canopy: Race and Civility in Everyday Life.* New York: W. W. Norton.

Angotti, Tom. 2008. *New York for Sale: Community Planning Confronts Global Real Estate.* Cambridge, MA: MIT Press.

Armstrong, Elizabeth A., and Suzanna M. Crage. 2006. "Movements and Memory: The Making of the Stonewall Myth." *American Sociological Review* 71: 724–51.

Bahr, Howard M. 1973. *Skid Row: An Introduction to Disaffiliation.* New York: Oxford University Press.

Bakalian, Anny, and Mehdi Bozorgmehr. 2009. *Backlash 9/11: Middle Eastern and Muslim Americans Respond.* Berkeley: University of California Press.

Barbaro, Michael. 2011. "Behind N.Y. Gay Marriage, an Unlikely Mix of Forces." *New York Times.* June 25.

Bayor, Ronald H., and Timothy J. Meagher (eds). 1996. *The New York Irish.* Baltimore: Johns Hopkins University Press.

Berger, Joseph. 2001. *Displaced Persons: Growing Up American after the Holocaust.* New York: Washington Square Press.

———. 2007. *The World in a City: Traveling the Globe through the Neighborhoods of the New New York.* New York: Ballantine Books.

Bernstein, Roslyn, and Shael Shapiro. 2010. *Illegal Living: 80 Wooster Street.* New York: Jonas Mekas Foundation.

Beveridge, Andrew A. 2008. "A Century of Harlem in New York City: Some Notes on Migration, Consolidation, Segregation, and Recent Developments." *City and Community* 7: 358–65.

Bloom, Nicholas Dagen. 2008. *Public Housing that Worked: New York in the Twentieth Century*. Philadelphia: University of Pennsylvania Press.

Brawarsky, Sandee, David Hartman, and Mick Hales. 2002. *212 Views of Central Park*. New York: Stewart, Tabori and Chang.

Burrows, Edwin G., and Mike Wallace. 1999. *Gotham: A History of New York City to 1898*. New York: Oxford University Press.

Chast, Roz. 2017. *Going into Town: A Love Letter to New York*. New York: Bloomsbury.

Chung, Thomas. 2017. "From the Five Points to Five Star Ratings on Yelp: The Lower East Side in 2017." Research paper. Department of Sociology, City University of New York Graduate Center.

Churchill, Winston S. (1906) 2013. *For Free Trade*. New York: Rosetta Books.

Cimino, Richard. 2011. "Neighborhoods, Niches, and Networks: The Religious Ecology of Gentrification." *City and Community* 10: 157–81.

Clinton, Bill. 2004. *My Life*. New York: Alfred A. Knopf.

Cruz, Angie. 2005. *Let It Rain Coffee*. New York: Simon & Schuster.

Currid, Elizabeth. 2007. *The Warhol Economy: How Fashion, Art, and Music Drive New York City*. Princeton, NJ: Princeton University Press.

Davidson, Justin. 2017. *Magnetic City: A Walking Companion to New York*. New York: Spiegel & Grau.

De Avila, Joseph. 2011. "Downtown's Big Shift: Lower Manhattan Has Transformed into a Place to Call Home in the Past Ten Years." *Wall Street Journal*, September 8.

Duneier, Mitchell. 1999. *Sidewalk*. New York: Farrar, Straus and Giroux.

———. 2016. *Ghetto: The Invention of a Place, the History of an Idea*. New York: Farrar, Straus and Giroux.

Ellen, Ingrid Gould, Amy Ellen Schwartz, Ioan Voicu, and Michael H. Schill. 2007. "Does Federally Subsidized Rental Housing Depress Neighborhood Property Values?" *Journal of Policy Analysis and Management* 26: 257–80.

Emoto, Masaru. 2004. *The Hidden Messages in Water*. Hillsboro, OR: Beyond Words.

Florida, Richard. 2017. *The New Urban Crisis: How Our Cities Are Increasing Inequality, Deepening Segregation, and Failing the Middle Class—and What We Can Do about It*. New York: Basic Books.

Foner, Nancy, ed. 2005. *Wounded City: The Social Impact of 9/11*. New York: Russell Sage Foundation.

Gentry, Kendra. 2009. "Then and Now: An Exploration of Manhattan Valley." Research paper. Department of Sociology, City University of New York Graduate Center.

Grynbaum, Michael. 2012. "Amateur Mapmakers Redraw Boundaries, Working Online." *New York Times*, September 9.

Gurock, Jeffrey S. 2016. *The Jews of Harlem: The Rise, Decline, and Revival of a Jewish Community*. New York: New York University Press.

Hallman, Howard H. 1984. *Neighborhoods: Their Place in Urban Life*. Beverly Hills, CA: Sage Publications.

Hassell, Malve Von. 1996. *Homesteading in New York City, 1978–1993: The Divided Heart of Loisaida*. Westport, CT: Bergin and Garvey.

He, Jingjing. 2017. "Little Senegal." Research paper. Department of Sociology, City University of New York Graduate Center.

Helmreich, William B. 2013. *The New York Nobody Knows: Walking 6,000 Miles in the City*. Princeton, NJ: Princeton University Press.

———. 2016. *The Brooklyn Nobody Knows: An Urban Walking Guide*. Princeton, NJ: Princeton University Press.

Hodges, Graham. 2007. *Taxi! A Social History of the New York City Cabdriver*. Baltimore: The Johns Hopkins University Press.

Israelowitz, Oscar. 2014. *Secrets of Jewish New York City*. New York: Israelowitz Publications.

Jackson, Kenneth T. 2010. *The Encyclopedia of New York City*. 2nd ed. New Haven, CT: Yale University Press.

Jacobs, Jane. 1961. *The Death and Life of Great American Cities*. New York: Vintage Books.

Jerolmack, Colin. 2013. *The Global Pigeon*. Chicago: University of Chicago Press.

Kasinitz, Philip, Gregory Smithsimon, and Binh Pok. 2005. "Disaster at the Doorstep: Battery Park City and Tribeca Respond to the Events of 9/11." In *Wounded City: The Social Impact of 9/11*, edited by Nancy Foner, 79–105. New York: Russell Sage.

Kornblum, William. 2002. *At Sea in the City: New York from the Water's Edge*. Chapel Hill, NC: Algonquin Books.

Kwong, Peter, and Dusanka Miscevic. 2005. *Chinese America: The Untold Story of America's Oldest New Community*. New York: New Press.

Lowenstein, Steven M. 1989. *Frankfurt on the Hudson: The German-Jewish Community of Washington Heights, 1933–1983, Its Structure and Culture*. Detroit: Wayne State University Press.

Marable, Manning. 2011. *Malcolm X: A Life of Reinvention.* New York: Viking.

Martin, Douglas. 1997. "A Village Dies, A Park Is Born." *New York Times,* January 31.

Min, Pyong Gap. 2008. *Ethnic Solidarity for Economic Survival: Korean Greengrocers in New York City.* New York: Russell Sage Foundation.

Mollenkopf, John, ed. 2005. *Contentious City: The Politics of Recovery in New York City.* New York: Russell Sage Foundation.

Murphy, Tim. 2016. *Christodora.* New York: Grove Press.

Ocejo, Richard E. 2014. *Upscaling Downtown: From Bowery Saloons to Cocktail Bars in New York City.* Princeton, NJ: Princeton University Press.

Quercia, Daniele, Luca Maria Aiello, Rossano Schifanella, and Adam Davies. 2015. "The Digital Life of Walkable Streets." ACM 978-1-4503-3469-3/15/05. Online

Podhoretz, John. 2010. "The Upper West Side, Then and Now." *Commentary.* May 1.

Putnam, Robert D. 2000. *Bowling Alone: The Collapse and Revival of American Community.* New York: Simon & Schuster.

Reed, Henry Hope, and Francis Morrone. 2011. *The New York Public Library: The Architecture and Decoration of the Stephen A. Schwarzman Building.* New York: W. W. Norton.

Remeseira, Claudio Ivan, ed. 2010. *Hispanic New York: A Sourcebook.* New York: Columbia University Press.

Remnick, Noah. 2016. "With Closing of East Village Shop, Little Ukraine Grows Smaller." *New York Times,* June 6.

Rhodes-Pitts, Sharifa. 2011. *Harlem Is Nowhere: A Journey to the Mecca of Black America.* New York: Little, Brown.

Rizek, Barbara, Martin Rizek, and Joanne Medvecky. 2004. *The Financial District's Lost Neighborhood: 1900–1970.* New York: Arcadia.

Roberts, Sam. 2010. "No Longer Majority Black, Harlem Is in Transition." *New York Times,* January 5.

———. 2013. *Grand Central: How a Train Station Transformed America.* New York: Grand Central.

———. 2014. *A History of New York in 101 Objects.* New York: Simon & Schuster.

———. 2017a. "Frank Pellegrino Sr., 72, Is Dead; Proudly Rebuffed Would-Be Diners at Rao's." *New York Times,* February 1.

———. 2017b. "200 Years Ago, Erie Canal Got Its Start As Just a 'Ditch.'" *New York Times,* June 26.

Schulz, Bill. 2016. "Small Relics of a Colossal Disaster." *New York Times,* June 10.

Shapiro, Julie. 2011. "Financial District Residents Want to Rename Neighborhood 'SoMa.'" https://www.dnainfo.com/new-york/20110408/downtown/financial-district-residents-want-rename-neighborhood-soma.

Sherman, William. 1973. "Pair of Medicaid Kings with a Midas Touch." *New York Daily News,* February 1.

Singer, Barry. 2012. *Churchill Style: The Art of Being Winston Churchill.* New York: Abrams Image.

Smith, Christopher M., and Hilda E. Kurtz. 2003. "Community Gardens and Politics of Scale in New York City." *Geographical Review* 93: 193–212.

Snyder, Robert. 1996. "The Neighborhood Changed: The Irish of Washington Heights and Inwood since 1945." In *The New York Irish,* edited by Ronald H. Bayor and Timothy J. Meagher, 439–60. Baltimore: Johns Hopkins University Press.

———. 2015. *Crossing Broadway: Washington Heights and the Promise of New York City.* Ithaca, NY: Cornell University Press.

Sorkin, Michael. 2009. *Twenty Minutes in Manhattan.* New York: Reaktion Books.

Spiegelman, Willard. 2016. "Retire to Manhattan: Live Long." *New York Times,* Sunday Review, September 3.

Stern, Robert A. M., David Fishman, and Jacob Tilove. 2006. *New York 2000: Architecture and Urbanism between the Bicentennial and the Millennium.* New York: Monacelli Press.

Stoller, Paul. 2002. *Money Has No Smell: The Africanization of New York City.* Chicago: University of Chicago Press.

Toy, Vivian S. 2009. "The Financial District Attracts Families." *New York Times,* February 20.

Vergara, Camilo Jose. 2009. "125th and Lex." *Slate,* December 3. http://www.slate.com/articles/arts/.

Waldinger, Roger. 2015. *The Cross-Border Connection: Immigrants, Emigrants, and Their Homelands.* Cambridge, MA: Harvard University Press.

Wertz, Julia. 2017. *Tenements, Towers, and Trash: An Unconventional Illustrated History of New York City.* New York: Black Dog & Leventhal.

White, Norval, and Elliot Wilensky. 2000. *AIA Guide to New York City*. 4th ed. New York: Crown.

Whyte, William H. 1988. *City: Rediscovering the Center*. New York: Doubleday.

Williams, Alex. 2016. "The Interloper on Avenue B." *New York Times*, September 1.

Wynn, Jonathan R. 2011. *The Tour Guide: Walking and Talking New York*. Chicago: University of Chicago Press.

Zukin, Sharon. 1982. *Loft Living: Culture and Capital in Urban Change*. Baltimore: Johns Hopkins University Press.

———. 2010. *Naked City: The Death and Life of Authentic Urban Places*. New York: Oxford University Press.

INDEX